Praise for *One More Croissant for the Road*

'Felicity Cloake is the perfect travelling companion – curious, funny, philosophical, and, best of all, imperishably greedy.'

Matthew Fort

'A highly entertaining, tough-minded and enchanting book where the spirit of freewheeling travel writing is grounded perfectly with Felicity's sure-fire recipes. I had great trouble putting it down.'

Caroline Eden

'Whether you are an avid cyclist, a Francophile, a greedy gut, or simply an appreciator of impeccable writing – this book will get you hooked.'

Yotam Ottolenghi

'Such a brilliant book, funny, captivating and wonderfully written. I feel like I was packed up in Felicity's pannier for the ride (with a croissant to snack on obviously).'

Anna Jones

'Felicity writes about food and places with an infectious and hearty appetite. Whether you are a cyclist or not, she is the perfect travelling companion: witty, observant and warm.'

Bee Wilson

'This is the kind of food book I thought people had stopped writing. A journey with stops for lunch (and coffee and dinner) which ultimately provide the recipes. And in France! I loved it.'

Diana Henry

'Felicity Cloake combines the authority and lyricism of a young Elizabeth David with the determined eccentricity to eat her way through France on a bike. Brilliant and bonkers.'

Tim Hayward

'Felicity Cloake is the new Wainwright, only much funnier and in France with a bicycle and an appetite. This is a joyful hunger-stoking and eye-opening journey across France.'

Meera Sodha

'An evocative, infectious, and at times utterly hilarious adventure that will make every food lover, and even the most lapsed of cyclists, want to jump on their bike, and on a ferry to France, immediately.'

Rosie Birkett

'Completely delicious. I scarfed down it down as if every paragraph was a freshly baked croissant. Cloake's writing is as mouth-watering as the food she selflessly eats on our behalf.'

Hadley Freeman

'Felicity Cloake's writing always targets the taste buds with unnerving precision, but "Perfect" fans are about to discover how much fun Felicity is out of the kitchen. Impossible to imagine better company for this sweary, cheese-happy, gastronomic odyssey. What a ride!'

Rhik Samadder

'A deliciously entertaining book chronicling the journey, by bike, from Cherbourg to Paris. You wish you were cycling with her in order to eat an Omelette Soufflée of exquisite lightness and beauty. Brilliant.'

Rachel Roddy

FELICITY CLOAKE

Red Sauce Brown Sauce

A BRITISH BREAKFAST ODYSSEY

MUDLARK

Mudlark
HarperCollins*Publishers*
1 London Bridge Street
London SE1 9GF

www.harpercollins.co.uk

HarperCollins*Publishers*
Macken House, 39/40 Mayor Street Upper
Dublin 1, D01 C9W8, Ireland

First published by Mudlark 2022
This edition published 2023

13 5 7 9 10 8 6 4 2

Text © Felicity Cloake 2022
Illustrations © Hannah Riordan/The Artworks 2022
Map by Liane Payne © HarperCollins*Publishers* 2022

Felicity Cloake asserts the moral right to
be identified as the author of this work

A catalogue record of this book is
available from the British Library

ISBN 978-0-00-841366-8

Printed and bound in the UK using 100%
renewable electricity at CPI Group (UK) Ltd

All rights reserved. No part of this publication may be reproduced,
stored in a retrieval system, or transmitted, in any form or by any means,
electronic, mechanical, photocopying, recording or otherwise, without
the prior written permission of the publishers.

MIX
Paper | Supporting
responsible forestry
FSC™ C007454

This book is produced from independently certified FSC™ paper
to ensure responsible forest management.

For more information visit: www.harpercollins.co.uk/green

'When you wake up in the morning, Pooh,' said Piglet, at last, 'what's the first thing you say to yourself?'

'What's for breakfast?' said Pooh. 'What do you say, Piglet?'

'I say, I wonder what's going to happen exciting to-day?' said Piglet.

Pooh nodded thoughtfully.

'It's the same thing,' he said.

A. A. Milne, *Winnie the Pooh* (1926)

It's only after a bit of breakfast that I'm able to regard the world with that sunny cheeriness which makes a fellow the universal favourite. I'm never much of a lad till I've engulfed an egg or two and a beaker of coffee.

P. G. Wodehouse, *Jeeves and the Unbidden Guest* (1916)

For Hamish, who also loves sausages

The Great Egg-spedition

Carrbridge

Arbroath
Glenshee
Ski Station
Dundee
St Andrews

Glasgow
Edinburgh
Holy Island

Ballymoney
Newcastle

Belfast
Malton
Isle of Man
Harrogate
York

Liverpool
Spalding
Stoke-on-Trent
Peterborough
Wisbech
Aberdyfi
Burton-on-Trent
Corby
Aberystwyth
Birmingham
New Quay
Cambridge
Southwold

Ipswich
SECOND FALL!
Usk
Chelmsford
Swansea
Malmesbury
London
Port Talbot
Bath
Windsor
Croydon
FIRST FALL!
Glastonbury
Richmond

Exeter

Plymouth

Falmouth

Contents

INTRODUCTION

The English-speaking peoples are differentiated from the other nations of the earth by the peculiar and substantial character of their breakfast ... to the nation as a whole the British breakfast remains as sacrosanct as the British constitution.
– F. Marian McNeill, 1932

Many people spent 2020 homeschooling their children, or trying to work at the same kitchen table as their four flatmates. I spent it holed up with a taciturn cairn terrier and a huge map of the UK.

When I say huge I mean that, once pinned to a corkboard and balanced precariously in the only space large enough to accommodate it, the map helpfully blocked out much of the light while also serving as a constant, depressing reminder of what I would be doing – cycling around it eating fry-ups – if it weren't for the minor inconvenience of a global pandemic.

Although this book was conceived back when coronavirus was Something Happening Elsewhere, the ink was barely dry on the publishing contract before it became clear I wasn't going anywhere fast. (Fortunately I didn't know that this would be the case for another 14 months or I might have wrestled the British Isles out of the window, pins and all.)

Yet had circumstances been different, it would have been a useful tool given that I'd planned to spend the summer riding around Britain, attempting to recreate 2018's two-wheeled tour of French culinary classics on home soil. In place of croissants and chocolat chaud I'd decided to focus on our own greatest breakfast hits – an idea that comes to me while cycling the length of the Outer Hebrides the next year.

My old cycling buddy Caroline and I ate a lot of 'breakfast' en route from Vatersay to the Butt of Lewis – morning fry-ups, petrol station lunches of soft rolls filled with the famous local black pudding (dry as dust after hours under a heat lamp), battered haggis from the chippie in Stornoway washed down with cans of Tennent's to celebrate our achievement.

It's while arguing with her about the question of chips before noon on the ferry back to the mainland (she's pro, I'm vehemently anti) that I realise what I've been put on this earth to do. Just as long, dreamy days pedalling from Brittany to the Med in 2017 inspired me to eat my way around France the following summer, a wet week of porridge and puddings in the Western Isles have left me convinced that the Great British* Breakfast merits a similar commemorative tour.

Even examined in the cold and breezy light of the boat's stern deck, the concept seems watertight. Without wanting to get too Nigel Farage about it, our breakfasts are clearly world class – 'certainly one of the best things about British cuisine, mate', Caroline, who is half French, agrees – superficially celebrated yet rarely given the respect they deserve.

I blame the strange reverse snobbery that persists around food in this country, and is arguably never more apparent than

---

* Strictly speaking, given the supremacy of the Ulster Fry, it's UK breakfasts, but that's less alliteratively pleasing, so forgive me, good people
  of Northern Ireland – I love your potato bread too much to be barred.

in the morning, when any pretensions to quality are given short shrift. 'Even Nigel Slater prefers his bacon sandwiches cheap and nasty!'* I squawk into the wind. (By this point, a Manx shearwater is paying me more attention than Caroline, concentrating hard on her slopping cup of tepid coffee.)

I explain earnestly (as the sea tosses us so vigorously that people around us flee for the lounge) that I'm going to change this, to yank the British breakfast out of its cosy niche as a cultural artefact and examine it as a living culinary tradition – historic, yes, but still evolving. I'll give it the same loving attention that I lavished on the French stuff; explore why this meal has come to define us, what's behind the famous regional differences (and whether they still exist now every café in London offers porridge) – and of course, establish once and for all what makes a perfect fry-up.

Naturally I'll visit all four home nations in my quest, and leave no stone unturned and no cuppa undrunk in pursuit of this noble goal – for what better way, I say (with a flourish that sends thick orange tea flying over the rail), to see the UK than through the prism of the one thing we all have in common – a love of breakfast? Probably I'll get an OBE or something, for services to my country.

I'd like to say Caroline is as excited as me to be there at the Moment of Revelation but actually she just jams her woolly hat down further over her ears and says she's going back inside for a nap.

———◆◆———

* 'No cheque on earth would ever get me to eat a thick-crust pizza or a cheap doner kebab ... give me a greasy spoon bacon sandwich on the worst plastic white bread and I'll be yours for life.' Nigel Slater, writing in the *Guardian* in 2014.

The more I think about the idea as I cycle east from Ullapool that afternoon in search of a railway station, the better it seems. For all our cakes and buns and comforting stews, our pies and potatoes and mad fixation with putting everything and anything on toast, Britain is a country that runs on breakfast.

And though we may abuse, neglect and generally take this glittering gem in our modest culinary crown for granted, a truly great breakfast is more complex than it looks. Having investigated the best way to prepare porridge, to make kedgeree, even to fry the perfect egg* in my *Guardian* cookery column over the years, I should know.

Occasionally commenters online will tartly enquire, under some recipe they deem insufficiently sophisticated, 'what next, perfect toast?'† – and I always think, yes, if my editors would allow me, I think I could write a lot about toast: the ideal thickness, staleness, degree of heat; how sourdough demands a different treatment to a soft white bloomer, perhaps, or why you should double, if not triple, cook a crumpet. In fact, I have quite a lot to say about toast, and butter, and jam too – and an inexhaustible appetite for finding even more. (Who on earth invented those conveyor-belt toasters you get in hotels, for example ... and can they be held accountable?)

This, in fact, is surely the task I was born for, because if there's no better way to see Britain than through its breakfasts, there's no better way to see anywhere than by bike. As I discovered in France, it's a conveyance uniquely suited to nosiness; a mode of transport slow enough to reveal the little details, but fast enough for the traveller to notice them changing. A cyclist can cover more ground than a walker while remaining equally flexible: unlike in a

* Not as simple as it sounds: see page 338.
† See page 170 for more on this.

car, you don't need to do a handbrake turn to find a parking space when you spot a promising-looking bakery, you can just stop and lean your handlebars annoyingly against the window. Best of all, pushing those pedals around gives you a large, and often completely baseless, appetite, which I sense will come in useful.

Back in London, as the Scottish wind burn on my face fades to a mere cheery blush, I waste no time in getting started on a book proposal, watched over by an inspirational quote from the late great A. A. Gill, scrawled on a sticky note that is to remain on my wall for two years: 'Breakfast is everything. The beginning, the first thing. It is the mouthful that is the commitment to a new day, a continuing life.'

It's also, I realise, as I try to get across the importance of my Great Idea without coming across as genuinely unhinged, the one thing that truly unites this fractured country. However we vote, whichever team we support, and even if we rarely actually eat before noon, we're an island of breakfast worshippers next to a continent largely content with a coffee and a pastry on the hoof.

I exaggerate of course (why, the doughty Dutch like to start the day with bread and chocolate sprinkles), but truly nothing brings Britons together like arguing about baked beans, or slagging off a badly cooked egg. Witness the Fry Up Police, an account dedicated to rating other people's breakfasts,* boasting 75,400 followers on Instagram, which is significantly more than the Churches of England, Ireland, Scotland and Wales put together.

While I'm not saying breakfast is the national religion – my mum might read this, for a start – I might go as far as to call it a

---

* Sample comment on a plate of eggs, bacon and undercooked crumpets: 'There should be a list for people like you that have to report to police every other week and that you have to tell people in your street you're a fry-up molester and you should be court ordered to never do this again or face 25 to life in England's worst prison.'

cult. Our devotion certainly borders on the fanatical: the come-
dian David Baddiel was astonished by the strength of people's
reactions when he began posting pictures of the breakfasts he ate
on tour. One particular fry-up in Doncaster featuring beans in a
little cup of toasted bread, and a tomato cut like a coronet, 'got a
lot of weird political hate: people, as ever, calling me a member
of the metropolitan liberal elite who clearly has no idea what
constitutes a good, proper, working-class full English breakfast'.

As he's discovered, breakfast is more than just a meal, it's a
badge of identity, a declaration of self. Krishnendu Ray, Associate
Professor of Food Studies at New York University, told the *Atlan-
tic* a couple of years ago that if all food is the domain of habit,
that habit is strongest at breakfast time: 'People are just waking
up, and they need their caffeine-delivery system and they need
their cereal and they don't want too much thinking about it.'

In other words, familiarity rather than novelty is prized
before 9 a.m. Most of us favour the flavours we grew up with,
whether cornflakes or corn tostadas, so to criticise someone
else's breakfast habits is to attack their culture, even, in many
cases, their mothers. No wonder we feel such fierce loyalty to
our favourite brand of tea, or choice of breakfast condiment.

But such small details define us: the *Daily Mail* ran a feature
from 'etiquette expert' William Hanson back in 2016, which
explained in great detail 'how the first meal of the day reveals
your social class' (spoiler: 'being seen walking down a street
with a takeaway cup of coffee is . . . a fast-track ticket for entry
into society hell'), the upshot of which seemed to be that the
aspirational should eat more kedgeree.

Equally, your taste in bacon can betray your origins as surely
as the accent in which you order it: Jilly Cooper* (the source of

---

* *Class: A View from Middle England* (1979).

so much wisdom in life) quotes a butcher as saying, 'When a woman asks for back I call her "madam"; when she asks for streaky I call her "dear".'

Perhaps most divisive of all, however, is our choice of breakfast condiment, as I found shortly before publication when the *Daily Star* made my own 'barmy' predilection for marmalade front page news – 'the world as we know it is well and truly broken', the tabloid concluded. That contestants in Radio 5 Live's Sausage Sandwich Game (in which callers had to guess a celebrity's sauce of choice) often felt able to argue their case on the grounds of the guest's accent or reputation confirms my suspicion that many of us feel tied to red or brown sauce as we might a football team – as a marker of geographic or class solidarity.

This hypothesis is backed up by a 2011 YouGov poll, which found the nation evenly split, with brown more popular with men, northerners, Scots and the over-sixties, and red gaining ground with the young, and in the South, Midlands and Wales. Showing a severe lack of collective imagination, only 4 per cent opted for a different sauce, with 14 per cent of respondents instead preferring no sauce at all.

Tea Break: ONE NATION. UNITED BY BREAKFAST

Well, not quite. Here are the generally, though never universally, agreed components of each home nation's 'traditional full breakfast' as laid down in the mid twentieth century – a meal that, give or take a chop or two, might previously have been eaten at any time of day under the guise of a 'mixed grill'.

Note that in all cases bacon is almost always back, and the eggs are usually fried. (In for a penny, in for a pound, as my grandma always said.) Tomatoes – fresh and grilled, or warmed from the tin – fried mushrooms, baked beans and hash browns are all very much optional extras wherever you are: this isn't a salad. Chips, for some reason, are only acceptable if you're wearing a high-vis jacket, or you're so hungover you don't care.

Full English – bacon, eggs, sausage, black pudding, fried slice (of bread). In the West Country it may also include hog's pudding as well, or instead of the black pudding. In the South East, bubble and squeak is traditional but sadly rarely seen these days.

Full Scottish – bacon, eggs, sausage (often lorne, or square sausage rather than 'links'), black pudding and tattie scones. If you're really lucky you might also get white pudding, fruit pudding and/or haggis too.

Ulster Fry – bacon, eggs, sausage, black pudding, white pudding (I must add this is disputed), potato and soda breads.

Full Welsh – bacon, eggs, sausage, cockles, laverbread, fried slice.

✦✦✦

Patrick Kidd, writing in *The Times* in October 2016, four months after the Brexit referendum, noted that 'Politicians . . . want to talk about Britain leaving the EU but instead they keep mentioning their morning meal . . . To say breakfast instead of

Brexit once is a misfortune, to do it twice careless. But to do so three times in five minutes* looks like peckishness.'

It's a shame our elected leaders didn't learn something from this collective Freudian slip. Our national obsession with the concept suggests 'breakfast means breakfast' is a slogan, and a manifesto, 100 per cent of us could have got behind – though if we're honest, few of us eat a 'full' one every day. A 2020 survey found that almost one in five under-thirties claimed to never have even tried a Full English, yet such is its place in the collective psyche that a British hotel provides a mere 'continental' version at its peril.†

In fact, Brits expect to be offered at least a nod to a 'proper' breakfast on planes, trains and in automobile service stations; in holiday resorts and high street cafés – whether or not we actually order them, it's important to have the choice. There's nothing I like more than watching my people washing down their airport fry-ups with a 6 a.m. pint ... as long as I don't end up sitting next to them for the next 12 hours.

George Orwell's words back in 1946, in an unpublished essay on British cookery, still ring true: 'Ideally for nearly all British people, and in practice for most of them even now, this is not a snack but a serious meal.' Wherever you eat it, and however you define it, making a good breakfast is still a source of national pride.

Tempting as it is, however, to mistily imagine our forerunners on these islands tucking into a Viking Fry at their

---

* All credit to the Labour shadow chancellor at the time, John McDonnell.
† It took me just ten seconds to find a one-star review on Tripadvisor, apparently awarded because an establishment in Surrey did not supply a 'fully cooked breakfast . . . maybe minor to some but a matter of principle and important to me'.

wattle-and-daub breakfast bars, the 'full' cooked breakfast is, like the cream tea and the ploughman's lunch, a relatively recent creation – the term Full English doesn't pop up until 1933, in a cookery book that, with a brass neck typical of the period, declares it 'the best breakfast in the world' and, less disputably, 'the best meal of the day in England'.

Indeed, for a long time the British did not really go in for breakfast – the word itself does not come into use until the fifteenth century, suggesting that either it was not much taken, or it was so little regarded that no one bothered to record it. Not entirely coincidentally, the medieval Church, so officially censorious of any pleasures of the flesh, frowned upon anything more than two meals a day as self-indulgence; the thirteenth-century philosopher Thomas Aquinas lists *praepropere*, or eating too soon, as coming under the deadly sin of gluttony.*

The few exceptions allowed to gulp down some gruel – the very old, the very young, the very ill, and those claiming to have a hard day of physical toil or travel ahead† – meant that breakfast, as it was not yet known, was far from a fashionable meal. 'It was presumed,' Heather Arndt Anderson writes in her book *Breakfast: A History*, 'that if one ate breakfast, it was because one had other lusty appetites as well.'

Even once it became commonplace in the seventeenth century, fry-ups were not on the menu – bread, beer or wine and cheese seem to have been typical, with many subsisting on what the Restoration-era civil servant Samuel Pepys called 'the morning draught' of ale, a ritual enacted in many a Wetherspoons to this day.

---

*   Oh dear.
†   The rich, of course, could afford to bend the rules; that handy travel
    dispensation allowed Henry III to have six tuns (about 1,500 litres) of wine
    delivered to St Albans cathedral for his breakfast while on pilgrimage there.

Though the menu slowly became more elaborate for those that could afford it, even in Jane Austen's day breakfast, as recorded by her mother on a visit to wealthy relatives, consisted of 'Chocolate, Coffee, and Tea, Plumb Cake, Pound Cake, Hot Rolls, Cold Rolls, Bread and Butter and dry Toast' – not an egg in sight.

For most of history breakfast seems not to have had any special foods associated with it, as continues to be the case in many other culinary cultures. When you think about it, it is a bit bizarre that a bowl of porridge is considered the perfect thing to eat at 8 a.m., but deeply weird just four hours later – a disconnect born out of the very modern luxury of choice. As recently as 1946 the MP for Perth and Kinross protested the proposed introduction of rations on oatmeal on the basis that Scottish farm workers ate porridge twice a day.

In his diaries Pepys mentions breakfasting on such things as oysters, turkey pie, the hashed remains of last night's supper, cold roast beef or pork, brawn, herrings and sweetmeats – it wasn't until the nineteenth century that what the writer Wyvern describes as 'the ding dong monotony of "bacon and eggs" alternated with "eggs and bacon"' set in.

I say monotony: to read Victorian cookbooks is to goggle at the range of dishes suggested as suitable for the breakfast table in a country house, or those aspiring to recreate one in more humble surrounds. Kidneys, ptarmigan, salmon, 'curried bones', rump steak, veal and ham pies, roast larks, devilled turkey, muffins, periwinkle patties, pickled oysters, Russian caviar and hot-house fruits to name but a few of the options presented, a selection of which would be left in chafing dishes for guests to help themselves to as they pleased, breakfast being the one meal where servants* were not employed in the dining room. (Unsurprisingly, given the corsets they had to be crammed into, Victorian ladies were permitted to take their breakfast in bed, though it was considered extremely effeminate for men to do the same.)

A letter home from the American ambassador in 1867 suggests that such 'fabulous feasts' were already a distinctively British phenomenon: 'When I reflected that all these people would lunch at 2 and dine at 8,' he wrote, 'I bowed my head in humiliation and the fork dropped nerveless from my grasp.'

That breakfast really came into its own in this period probably has something do with the emergence of a substantial middle class, who suddenly found themselves with a newfangled thing called leisure time with which to while away the morning drinking coffee and harrumphing over the newspapers. Certainly the average man or woman on the street didn't enjoy so much choice, yet it seems all but the poorest families breakfasted on eggs and bacon by the late nineteenth century, even if just once a week and for the man of the house alone – the woman and children, one assumes, would probably have made do with bread and dripping. Yet despite the differences in scale, in so doing, the historian Kaori O'Connor writes, 'all felt they were eating the English Breakfast'.

It wasn't a change in appetites that did for the practice, but a change in employment habits after the Second World War: without paid servants, or, increasingly, an unpaid wife at home, convenience foods began to gain ground. In a household where everyone was going out to work, cornflakes or bread and jam

---

* They would have already eaten a more modest repast – porridge and toast, perhaps – in the servants' hall between sweeping the grates and washing the steps.

were things even children could be trusted to provide for themselves, and fitted in well with the low-fat mantra of the final decades of the century.

According to figures from January 2021, toast, once mere hand luggage to the main event, has become our second-most popular breakfast after the even quicker bowl of cereal. Yet a YouGov survey from 2016 found that almost three-quarters of us still top it with butter rather than margarine, and that the jams and marmalades that have been on the breakfast table for centuries are still significantly more popular than chocolate spread and peanut butter. (My own beloved Marmite sits somewhere in the middle; the arriviste avocado doesn't merit a mention.)

The modern British breakfast has two faces: the rushed weekday meal – the toast on the school run, the drive-thru on the way to work, the cereal al-desko – and the feast we enjoy at weekends, or when we treat ourselves at one of the greasy spoons still holding firm against the relentless assault of American-style coffee shops on our high streets – what we secretly think of as a real breakfast. Greedy, rather than particularly discriminating, I'm looking forward to getting better acquainted with both in the name of research.

Having had the bright idea of writing a travel book just before travel is outlawed for the best part of 14 months, I get an extra year to put together an itinerary that takes in the best-loved breakfast foods from around the UK, both ancient (porridge) and modern (Marmite), to worry endlessly that I've missed some niche regional treasure and spend hours staring vacantly at that giant map, trying to spot the flaws in my plans.

Starting off in London, with a classic metropolitan millennial breakfast of smashed avo on toast, I'm planning to head down to the West Country first, via the mustard makers and butter churners of Somerset, to find out more about the hog's pudding traditionally found on breakfasts in Devon and Cornwall. From there, I'll cross the Bristol Channel into Wales for some cockles and laverbread before returning to England for Midlands favourites like Staffordshire oatcakes, Weetabix and, yes, Marmite.

The North West offers up Bury black pudding and the world's biggest baked bean factory for inspection, as well as being a handy jumping-off point to the Isle of Man – for kippers, naturally – and thence to Northern Ireland for a carbolicious Ulster Fry. Scotland, a ferry ride from Belfast, is almost too full of possibility, but Ayrshire bacon, porridge, marmalade and Arbroath smokies form a neat loop to take me back down the east coast for a Geordie stottie.

After a small diversion to Harrogate for tea and crumpets, I'll return to London for bubble and squeak by way of East Anglia, and Newmarket sausages, Suffolk bacon and Tiptree jam. It's not a comprehensive picture of the nation at breakfast – I regret not having more time to make a proper study of sausages, or to hop back across to the Hebrides for black pudding – but had I known when I made these plans how thoroughly they would be scrambled by continuing Covid restrictions, I'd have realised this was the least of my worries.

In spring 2021, with the government's 'roadmap to freedom' graven on every heart, and just as I'm feeling confident enough to dig out my mothballed Lycra to see if it's still decent, news of the 'delta variant' arrives in Britain . . . and casually sets about creating chaos.

Unilever decide it's too risky for me to visit the Marmite factory as planned. Heinz baked beans follow suit. The entire Isle of Man opts to remain shut to all visitors, even those who only want to commune with kippers. Several Post-it notes, so optimistically pinned to the map the year before, gain a tentative question mark, and I take to ringing my sister in Edinburgh daily to interrogate her about Nicola Sturgeon's probable intentions, steeling myself for the necessity of putting the trip off for yet another year.

But in late March I wake up in the middle of the night and a cold sweat, and decide I can wait no longer: if it's legal, I'm going. The stout little dog, who has shown no interest in the map since it fell on his head in early 2020, must regretfully be left at home – much as Wilf would enjoy the breakfast element of proceedings, the idea of him rampaging around in my tiny tent is too terrifying to countenance.

Having arranged his bed and board with two of his favourite people in the world – Kaj, a Finnish friend who boasts underfloor heating and takes him for long pub lunches, and Gemma, who boasts several battered footballs and takes him for long walks up mountains – I'm able to make my own, more tentative arrangements with breakfast experts from South Wales to the Scottish Highlands.

I buy a camping stove in case I have to cook my own breakfasts, take the faithful Eddy,* my two-wheeled partner in grime, to a genial, gently stoned Polish bike mechanic in Hackney for a service and, the evening before I leave, finally remember to pack my bags.

Oh, and before we go any further, I'm neutral on the question of red sauce or brown sauce: *personally* I like my breakfast with English mustard and my bacon sandwiches with marmalade. Draw your own conclusions.

---

* Named after the great Belgian bike racer Eddy Merckx, who once famously said, while grabbing some viennoiserie from a hotel buffet, that it wasn't the pastries that hurt, it was the climbs.

◆◆

Tea Break:
PACKING LIST

Because people sometimes express a rather prurient interest in the contents of my panniers . . . here's what I started out with, divided between two waterproof bright yellow Ortlieb bags, one handlebar pack, and a small frame bag that proves to obstruct my water bottles so effectively that I abandon it in Cornwall:

Tent
Sleeping bag
Roll mat
Eyemask and earplugs
Camping stove, pans and gas
Spork
Mug
Knife
Corkscrew
Marmite
Hipflask of damson gin

Dry bag 1:
2 × bib shorts (the ones with ridiculous shoulder straps like Eighties salopettes, which make it a right pain to go to the loo, but, on the plus side, never fall down)
1 × bib tights (ditto, also keep you very warm)
2 × cycling jerseys (the things with the big pockets in the back for bananas and old toffee wrappers and whatever I'm sure they're actually designed for)

2 × cycling socks (this just means they're thin and come in nice neon colours)

2 × sports bras

1 × windproof jacket

1 × windproof lightweight gilet (shades of Alan Partridge)

1 × waterproof

1 × pair of sleeves (believe me, once you've experienced these cut-off tights for the arms, you'll never go back)

1 × snood

Dry bag 2:

1 × pair of jeans

1 × pair of shorts

1 × wool jumper

1 × T-shirt

1 × pair of leggings

1 × merino vest

1 × ordinary socks

2 × knickers (look, you're not wearing them most of the time)

2 × masks

1 × woolly hat

1 × cotton shawl that does as both a towel and a scarf

Swimming costume

1 × helmet

1 × cycling shoes

1 × pair of Converse

Flip-flops (useful on campsites)

1 × bike lock

2 × bike lights

1 × bike pump

1 × inner tube

1 × patch kit

1 × chain oil

1 × multitool

2 × water bottles

Shampoo

Conditioner

Soap

Deodorant

Moisturiser

Suncream

Lip balm

Painkillers

Insect repellent

Water-based eco face wipes (did I mention I write for the *Guardian*?)

Comb

2 × hairbands

Lateral flow tests

1 × book (J. D. Taylor's weighty *Island Story*, which got exchanged, with some relief, for Emma Hughes's *No Such Thing as Perfect* in Edinburgh)

1 × notebook, which I'll hopefully remember to write notes in this time

1 × pencil

1 × smartphone (most-used apps: Komoot, a navigation tool slightly less likely than Google Maps to send cyclists across ploughed fields or on motorways; Strava, to record every metre pedalled; and Instagram, to share all those breakfasts)

1 × charger plus leads to recharge lights, phone, etc.

1 × battery pack

1 × lighter, because you never know when one might come in useful

◆◆

I
LONDON TO EXETER
Sauce

I believe mustard to be one of the most amazing condiments.
– Justin Timberlake, 2009

It's grey, and chilly for late spring when I stumble crossly out of bed the next morning after a luxurious almost three hours of anxious, broken sleep I can't even blame on the dog, who trotted off with Kaj last night without so much as a backward glance. Apparently they had a date with *RuPaul's Drag Race*.

Pulling on my Lycra workwear, I haul my startlingly weighty bags up to street level, where I half hope they'll be stolen as I'm bringing up the bike. As they're not, I then face the problem of how to get them onto the new pannier rack, something I now realise I could have investigated in advance had I not been in denial that this was actually happening.

Eventually I work it out, at which point there's nothing for it but to leave, though, worried I'm going to overbalance after so long riding without luggage, I scuttle across the main road on foot first. Not the most noble start to the expedition but I'm nervous enough without being run over by the 17 bus.

I'm still a bit wobbly when I get to the Australian café in Paddington Basin where I'm meeting my first travelling companion, the aforementioned Caroline (who's coming with me as far as South Wales) and two well-wishers, my school friend Lucinda, and my 'book club' friend Claire.*

I've chosen Bondi Green for my first breakfast of the trip not only for its proximity to the railway station, but because of the glorious absurdity of its menu – I sense[†] I'm unlikely to find anywhere else offering gluten-free celeriac 'toast' for the next seven weeks. As a fair dinkum Aussie, Claire has kindly offered to act as translator and cultural consultant, in which capacity she's quick to assure me they do have 'actual toast, made out of bread' in the Antipodes as well.

Apparently so, I say, regarding my smashed avocado on cold-fermented activated charcoal sourdough (I swear I'm not making this up) with house labne, Aleppo chilli and a poached egg. Though I try not to eat it often for the reasons mentioned below, when the avocados are as soft and yellow as butter, and just as generously salted, avocado toast can be a beautiful thing. That said, I suspect a large part of the dish's appeal is how great tragically underripe examples look in photos, all fresh and green and crunchy, perhaps accessorised with a sprinkle of red chilli for a few extra likes . . . not to mention the shameful craze for carving the noble fruit of the Aztecs into hard, watery roses for the benefit of social media.

Of course, every trend has a curve, and you know something's on its way out when even Wetherspoons ditches it from the menu. I'd like to think it's because of sustainability

---

concerns around this water-thirsty crop or because they've heard many of those who grow avocados can no longer afford to eat them . . . but I suspect they were just too much faff to prepare.

Lucinda, horrified by my blackened bread, asks Claire if toast is always served this burnt Down Under – but washed down with a tepid flat white (you guessed it, 'it's meant to be like that') and a green juice to offset any future bacon roll consumption, it's not bad, the richness of the eggs balanced by the zingy lime and chilli-spiked avocado underneath. The mound of salad on the side, however, should probably be illegal.

•••

Tea Break:
OR SHOULD THAT BE CHAI?

Of course, we've never all eaten the same thing for breakfast – no doubt those pesky Romans put a few backs up when they insisted on starting the day with garlicky cheese and honey. Britain has always been a population in flux, each wave of arrivals enriching our cuisine with their own traditions, and my narrative would be much the poorer without them.

Some of them have become so ingrained we claim them as our own – the cold smoked salmon brought by Jewish emigrés from Eastern Europe in the late nineteenth century – or bear little resemblance to the original dish that inspired them, like Anglo-Indian kedgeree (of which more in Chapter 8), while others are still thrillingly novel, like Tunisian shakshuka, a beneficiary of 'the Ottolenghi effect'.

Should you have a yen to widen your breakfast horizons, here's something to try from each of the top ten countries of origin for overseas-born Britons according to 2020 figures:

1. **India:** appam – fluffy rice and coconut pancakes popular in the southern state of Kerala – with mutton curry or vegetable stew.
2. **Poland:** naleśniki – thin pancakes with fresh cheese and sugar or fruit compote.
3. **Pakistan:** halwa puri – flaky fried flatbreads with sweet, nutty semolina porridge, often served with chana masala and spicy potatoes too.
4. **Ireland**: a full Irish, with black and white pudding, and potato farls.
5. **Romania:** mămăligă cu lapte – thick cornmeal porridge (polenta) served in a bowl of hot milk. (An old-fashioned breakfast now, I'm told.)
6. **Germany:** Bavarian Weisswurst sausages with sweet mustard.
7. **Nigeria:** akara – spicy black-eyed pea fritters served with bread, corn custard or millet porridge.
8. **South Africa:** mieliepap – maize porridge served with tea or coffee.
9. **Italy:** biscotti with milky coffee.
10. **Bangladesh:** sobji porota – mixed spiced vegetables with a flaky flatbread.

• •

I won't be sorry to leave problematic avocados and activated bread behind me, though – in fact, I'm eager to get going before I can change my mind. We pose for Official Pictures outside, and then Caroline and I head for the train that will take us to Wiltshire, and the first stop on my tour: the Tracklements condiment factory.

First we have to find the right platform, hoisting the laden bikes up one flight of steps and down another, me skidding precariously in my stupid, gripless shoes,* unused to the weight behind me. 'How have you got so much luggage, mate?' Caroline asks as, giving up on finding the allocated cycle spaces once on board, we prop them in a corridor.

I look at her unusually svelte packing and fight the urge to chuck my jolly yellow panniers out of the window – this is more than I took to France, and that included a passport. New bags, I say by way of explanation. The first rule of bike touring, we decide, is that stuff always expands to fit the space available.

My mood is improved by the appearance of a cheerfully whistling train conductor with a broad Bristol accent who, after explaining that the missing bike spaces are thanks to Great Western sending five carriages instead of the expected ten, pauses to tell us about his own cycling adventures, including a trip around Ireland with a friend with a £50 bike: 'Rosslare to Killarney, and we didn't pass a pub, put it that way. That were fun.' Excitingly, unlike in France I'm able to engage in witty repartee at a level slightly above that of your average three-year-old. It strikes me that, given my modest fluency in English, there might be benefits to staying closer to home – though sadly the cost of train travel is not likely to be one of them.

We disembark in Chippenham, a busy commuter hub about halfway between Swindon and Bristol and 20km south of the

---

* There is a good reason cyclists waddle around in this hard-soled footwear – difficult as it is to walk in, each shoe clips into specially designed pedals, which makes riding easier . . . as long as you remember to unclip before coming to a halt. Of which more later.

Tracklements HQ. The first 10 minutes of riding are, as ever in my experience, a despondent slog – not only is traffic faster and less predictable out here, but merely turning the pedals feels like hard work. Trying to take comfort from my triathlete friend Rob's airy assurance that training is overrated and I'll get fit en route, I nevertheless can't help a rush of profound regret. How am I going to survive almost two months of this? I wonder glumly, struggling to keep up with Caroline. Why did I ever think cycling was enjoyable?

And then we turn off the main road, and it all makes sense again. The sun's out, the scenery is glorious, frothy with hawthorn blossom, every leaf soft and new, and the villages boast names like Tiddleywink and Knockdown and Lower Stanton St Quintin. Chancing our luck on a closed road, fate smiles upon us and the municipal hedge cutters are happy to wave us through. In the kind of swift change of mood that seems to happen more often on expeditions than in real life, I honestly can't think of anywhere I'd rather be this Tuesday morning. I even start singing, before remembering Caroline is Musical, and my voice probably causes her active pain.

It's then that Google springs another surprise upon us by taking us down the excitingly named Fosse Way, the Roman road that once linked Isca Dumnoniorum (Exeter) to Lindum Colonia (Lincoln) but is now, perhaps unsurprisingly, in rather bad nick. Despite the buckled cat's eyes poking out of the mud as a bonus skid hazard (a recycled piece of motorway, I later discover), this ancient route has decayed into little more than a track, and eventually I have to get off and push, cursing my narrow tyres and heavy panniers. By the time we see the gate blocking the other end, I'm covered in mud and chin-deep in high dudgeon again – until I suddenly smell it.

ONIONS! I shout triumphantly. Startled out of her reverie, Caroline looks momentarily terrified. Can't you smell them? I ask, now worried she might have Covid. Clearly she's thinking the same thing, because she shouts, 'YEESSSSSSS, MATE!' Birds scatter in terror as we turn into a light industrial estate, following our noses to the Tracklements* factory, somewhat incongruously sited amid the Nissan huts of a Second World War prisoner-of-war camp.

———•◆•———

It feels fitting that a sauce factory should be my first stop, given it's the thing that ties the disparate elements of a fry-up together, and here, owner Guy Tullberg confirms, as we obediently pause to have our temperatures taken, they make them all: ketchup, brown sauce and mustard. In fact, they specialise in mustard, producing eight varieties plus a mustard ketchup.

Before you throw down this book in disgust, accusing me of pro-mustard bias, I assure you that I would have visited Heinz Ketchup and HP Sauce too, but they're both made abroad these days. The fact that conversation on our visit revolves almost solely around my own preferred breakfast condiment is purely coincidental, but if you're miffed, please accept my apologies in the form of a brief skip through more populist options.

◆◆◆

Tea Break:
RED. BROWN . . . OR YELLOW

Strictly speaking, both red sauce and brown sauce are ketchups, the generic name for what the *Oxford Companion to Food*

---

* The name came from the founder's Lincolnshire grandmother, who used it to refer to any sort of accompaniment, from piccalilli to potatoes.

describes as 'a range of salty, spicy, rather liquid condiments': western but with their roots in the east. The word probably comes from the Amoy Chinese word *kêtsiap* (fermented fish sauce), and arrives in English via the Malay *kecap* (kecap manis, keen cooks will know, is a thick, sweet soy sauce), though the recipe itself has changed more than its name.

Oyster, mussel and many other flavours of ketchup have come and gone, squashed in the path of Big Tomato. Though early tomato ketchups struggled with spoilage, Heinz solved the problem by dramatically upping the vinegar content, changing the flavour so significantly that people began to lose their taste for the homemade variety.

Launched in the States in 1876, it reached the UK a decade later, and was produced here from the 1920s – with a brief break during the war, when consumers had to be content with salad cream instead – until 1999, when production went abroad. Heinz isn't the only brand of tomato ketchup of course, but it does hold by far the largest market share.

I suspect brown sauce bears more resemblance to early homemade ketchups, being also tomato based, but so heavily seasoned with dates, molasses, tamarind, vinegar and spices that you wouldn't know it. The most famous brand, HP, or Houses of Parliament sauce, is said to have been originally developed in Leicestershire to go with the famous local pork pie; it acquired its current name when a subsequent owner discovered his 'banquet sauce' was gracing tables at the Palace of Westminster. These days, HP is also made by Heinz-Kraft, in the Netherlands. Again, other, arguably more delicious, brands are available.

English mustard, whose history is elaborated below, is, of course, the king of breakfast condiments, being possessed of a clean, sharp heat – vinegar-spiked Dijons or crunchy wholegrain* are, in my opinion, both too acidic to be enjoyable first thing.

❖❖

Suitably kitted out in hairnets and shoe covers (if you take one piece of advice from this chapter, it's don't enter a food factory in cycling shoes unless you actively enjoy skittering around in the vicinity of bubbling pans of chilli jam), Guy takes us behind the scenes. Though this is not my first rodeo, having poked my nose in everywhere from Japanese koji distilleries to Norwegian cod-processing plants in the name of 'work', I find Tracklements particularly fascinating because, unlike many factories I've visited, it reminds me of a shinier, noisier, scaled-up version of a home kitchen.

The ingredients store is stacked full of vast tubs of spices and sugar, vats of vinegar and sacks of different mustard seeds. The yellow ones, we learn, grown for them in Suffolk, give the mustard its rounded flavour, while the brown, which come from Canada, supply the heat that gets up your nose. 'We joke that it was the Romans who brought the mustard here first,' Guy says, striding ahead (at six foot six, he's hard to keep up with). 'There's a Roman camp down at the bottom of the dip there – you'll have come past it probably – and they always travelled with mustard seeds.'

As it dawns on me that the annoying bog I struggled to wheel Eddy through was in fact a Romano-British village, Guy's already skipping forward a few hundred years to tell us that every important household and monastery used to have its own mustardarius, whose job it was to oversee the

---

* Broadcaster John Humphreys' breakfast condiment of choice.

production of mustard, and reminding us of Falstaff in *Henry IV, Part II* dismissing his rival as 'as thick as Tewkesbury Mustard'. Once, he says, England was peppered with small-scale mustard makers; now they're almost as thin on the ground as Romans. 'I can't work out why, when we managed to hang on to so many of our breweries, we didn't keep the mustard factories too.'

He scoops a few seeds out of a large tub for us to try – 'I love the nuttiness of the yellow seeds – go on, get some between your molars!' – explaining that they don't release their flavour until they come into contact with liquid, whether that's in your mouth or in the large blue barrels at our feet.

The sudden rumble of a stone grinder, a solid, Victorian-looking machine named Mick (the other is Keith – 'after the least organic of the Rolling Stones') distracts me from the party popping off on my tongue. Guy beckons us over to where a hopper of brown and yellow mustard seeds, allspice, black pepper and dried chillies is being crushed into submission for the wholegrain mustard that launched the business way back in 1970.

In those days Guy's father, William Tullberg, was working for a large sausage manufacturer. The only mustard readily available was, 'Colman's yellow or brown, ready made in little pots', he's said in the past. 'Professionally I had to taste a great many sausages and pies … and my palate needed something better to accompany them.'

So, when Tullberg Sr came across a 270-year-old recipe for wholegrain mustard in the writings of horticulturalist and ardent salad fancier John Evelyn, he decided to give it a go, though lacking the cannonball Evelyn recommended to crush the seeds, William employed a home coffee grinder instead. The results went down so well at his regular Saturday-morning sausage and mash parties* that he purchased a commercial coffee mill to make up larger batches for friends and the local pub.

When he left the sausage business, after an unspecified 'disagreement with my employer', and set up a restaurant, his homemade mustard featured on the menu, which meant more people wanted to buy it . . . and lo and behold, almost half a century later I'm standing in a factory that exports the stuff to China, watching Mick bump and grind.

Having been squashed to release the oils, the seeds are poured into barrels, mixed with water and cider vinegar and left to sit for a week, with the occasional stir. 'Colman's say to leave their mustard powder for 10 minutes to let the flavour develop,' Guy says dismissively. 'I think you need five days, at the very least.' We take a lusty sniff of some already under way, and all sneeze on cue.

On the way out, I reluctantly turn the conversation to mustard's johnny-come-lately rivals, ketchup and brown sauce. Tracklements' ketchup, I discover, is more savoury than the leading brand, with onions and spiced vinegar – cloves, allspice, peppercorns – plus chillies: 'the king of ketchups!' Guy's own preference, however, is brown sauce, made 'as the gods intended', tangy with tamarind, cider vinegar and lemon juice, the spices, surprisingly, restricted to just chilli. Unlike HP, it contains onion and garlic, giving it a fuller, more rounded flavour that points up the rather one-dimensional sweet and sour profile of the version I'm familiar with. I could, I say, get used to this one with sausages. You never know, it might even turn me.

Nevertheless, I gratefully accept Guy's offer of a jar of their Tewkesbury mustard for the road: I suspect it will come in handy

---

* I like the sound of Guy's dad.

given that the connoisseur's choice of breakfast condiment is a somewhat recherché pleasure in the land of red or brown.

TOMATO KETCHUP

Based on an 1857 recipe from Tendring Hall in Suffolk, demolished in the 1950s, this fiery and intensely savoury roasted tomato ketchup is a good way to use up even anaemic, underripe tomatoes. It doesn't keep quite as well as more vinegar-heavy commercial versions, so I've kept the quantities small; if you're a heavy user, as it's known in the trade, I'd suggest doubling or tripling the recipe.

Makes 1 mini jar
1kg tomatoes
1 long shallot, peeled and squashed with a knife
2 garlic cloves, peeled and squashed with a knife
2 dried chillies, as hot, or not, as you like
4 tbsp soft dark brown sugar
4 tbsp cider vinegar
Salt, to taste

1 Heat the oven to 180°C/160°C fan/gas 4. Arrange the tomatoes on a lightly greased baking sheet and bake for about 30–40 minutes, until very soft and beginning to collapse.

2 Push the tomatoes through a sieve into a saucepan; scrape the underside of the sieve regularly and make sure you get as much of the flesh through as possible. You should be left with just skin and seeds.

3 Add the shallot, garlic, chillies, sugar and vinegar to the pan. Bring to the boil and simmer for 20–25 minutes until thick, stirring regularly.

4 Allow to cool, scoop out the shallot, garlic and chillies and discard, stir in salt to taste and store in a clean jar.

BROWN SAUCE

Richer and mellower in flavour than leading brands (ahem), this takes brown sauce back to its fruity roots. It is, I must say, outstanding with sausages in particular, but also works well with cheese – try it with the Glamorgan sausages on page 297.

Makes 2 medium jars
500g tomatoes
¼ tsp fine salt
1 cooking apple, peeled, cored and roughly chopped
75g stoned dates, roughly chopped
1 small red onion, roughly chopped
1 garlic clove, finely chopped
5cm root ginger, peeled and roughly chopped
400ml apple juice
50ml tamarind paste (this varies; if very thick and dark, halve this then add to taste)
100ml cider vinegar
2 tbsp treacle
2 cloves, crushed to a powder
¼ tsp ground allspice
⅛ tsp ground cinnamon
½ tsp black mustard seeds, crushed to a powder

1 Roughly chop the tomatoes, put in a bowl, sprinkle with the salt and leave for at least an hour. Drain off the salty liquid and discard.

2 Put the tomatoes into a large pan with the apple, dates,
   onion, garlic and ginger. Add the apple juice, tamarind
   paste, cider vinegar, treacle and 100ml of water. Bring to the
   boil and allow to bubble away vigorously for 5 minutes, then
   reduce the heat and simmer gently for 45 minutes, until the
   contents of the pan are soft and pulpy.

3 Whizz with a stick blender, or in a food processor, until
   smooth, then stir in the spices. Bring back to the boil and
   simmer for about 30 minutes, until thickened to your liking,
   stirring regularly. Allow to cool slightly, then season to taste.
   Store in clean jars.

SINUS-CLEARING MUSTARD

*Making your own mustard is both fun, and one way to guarantee
it'll blow your socks off – prepared mustard decreases in potency
over time, so I've kept amounts small. Try it in a bacon sandwich
(pages 311–314) with the marmalade on page 219. (Though I like to
keep my mustard simple, do play around with different vinegars,
spices, and sweeteners like honey; this is just a template.)*

Makes 1 small jar, but is easily doubled or tripled
2 tbsp yellow mustard seed
1 tbsp brown mustard seed
1 tbsp cider vinegar
½ tsp flaky salt
A pinch of cayenne pepper (optional)

1 Grind the seeds finely in a spice grinder or a pestle and
   mortar.

2 Stir in 1 tablespoon of cold water to make a paste. Leave to
   sit for 15 minutes.
3 Stir in the vinegar, salt and cayenne pepper to taste.

After a feast of cold cuts, pork pies and cheeses served with a
condiment selection that stops conversation for at least
five minutes, Guy offers to escort us some of the way to Bath,
where I'm hoping to try a bun or two tomorrow. 'I ride to work
every day, rain or shine,' he says, wheeling out a battered-
looking mountain bike. 'If you can believe it on this.'

The grey clouds that have been quietly massing overheard
begin to unload their watery burden, but our guide is undaunted,
waxing lyrical as we head west, on the pleasures of his commute,
whatever the weather, a chance, he says, to clear the head and
soothe the soul. 'These horses, I always say hello to them.' He
nods cordially as we pass. 'Every single morning.'

A little later, I see my first hare for years, frozen on the
tarmac for the briefest of moments before it takes off again – a
truly magical sight. Despite the grim conditions, I find myself
grinning at nothing in particular, and Caroline, up front
chatting to Guy, looks like she's having the time of her life. I
remember, with a rush of affection, why I enjoy cycling with
her so much: unfailingly stoic, with a sense of humour that's
drier than a dead dingo's donger,* she's pedalled through worse
weather in the Hebrides and we've both still come out giggling
at ourselves. Or, more often, each other.

---

* Can you tell I watched a lot of *Married at First Sight Australia* during
   lockdown?

The gently swooping lanes of Wiltshire become hillier as we approach Bath, narrower and more closed in by trees. Rain is dripping steadily from the tip of my nose, and I've got the beginnings of a headache, always a sure sign that the cap I wear inside my helmet – Allez! this one says, somewhat incongruously – is beginning to shrink around my skull. It's with no little relief that I spy signs for the Kennet and Avon Canal: towpaths, like old railway lines, are reliably flat things, and this blessed one takes us, via various honey-stone tunnels and bridges, right into the centre of Bath (which, today, aptly, appears to be entirely full of water).

Our knight in shining armour, refusing all offers of a drink, soggily peels off in the direction of the station to make his way home, and Caroline and I point ourselves in the direction of ours for the night, the YHA hostel, ominously situated on Bathwick Hill. Or, more accurately, up Bathwick Hill ('What is this, Ben fucking Nevis?' Caroline grumbles behind me), though the hostel itself is so absurdly grand it's almost worth the climb. Only in Bath could your £14.50 bunk bed be in an Italianate villa – and thanks to Covid restrictions, we have a six-person dorm all to ourselves.

Having stowed the bikes in a shed crammed with laundry awaiting collection, we turn the heating up, spread our soaking kit out on the empty bunks to dry, and lie spread-eagled on the carpet, filthy but happy, eating Caroline's Emergency Saucisson and drinking damson gin from my hipflask – and as ever in such situations, nothing, at this exact moment, could taste any better.

By the time we've mustered the energy to go out and forage for dinner, it's finally stopped raining, and the beauty of Bath is laid out in front of us, shyly glowing in the evening sunshine. Last time I was here it was to review an excellent vegan restaurant, but Caroline's Gallic honk when I tentatively mention this fact is enough to steer us in the direction of the nearest pub, whose sole draw is the fact that it has a free table and can serve us cold beer and hot chips. Those necessities despatched, we find a better pub. In fact, it may be the best pub full stop, and I do not say those words lightly.

The Star Inn, which we stumble across quite by accident, has been in business since the seventeenth century, and it seems entirely possible that the man on a wooden settle by the bar has been there even longer; with his long grey beard, Simon looks disconcertingly like a Druid. When I return from the loo, he's cheerfully informing Caroline that the bench is known as 'death row' because it's where all the old boys sit: 'The closer you are to the bar the closer you are to creating a vacancy, if you understand me.'

There are three Simons in tonight, he helpfully adds after introducing himself, lest we should lose him in this tiny rabbit warren of a place – 'though he doesn't count, that one over there. He's a fruit bat.' The fruit bat, who is holding court to a largely silent, and possibly non-consensual, companion in the adjoining room, appears wholly human, if somewhat lightly furnished in the dental department.

Thanking Simon No.1 for this advice, we take our pints of Bellringer, brewed a few hundred yards away, and packets of Golden Wonder to a little table in the snug, a safe distance from the fruit bat and his strong opinions on smartphones, and sneakily google restaurants – it's almost nine o'clock, and this is the kind of pub that actively prides itself on not doing food. Barely 90 minutes later, having consumed our weight in kebabs and naan, I'm smug in my bunk bed, feeling a lot less anxious than I did this morning. The adventure is under way. There's no going back now.

Digging our bikes out of an overnight avalanche of dirty linen, we career back down the terrifying hill to the much-recommended Landrace Bakery for warm, sticky cardamom buns. Sunning ourselves on a bench outside, we bump into baker, food writer and *Great British Bake Off* quarter-finalist Benjamina Ebuehi – here, she says, on a little solo mini-break.

Shyly, I ask her about Bath's most famous baked good, the Sally Lunn bun, which I'm hoping to make our second break-fast, and she shakes her head, laughing. 'I was so disappointed! It's LITERALLY A ROLL.'

Undaunted (because I always kind of think I know best about everything anyway), I insist to Caroline we see for ourselves at Sally's eponymous tea shop in one of the oldest houses in Bath, where they've been serving up literally rolls since 1680. (To be fair, the menu concedes bun is 'an unhelpful description. There is no truly useful common English word to describe a Sally Lunn bun as it is part bun, part bread, part cake . . . A large and generous but very very light bun; a little like brioche.')

After the hip Landrace, the panelled tearoom, with its open fireplace and decorative china, is more like the self-consciously quaint Bath I'm more familiar with, but the thing identifying as a bun is unexpectedly delicious. Yes, it's plain, but it's also soft and surprisingly light, and comes slathered in so much salty butter that it leaves a puddle on the plate below. It may taste like an anachronism in this Instagram age, but quite honestly I find the less-is-more approach rather restful.

Caroline comes back from the loo smirking. 'Mate, you've got to go downstairs, there's an amazing museum.' Obediently I clip-clop down and find a couple of dusty and faintly terrifying mannequins engaged in bun production in the cellar kitchen. Opposite, a mummified archaeologist is peering into an ancient oven with, and this is a nice touch, a packed lunch of Wotsits and sandwiches waiting for him on the side. As I wait to go back up, I wonder to myself how often they replace the Wotsits.

—•◆•—

Fortified by this two-carb breakfast, we leave Bath and head west, through carpets of wild garlic and long, dark, drippy railway tunnels, heading for Glastonbury, where I've booked a campsite for the evening.

We haven't been cycling more than 45 minutes when, coming down a single-track lane, hedged about with cow parsley at its majestic peak, I spot an exciting sign for a bona fide Ancient Monument. Enjoying the luxury of being in no particular hurry, I wheel Eddy across a little wooden bridge in the direction it indicates, while Caroline attempts to befriend the horses in the neighbouring field.

The Stoney Littleton long barrow (which I later discover is one of the country's finest neolithic tombs) isn't immediately visible from the other bank of the stream, and I'm certainly not wearing the right shoes for clambering around in muddy fields, so I regretfully turn back. Unfortunately, it turns out I'm also not wearing the right shoes for falling off a bridge. Coming off the other side, I step onto a deceptively trustworthy-looking tuft of grass and plummet downwards, coming to a halt with one foot wedged in the slats of the bridge and the other dangling in the weeds several feet below. The splits are not a position my legs have found themselves in for a while, and I feel something in my bum snap in protest as my left foot hits cold water, and then a blow to the chest as Eddy tumbles on top of me.

There's an agonising pause, and then a high, squeaky OH MY GOD! and the sound of running feet. Caroline's horrified head appears. I reassure her I'm alive – but realise I have absolutely no idea if I can move. 'Just give me a minute,' I say as she lifts poor Eddy clear. Thirty seconds of deep breathing later, I ask her to take off the shoe high above my head so I can return my legs to their more natural parallel state, and she then hauls me up the bank, where I lie on my stomach like a beached whale in a Marmite jersey, laughing slightly hysterically at the ridiculousness of it all, and wondering, with detached curiosity, if this is game over already.

Something definitely hurts, but it doesn't feel terminal, so after a few minutes of listening to Caroline recount the terrifying moments between hearing a muffled squawk, and working out where I'd gone – 'All I could see was the bike, mate!' – I gingerly regain the vertical, and put myself back on board. Pedalling is just about bearable but, I quickly discover, putting any more strain on the top of my right hamstring – by going uphill, for example, or failing to unclip my foot from the pedal fast enough when I stop – is agony. I begin to feel nervous at the mere possibility of braking.

This anxiety prompts my next fall, in front of a goggling queue of stationary cars, as I slam them on too fast and topple, still clipped in, into a viciously spiky bush. Caroline picks me up for the second time in an hour, and, though now shaking like a jelly, I insist I'm fine apart from a few scratches and a large brown thorn sticking out of the stout padded material of my glove.

It's easily and cleanly removed, and though the area feels strangely bruised, I'm more immediately concerned with the new claw-like slashes across my bare shins. When we stop at a café, I swap my clip-in shoes for ordinary trainers – not being attached to Eddy feels safer in the circumstances – and, loading up on provisions at Waitrose in Wells, pop a packet of ibuprofen in the basket on top of a medicinal gin in a tin.

Panniers bursting with ham, bread and cheese, and with a bottle of wine strapped precariously on top of Caroline's bag, we wiggle through the Somerset Levels (which aren't, my hamstring informs me, entirely level) towards Glastonbury Tor, sticking out of the landscape like a green pyramid, the late-afternoon light golden on the lush grass and lichen-clad stone walls of the West Country.

Though I've booked and paid in advance, I can't rouse anyone at the house opposite the lumpy field that apparently serves as the campsite, so we pitch in the least sodden spot we can find, reminiscing about the disastrous night we spent wild camping on Benbecula in a proper Scottish gale, and shiver our way through our picnic, watched by fellow campers, snug and smug in their cars. As the sun sinks below the Tor it becomes increasingly chilly, and, barely able to string a sentence together, I retire to my sleeping bag in full Hebridean woolly hat, coat and snood. It's not even properly dark yet but I'm soon out cold.

———◆———

I do not sleep well, and am woken at 5.30 a.m. by what sounds like heavy rain, but – I touch the side of the tent – isn't. The noise is repeated an hour and a half later, at which point I stick my bleary head out, grimacing at the pain in my bum, and spot a black-and-white train of Friesians returning from their morning milking on the other side of the hedge. As I wincingly bend down to pull out my tent pegs, Caroline notices the thorn puncture wound in my wrist is red and swollen, and makes me promise to consult a chemist in Glastonbury – 'before breakfast', she says firmly.

Thankfully, alongside the many and varied alternative health practitioners in that world-famous festival town is a comfortingly prosaic branch of Boots, not far from the Chocolate Love

Temple and the Wonky Broomstick wicca store. The pharmacist takes one look at the offending area and directs me straight to the cottage hospital. I'm grateful that Caroline, who's declared herself a 'semi-professional medic' due to her close friendship with various formally qualified examples, allows me to have my breakfast first.

She comes back from a scouting mission down a narrow passageway incredulous. 'Everyone in the café turned and stared at me when I went in there wearing a mask,' she reports, 'but we can sit in the courtyard.' Despite the definite scarcity of legally required face coverings, the vegan breakfast (hash browns, beans, tomatoes, lightly sautéed spinach, mushrooms, sausages of unknown but reassuringly plant-based origin) is actually pretty good, especially with a dollop of Guy's mustard to lift it. I treat myself to an allegedly anti-inflammatory 'turmeric latte' alongside my double espresso as Caroline busies herself attempting to book flights back to France to see her family for the first time in over a year.

'DONE!' She slams her phone down on the table. I frown at her.

'What?'

In response, I swivel my eyes meaningfully left, in the direction of four women who have been slagging off the concept of vaccination for the past ten minutes. One of them, who is breastfeeding a large and chatty child, is of the opinion that Bill Gates isn't all he's cracked up to be. 'You have to ask yourself, why is he doing this?' she says to general murmurs of agreement.

Having never knowingly been in the presence of such convinced anti-vaxxers before, I'm fascinated, even when they move on to the importance of allowing toddlers to express themselves by choosing their own haircuts. As we pay, Caroline tells me a woman on the table behind them, wearing a sweatshirt branded 'SELF LOVE', has been sobbing quietly to herself for the last 20 minutes.

Even the two hours I spend waiting to be seen in the West Mendip Community Hospital are anything but dull thanks to the constant stream of traffic in the direction of the vaccination centre. One visitor, asked for his name, merrily shouts 'MATT HANCOCK!' Heads swivel in all directions as we try to get a look at a small, round person whose only similarity to the current Health Secretary is that he appears to be a man.

'Ooh, you had me there for a minute, my lovely!' the volunteer chuckles. 'Just down the corridor to the right.'

When I'm finally called in, to a room with an Eye of Horus sticker on the back of the door, the kindly nurse swiftly identifies a blackthorn wound (notorious, it seems, for becoming infected – to think of all the sloes I've gaily gathered over the years for gin, never realising the danger!) and sends me off with some antibiotics and many good wishes for the rest of the trip.

It feels like a new start, though having planned to cycle all the way to Exeter, where we're meeting a butter maker tomorrow morning, we have to cut short the expedition at Taunton at half six and train it the rest of the way; in fact, when we arrive at the coaching inn where we're staying for the night they strongly recommend we book a table for dinner immediately. 'Everywhere's just mad at the moment.' The empty pub when we come back down suggests this may be a creative interpretation of the truth, but just as I'm about to start my pint, Caroline, who is taking her role as team medic very seriously, demands to see my wrist. 'Oh my God, mate,' she says, taking a photo of it. 'I think it's tracking.'

'Tracking' sounds to me a rather sinister word for the faint pink line on my pallid arm, but she's already sent the picture to her friend, a nurse, who, without even waiting for any explanation of this random piece of flesh that's just arrived on her screen, replies, 'A&E now.' I demur, but Nurse Craig doesn't even let me finish my cider – I have to go straight back up to the room, collect a book and a phone charger and get a cab (alone – patients only at the hospital thanks to Covid) to the Royal Devon with a driver who wants to tell me how dangerous cycling is, a sentiment I'm unable to argue with. I'm tired, I'm hungry, and I'm really quite nervous, both about the looming prospect of almost certain death and the possibility of wasting the doctor's time. The only comfort I take, as I stand in the queue between a woman sobbing hysterically and a man whose entire hand is wrapped in a blood-red tea towel, is, well, at least it's all good copy.

Ridden: 167.72km
Climbed: 1,393m
Breakfasts eaten: 4 (smashed avo on activated
charcoal toast; cardamom bun;
buttered Sally Lunn bun; vegan fry-up)

RED SAUCE OR BROWN?

Caroline: 'Brown sauce, mate – ketchup is for chips. End of.'

Guy: 'In my book the quintessential accompaniment for a bacon butty is brown sauce – not any old brown sauce obvs! But when it comes to a Full English I can be persuaded to go with a proper tomato ketchup.'

Benjamina: 'For me, it's always going to be HP!'

2
EXETER TO PLYMOUTH
Butter

If I tried to tell you all the different ways butter was made in England, there would be room for nothing else in this book.
– Dorothy Hartley, *Food in England* (1954)

Having been fortunate enough not to spend a great deal of time in hospital, I'm unable to say for sure if the Royal Devon is particularly chaotic because of the Covid pandemic, but the challenge of trying to keep the statutory metre apart in a busy Accident and Emergency department certainly feels like it adds an extra frisson to proceedings.

On the plus side, I get a new mask, because my cloth one apparently isn't up to snuff. On the minus side, the receptionist is so busy inspecting masks she fails to actually book me in, which means that, after almost three hours, and starting to feel slightly shivery and faint (a symptom I both worry and hope is psychosomatic), I go up to the desk again and discover, as they have no record of me, I'm still at the back of the queue. To my lasting shame, I start to weep as I trudge back to my wobbly plastic chair. (Look, it's been a long evening, and my sister, who is messaging me at ever-decreasing intervals, appears to be genuinely convinced I'm going to die.)

At least this time I do get triaged within 20 minutes, courtesy of a brisk nurse who draws round the swelling with a biro and says it'll probably be another three and a half hours to see a doctor, and I can go home if I want, it's my decision. She shrugs. Feeling more like a fraud than ever, I take the advice of a doctor friend who reckons if I've waited this long I may as well actually get seen, and sit back down, treating myself to a bag of Wheat Crunchies from the vending machine, which is the only catering available. Even the coffee machine is out of order.

At 2.10 a.m., I'm called in, and the same nurse, looking impressed with my stubbornness if not my life-threatening condition, comes and kindly offers me a cup of tea. At 2.33 a.m. a very nice doctor arrives, interrupting the drama in a neighbouring cubicle where a teenage boy is explaining, in front of his mother and a doctor clearly doing his best not to laugh, how he sustained an awkwardly intimate injury in the shower.

Feeling foolish, I show her my wrist, which now looks somewhat less dramatic, and worried I'm mainly presenting as a hypochondriac, hurriedly find the photo that provoked such alarm in a nurse 200 miles away. She agrees it doesn't look very happy (though she may well just be humouring me) and sends me away with some stronger antibiotics. When I arrive back at the inn at 3.10 a.m., Caroline is fast asleep, a bin full of sad Chinese takeaway boxes outside the door.

Three hours later, the team doctor, having examined my wrist, which already looks more like its normal size thanks to the new drugs, pronounces herself satisfied that we can proceed. This is fortunate given that we have an 8 a.m. appointment with a butter producer in a village Google claims is a

32-minute ride outside Exeter (but is, in fact, more like 50) and which has already been pushed back from 7 a.m. at my request.

The reason it's so early is because that's when Quicke's make their butter, and by the time we finally turn up, 20 minutes late and frazzled from the aggressive rush-hour traffic, it's uncomfortably clear we've already held things up. But, much as I'd prefer to be in bed, you can't have breakfast without butter – the unsung hero of the plate. Toast is nothing without it, crumpets may as well not bother, even scrambled eggs are substandard with anything else. A knob is a happy addition to kippers and porridge, and the quickest way to improve a tin of baked beans . . . which is possibly the only cooking tip I've ever got from my brother. I suppose you'd get away with a butter-free bowl of cereal in extremis, but that's about the limit.

Tea Break: BUTTER

In simple terms, butter is just concentrated cream – the lower water content acts as a preservative, which means it's been made for as long as humans have kept dairy animals (though the ancient Greeks seem to have spread it on themselves, rather than their bread).

Cream is an emulsion of fat globules in water. When it's churned, these globules clump together into a solid mass floating in a watery liquid called buttermilk. That mass, drained and rinsed, is butter.

Though you can make butter from fresh cream, culturing it, or adding bacteria to convert some of its lactose sugars into lactic acid, will yield a more complex flavour – fresh cream butters are straightforwardly clean and milky, fermented ones might be tangy, or even faintly cheesy.

Salt was traditionally added to butter to improve its keeping qualities, which is why unsalted butter was once the preserve of the wealthy, who could afford to take the risk. These days, it's merely a matter of taste. (I prefer salted butter, though I admit cold sweet – as unsalted butter is traditionally known – butter is good on bread with salted anchovies and wafer-thin slices of onion.)

Clarified butter, which has been heated to separate out the milk solids (which spoil fast) from pure fat (which doesn't), keeps even better, which is why it's used to seal preserves like pâté and potted shrimps.

❖ ❖

Mary Quicke, the fourteenth generation of her family to farm this land, is not a woman to stand still listening to excuses about A&E – the efficiency with which she bustles us into our protective coats and hairnets explains, at least in part, how she's made such a success of the cheese business since taking it over from her mother, Prue, almost four decades ago. Not only has Quicke's clothbound Cheddar (which royal cheesemonger Paxton & Whitfield describes as 'rich and buttery [with an] outstanding depth of flavour') won a whole cupboard full of awards, but Mary herself boasts everything from an MBE to a 2019 Dairy Industry Woman of the Year gong.

Caroline and I scurry like contrite ducklings in her majestic wake across the yard as she tells us, talking as rapidly as she walks, that as soon as the farm began producing cheese again in the 1970s, her mother started making butter to subsidise it. Unlike Cheddar, which takes time to mature, butter could be sold immediately – 'in the old days,' she explains, 'the butter paid the cheesemaker's wages'.

Interestingly the physical act of cheesemaking, especially when large truckles of solid Cheddar are involved, is still a fairly male business, but butter, she says with a distinct note of satisfaction, tends to be made by women: 'The guys can do the paddling of course, but they're not as . . . patient.'

Quicke's, we discover, make their butter from whey, rather than fresh cream, once common practice in areas such as Lancashire and the West Country, using the watery liquid left over from the cheesemaking process. Because the milk has been 'cultured' – had a starter culture of bacteria added to it to begin the fermentation that will eventually turn it into cheese – it brings 'different and more complex flavours' to the resulting butter. 'To me,' Mary muses, 'it's almost nutty.'

CULTURED BUTTER

A satisfying little kitchen project; you can make this as strongly tangy or as mild as you like, and add other flavourings like chilli, seaweed and so on as suits your fancy (though if you'd prefer an even simpler uncultured butter, omit the yoghurt stage and start from step 2).

(If you happen to have whey left over from some other culinary endeavour, leave it to sit until a thick cream has risen to the top and use that, starting from step 2. Unless you have a lot of whey, however, I must warn you, you'll probably end up with quite a small amount of butter.)

Makes 1 × 200g pat
400ml double cream, at room temperature
2 tbsp live natural yoghurt
½ tsp flaky sea salt, or to taste

1 Put the cream and yoghurt into a large bowl (I use the bowl of a stand mixer, as I use it in the next step) and briefly whisk together. Cover, and leave in a warmish (comfortable room temperature is fine) place for 24–48 hours, depending on how strong you'd like the cultured flavouring, until thick and tangy and slightly sour-smelling.

2 Whisk the cream at a medium-low speed, either in a mixer or by hand (this is very much possible, but will take a while), scraping down the sides of the bowl as necessary, until it separates into a solid mass and milky liquid. Alternatively, shake it in a large jar until the same effect is achieved.

3 Once you have a solid clump of butter, drain it (keep the buttermilk to make soda farls (page 167) or pikelets (page 265), or drink it), then rinse it well under cold running water, squidging it with your hands to get as much butter-milk out as possible; the more you leave in the quicker it will spoil, so it's worth spending time on this step.

4 Knead in the salt to taste (½ teaspoon will give quite a salty result, so reduce it if you're less of a fan), then put the butter in the middle of a rectangle of parchment paper about 30cm wide. Using your hands, a spatula or butter paddles, beat into a flat rectangle about 12cm wide, then use the paper to roll up the rectangle into a sausage and twist the ends to seal.

Tracy – 'the Butter Lady!' as she introduces herself above the noise of a stainless-steel churn that sounds like a tumble dryer full of trainers – is apparently unperturbed to find a couple of women in Lycra shorts and paper coats popping in to watch her at work. Far from being born with a wooden paddle in her hand, Mary informs us that Tracy was a manager at Morrisons until the supermarket shed a layer of staff. 'She was recruited by someone who plays with her in the local darts team.'

'The boys pour the cream into the churn for me,' Tracy explains, 'which is a big help.' She adds water to bring the temperature inside to about 14°C (though in the summer she prefers it cooler, otherwise everything becomes a sticky mess) and then switches it on.

A sturdy lever indicates the churn's two speeds: fast, to 'break' the cream, and slow, to knead the solid butter that results. On it judders until the whey divides into butter solids and buttermilk – there's a little window in the side but Tracy says she doesn't really need to use it: 'I can hear it when it breaks, the noise changes.' Even I can sense the rumble becoming more liquid, swishy even, at which point the buttermilk is drained off (no market for it really, Mary says sadly, offering us a glass), and the solid butterfat is ready to be rinsed with cold water, kneaded and salted; 'not too much though, we want you to taste the butter'.

By this point, with a moisture content of just 12 per cent, the butter in the churn looks almost fluffy – possibly it's just last night's Wheat Crunchies wearing off, but I can't stop picking bits off the little cloud Mary has put in front of us as we talk. Unlike more provokingly tangy cultured butters I've tried, Quicke's version has a pure, sweet flavour, in keeping with Mary's desire that it taste as 'buttery' as possible: not cheesy, not sour, just 'of itself'.

Without warning, she moves the plate away from my greedy fingers – apparently it's time for us to take over from Tracy, who's moved on to deftly bashing little portions of fluff flat with two wooden paddles before curling it up, whacking it down and finally rolling it up into an elegant spiral of perfect yellow butter. ('That colour is because our cows are out on grass all the time,' Mary interjects. 'Paler butters often come from cows fed on maize.')

I watch Caroline, who proves annoyingly adept, turning out an almost perfect roll first time, and then confidently step up to produce something that appears to have been stepped on, possibly by a large cow. 'I only had three hours' sleep,' I say defensively, hiding it behind Tracy's. I'm kind of hoping it's so bad we might get to take it away with us to eat for breakfast, but it's still sitting there as we leave, a lasting record of my ineptitude.

Mary recommends we head to the busy little town of Crediton to eat. Still mourning the butter, which I could murder on a Sally Lunn right now, I tuck into baked beans on Marmite toast (definitely margarine on this, mate, Caroline says darkly) at a café on the market square. This is my default choice when the meat on offer is of unknown and unpromising provenance, and rarely fails to hit the spot, even when the toast is floppy and the beans insufficiently reduced in the pan, though this particular example is rescued by the deeply savoury Marmite, a special request that can usually be honoured by even the meanest British café.

We sit for a while in a sleep-deprived, carb-deadened trance listening to a folk duo playing Harry Belafonte's 'Day-O' to a small audience of unimpressed pensioners – possibly, we decide, it's hard to identify with the hardships of the banana business in rural Devon – before pushing on south towards Dartmoor, stopping for a ploughman's, a cider and a quick snooze in a pub garden on the edge of the moors in order to fortify ourselves for polite company.

'I'm not drunk,' I say to the waiter rather defensively when he comes to clear our plates and finds us both lying on the grass, 'just tired.' He shrugs. 'Do what you want, my lovely. No business of mine.'

—•◆•—

Thankfully we have two rest days ahead with my friends Lucy and Ned at their house near Chagford. This plan had seemed recklessly decadent so early in the trip, but now feels much needed given that I can barely manage any slope over about 5 per cent without an involuntary, but rather performative-sounding, squeak thanks to my unhappy hamstring. The rutted ski slope of a lane up to their house proves particularly problematic – I'm almost relieved to be driven into a hedge by a horsebox so I can finally get off and push.

My irritation melts away when we're met by a freshly made mojito and a slightly suspicious toddler. Juliet wasn't even a twinkle in her mummy's eye when Ned and Lucy joined me in Burgundy for my last book. As they moved down to Devon shortly before her birth, I've only met her once, on New Year's Eve 2019, when, at seven months old, she stole the lime out of my gin and tonic with a glorious gummy grin, but she's still a charmer ... once she's made peace with us pitching camp in the garden next to her play tent.

Given the past 36 hours it's bliss – I drift off, after a vast dinner, to the soft hooting of a distant owl, and wake late, or as late as you can sleep in a tent with the smell of bacon somewhere nearby. I follow it into the kitchen to find Ned has taken his duty to show me a proper West Country breakfast very seriously indeed.

As well as bacon, and the usual complement of eggs, tomatoes and beans, he's prepared local speciality hog's pudding and, to my surprise, a vast dish of macaroni cheese. He explains that macaroni cheese with roast potatoes and peas was one of the staples of his dad's repertoire when he was growing up – 'I loved it so much I asked for it for my birthday tea one year' – and that the family would have the leftovers with bacon for breakfast. Today, he's made a batch just for me. I'm absurdly touched.

Much as I love fried pasta at any time of day, however, it's the hog's pudding, another of his dad's signature meals, that I get really excited about. A cooked pork sausage that's somewhat spicier, in general, than the white puddings of Scotland and Ireland, hog's pudding is often claimed as a Cornish product, though in fact, like the county's signature pasty, it was probably once made far more widely, and is certainly still produced here in Ned's native Devon.

I regret the shrinking of the hog's territory because it's utterly delicious; fattier and saltier than black pudding, with a creamy richness offset by the warmth of the pepper, cloves and nutmeg. I'm privileged to witness Juliet try her first piece, dunked in copious amounts of ketchup. I stubbornly stick with my Tewkesbury mustard.

Between a trip to the village for hokey pokey ice cream, and a bracing dip in the River Teign, my other favourite riding companion Gemma arrives from Birmingham to join the peloton and keep Caroline on her toes. Since accompanying me through Alsace on an old mountain bike three years ago she's got into cycling in a big way, by which I mean she can quite happily sit on a static trainer in her kitchen for four hours pedalling her way up a virtual mountain. Having quickly established she did not get off and push on the hill outside, I'm immediately moved to show her my wrist, now merely bruised-looking thanks to the antibiotics, and tell her the story of my dramatic fall from the bridge. She turns to Caroline: 'I can't believe you didn't film it.'

I could stay here forever, being looked after by Ned and Lucy and watching Juliet lurch around the garden shouting at birds, but Gemma has not come to sit around drinking, nobly as she has borne it thus far, and I have a date with a hog's pudding producer 150km away in two days' time, so reluctantly, we roll up our sleeping bags.

Panniers on, Caroline's surprise puncture deftly repaired by Ned, Lucy plonks a pile of sausage sandwiches on the table, explaining that a friend asked if they could store a pig in her freezer, 'so I think we're allowed to eat some of it'. I note ketchup is being applied with rather more gusto than brown sauce by my fellow diners so, feeling sorry for the underdog, I dollop some on my plate, and find its spicy sweetness rather good with the salty, slightly charred meat. Not quite as nice as mustard, perhaps, but that's already been packed away.

—◆—

Our route to the coast takes us across Dartmoor itself, via the Miniature Pony Centre, where the hairy little inmates, lolling around underneath a tree, give me a sudden pang of longing for the hairy little dog – no doubt, at 11 a.m., still lolling around on Kaj's bed instead.

Waiting for Caroline and me at the top of the climb onto the moor, Gemma falls into conversation with a motorist on his way from Shrewsbury to the south coast. He tells us he and his family sat in traffic for four hours coming into Weston-super-Mare yesterday, and yet still can't resist the inevitable driver's quip as we pedal off – 'it's a lot easier in a car, you know!'

Less fun though; and this bit is a lot of fun, the wide open roads dancing us across the top of the moor, screaming with pleasure on the sweeping descents. We stop for a half at the third highest inn in England, pass the prison, still grim and grey, even in the sunshine, then freewheel down almost all the way to the sea.

The final stretch, riding into Plymouth along the old Plym Valley railway, is the same Caroline and I took last summer when we rode from coast to coast – we're even staying in the same chain hotel, Plymouth being short on characterful budget options in early summer. Last time we were here, as Caroline is quick to recall, I toppled over onto the pavement in front of the entrance. Keen to disabuse Gemma of the notion that I do this a lot, I hotly point out that it was because the cleat on the bottom of my shoe had become wedged in the pedal.

Fortunately thanks to my hamstring I'm in trainers today, a fact that makes me feel rather out of place when we head out for fish and chips. Plymouth is hopping this Sunday evening – the pubs around the marina throbbing with bass, everyone dressed up to the nines . . . and I wouldn't join them for all the tea in China. Instead, with an early start, and many miles through Cornwall on the cards tomorrow, Gemma, who seems to have assumed control of the situation to my quiet relief (I am not a born manager), suggests we lay in some supplies for a pre-dawn breakfast.

'You mean a first breakfast, right?' I say anxiously, buzzing around a Tesco Metro like a trapped fly. 'We'll stop again once we're on the road?'

She sighs. 'Just buy the bloody malt loaf.'

Ridden: 101.3km
Climbed: 1,630m
Breakfasts eaten: 3 (beans on Marmite toast;
full fry with hog's pudding and macaroni cheese;
sausage sandwiches)

RED SAUCE OR BROWN?

Mary: 'Neither, thank you: lots of Quicke's Whey Butter on the bread so that it lusciously melts when you put the bacon in.'

Tracy: 'Ketchup.'

Ned: 'Juliet and I are definitely on the red team; Lucy, I'm not sure . . . she does have brown with sausages . . .'

Lucy: 'I'm team red, but as Ned says, with the exception of a sausage and onion sandwich, for which I have 50/50.'

3

PLYMOUTH TO FALMOUTH
Hog's Pudding

*This morning I went to Sir W. Batten's about going to Deptford
to-morrow, and so eating some hog's pudding of my Lady's making,
of the hog that I saw a fattening the other day at her house.*
– From the diary of Samuel Pepys, 11 November 1660

No one speaks when the alarm goes off at 6 a.m. Plymouth is silent and though we were in bed by half ten, it still feels distinctly like the middle of the night. This feeling is not helped by the uneasy knowledge of today's ambitious route, across the Tamar, and down two-thirds of the south-Cornish coast in pursuit of a pudding. It involves three ferries, and should we miss the last one from St Mawes, we'll add a bonus three further hours to our ride. I'm afraid to say that, much as I love Cornwall, I am not excited by the prospect.

Gulping down muddy instant coffee and gummy malt loaf, I try not to think about the county's vertiginous villages and stunning cliffs; such things, so pleasingly dramatic on foot, hold less charm on a fully laden bike with an angry hamstring. Beggars can't be choosers, however, and having decided to take on one of the country's most popular tourist destinations during a half term when it's all but impossible to go abroad, and a fortnight before the G7 summit in Carbis Bay, I must pay the price in pain. We have beds at Gemma's parents' house in Falmouth, and by hook or by crook, that's where we'll be this evening. What time this evening, however, is less clear.

On the plus side, my wrist, though still a slightly unusual colour, has finally lost the tight, bruised feeling that made gripping the handlebars so uncomfortable, and it's bright and sunny as we head out to meet our fate. The roads are quiet, and the Torpoint ferry, a chain-link affair that hauls passengers across the Tamar river into Cornwall, turns out to be free for cyclists; a small but gratifying surprise.

The first few miles on the other side are unremarkable apart from Gemma falling off her bike while stationary, surprised by the first car we've seen for 10 minutes, which appears from nowhere as we stop to check the map in the tiny village of Antony. (The driver waits for her to pick herself up from the tarmac, then leans out of the window and says, 'You don't want to be doing that. You're supposed to be upright on them things,' chuckles at her own wit, and drives off. Fortunately Gemma's fine . . . or at least she claims to be; it's hard to tell with someone who eats injuries for breakfast before running an ultra marathon on them.) Second rule of cycle touring, Caroline intones solemnly from behind: there's always a bloody car.

The view, however, is beyond reproach: improbably blue skies, green tussocky fields hedged about with sticky goose-grass, pink vetch and dog roses, and a tormentingly calm, ink-dark sea that looks almost within touching distance as it shimmers far below us. It's already hot enough that we've all shed every layer going by the time we stop in Looe for a second breakfast. I order beans on toast (no Marmite, and I can't summon the energy to retrieve the jar from my bag, but the white toast is generously buttered, and they get points for putting one slice under the beans and the other off to the side, which almost makes it two meals in one), a double espresso and a chocolate milkshake. It's only 9.15, but we've already been going three hours and, somehow, barely covered 30km.

Coming out of Looe, we hit an unnecessarily unpleasant climb: both narrow, closed in on both sides by houses from which people emerge without warning, and so steep that it's impossible to see what's coming. I'm just about to admit defeat when a man walking his dog downhill says, 'Waoh, verrrry impressive, ladies,' in a thick Italian accent, which means I have to pant onwards for several metres before grabbing desperately at a wall for support, and then dismounting. Caroline carries on for a few more, but even Gemma is finally defeated by a bin lorry blocking our path, and we push up the steepest bit as a cross, sweaty trio.

The pay-off is that it's extremely pleasant to emerge from this humid humiliation and find ourselves sailing towards our second ferry of the day, which comes with trauma of the inverse variety, an absurd descent into Polruan, complete with a 16-per-cent gradient and crowds of happy holidaymakers thronging the road, oblivious, perhaps fortunately, to the fact that I couldn't stop if I wanted to. I resign myself to the fact that I'm going to end up in the harbour with a toddler attached to my handlebars, but end up merely scattering the queue for the boat, which flees obligingly in terror from my somewhat rapid approach.

This is not a ride-on, ride-off sort of ferry – the bikes have to be carted down some slippery stone steps and I'm glad I'm not in cycling cleats – but only the most jaded of souls could fail to smile at being on the water among so many jauntily bobbing dinghies. Grinding slowly back up the cliff on the other side I notice pedestrians, strolling along on their two perfectly functional feet, looking at us like we're mad, an opinion I must say I have some sympathy with.

We stop for lunch in St Austell, one of the largest towns in Cornwall, and known to me mostly because of its brewery, which is closed to visitors because of the pandemic. Instead we sit and have a pasty and a can of Lilt in the shopping precinct and Caroline enquires tentatively about our progress (I've been too scared to check). Gemma shows her the map. 'Oh, we're nearly there!' she says happily, lying back down on the bench. 'Only a couple of hours left.'

'That's a couple of hours of solid cycling,' Gemma says sternly. 'It doesn't include stopping every 10 minutes to have a piece of fudge.' Chastened, I offer the bag round now instead: if we don't make it to St Mawes in time to get the boat to Falmouth, we're going to have to ride the long way round, but either way I'm going to need all the help I can get.

Racing against the clock, we are not amused when Our Graham, as we've christened Komoot Man,* directs us across an actual beach near Pendowan. Having dragged Eddy through the dunes with very bad grace (for which I must belatedly apologise to Gemma, whose only crime was to volunteer to go in front), it's all worth it when road signs finally suggest – though I hardly dare look too closely at them – we're on the Roseland Peninsula. I happen to know that at the end of the Roseland Peninsula sits St Mawes. I only wish I also knew how big it was.

Still pedalling furiously, unsure how busy the ferry will be at the end of a sunny half-term afternoon, I note the increasing

---

*   My navigation app of choice. Sometimes I still cheat on Graham with Google, but he's much better at finding quiet roads that are roads, not footpaths or sets of steps, so I generally regret it.

frequency of white-washed stone cottages by the roadside. An empty horizon promises the sea somewhere ahead. There's a flash of blue glimpsed over a five-bar gate, a sharp right and we're twisting down through the steep streets of a little fishing village – but this time I'm relaxed about the whole braking thing because I can almost smell the gin and tonics from here.

Kind dads in bright chino shorts and pristine deck shoes compete to carry our bikes and bags down onto the busy Falmouth ferry, and soon we're stowed safely in the otherwise empty cabin. I'm sure the view from the deck is great, but all we want to do right now is lie supine on the wooden benches and talk about all the different ways things could have gone wrong but somehow didn't.

A warm welcome, a cold gin and tonic and a hot shower await us at Gemma's parents' house – in that order. The bikes go into the garage, and although it's only been a couple of days since we left Ned and Lucy's, I'm delighted to give them, and my legs, a rest.

—•◆•—

The first day of June dawns grey and drizzly, but, high on shots of Rosemullion Cornish spirit last night, Caroline and I publicly announced our intention to swim, and honour demands we both pretend we're still pumped about the prospect. 'After all, you never regret a swim,' I say brightly, with more conviction than I feel. Gemma and her mum Pam come down to the beach with us, huddled in fleeces; her dad John says he'll stay back to alert the RNLI if necessary.

Swanpool Beach, so blue and inviting the evening before, is looking a bit dull and choppy, and the only other swimmer is a large and enthusiastic golden retriever, who, I notice, is cheating in a fur coat. We waddle, squeaking, into the water (which isn't as cold as I'd feared) and immerse ourselves like fat, happy seals – I splash out to a buoy, rejoicing at how much easier swimming is than walking right now, turn round and see Caroline back on the beach shivering violently. As soon as I come out, so does the sun.

Annoying as this is timing wise, it does make breakfast on the Gylly Beach Café terrace more pleasant – naturally I order a full Cornish complete with hog's pudding from the very producer we're going to see this afternoon, served alongside her back bacon and chipolatas, baked beans, mushrooms, some shockingly yellow scrambled eggs and a rather delicious crispy potato cake. Bubble and squeak aside, I'm generally sceptical of the fried potato's ability to soak up grease (the main function of carbs in this context), but you can't deny they taste good.

I might have allowed the pallid pudding a little more time in a hot pan, but one bite confirms that yesterday's mammoth effort was not in vain. It's smooth and rich; milder and creamier than the Devon version served up by Ned, the spices more delicate – a quietly harmonious pairing with the buttery eggs in particular. They say the inner workings of sausages, like laws, are better not looked into too closely, but I can't wait to find out how these are made. To be honest, I'm not sure the other two are quite as excited; Gemma won't even try the stuff.

••

Tea Break:
THE PUDDINGS OF BRITAIN

To clarify, I do not mean the desserts of Britain, keen as I am on them, but pudding in the older sense, namely a collection of chopped items (meat, fish, cereals, pulses, vegetables – in fact, almost anything you can think of) simmered or steamed in a skin, cloth or pastry crust. It's a baggy grouping that includes everything from haggis to pease pudding, via steak and kidney and spotted dick, but you're only likely to come across a small handful on your breakfast plate:

- **Black pudding**, the best-known variety, is explored further in chapter 15. Often associated with the North West, black puddings are, according to *The Oxford Companion to Food*, 'probably the most ancient of all sausages and puddings' – they even get a mention in Homer – and were once made wherever people kept pigs. Even quite poor families might stretch to a single porker to keep them going through the winter, and not a single drop of the beast would have been wasted when her time came. Today, the most famous versions come from Bury in Lancashire – where, as well as the bleeding obvious (i.e. blood), they tend to use large chunks of back fat and plenty of pearl barley – and Storno-way, in the Outer Hebrides, where they go big on oats. As with all our sausages, British and Irish black puddings are unusual in their high cereal content. (Note, some black puddings, like the Irish Clonakilty, are made with cow's blood.)
- **White or mealie pudding**, which is basically black pudding, but with finely chopped meat and fat, generally pork, instead of blood. Found more in Ireland and Scotland than England and Wales.
- **Hog's or groats pudding**, a spiced variety of white pudding particularly associated with the West Country (though records suggest it used to be made more widely. That said, a Black Country groaty pudding is actually a beef stew).

- **Red pudding**, which is usually encountered encased in
  batter at chippies in the east of Scotland, and is more like a
  saveloy sausage, made from pork, pork rinds, suet, rusk and
  food colouring, and presented in a vivid red casing.
- **Fruit pudding**, another Scottish pudding, made from
  breadcrumbs or oatmeal, suet, dried fruit and spices. (I've
  found a 1930s Sussex hog's pudding containing currants, so
  this was clearly less unusual than it might sound to us now.)
- **Dock pudding**, a speciality of South Yorkshire and the
  Lakes, this vegetable porridge – made by cooking down
  bistort (a common meadow and hedgerow plant), nettles,
  onions and herbs into a purée, then adding oatmeal – is more
  like Welsh laverbread than any of the puddings mentioned
  above, and is usually served fried in bacon fat. It's only rarely
  seen for sale commercially, though a dock pudding festival is
  held in Mytholmroyd in the Calder Valley each spring.
- **Haggis**, which, though undoubtedly a pudding, I wouldn't
  have considered a breakfast item until I discovered that it
  pops up on many a fry north of the border. Made from
  sheep's pluck, or offal, minced up with oatmeal, onions,
  suet and plenty of pepper.

* *

We queue so long for a lunch of grilled mackerel baps on
Maenporth Beach, the fish blistered and deliciously charred,
the roll sweetish and generously buttered, that we end up
having to drive the 20km to our meeting with Primrose Herd
Pigs, purveyors of award-winning hog's puddings, rather than
cycling as planned. (Secretly, I'm rather relieved; being chauf-
feured by Gemma is considerably more pleasant than trying to
keep up with her on the bike.)

As passers-by are so fond of pointing out, things are indeed a lot quicker by car, but, we discover, it's also a lot harder to turn one round on a country road when you get lost. Sat nav isn't much use round here and we throw a few fun* 10-point turns on single-track lanes as one of us thinks we've spotted a pig, or the shape of an arc through the trees, 'Oh no, it's a cow, sorry.' Eventually I give up and ring Sally Lugg, Primrose Herd's founder and owner, who wearily guides Gemma into the farmyard.

Her exhaustion is not surprising when we discover she's been hard at work since 5 a.m. (could be worse, it's 4 a.m. on Fridays, when the deliveries go out, she adds quickly, lest we feel too sorry for her) and is likely to be here for a good few hours yet.

I'm grateful she's agreed to chat given how stressful life seems to be at the moment: half the roads are closed to traffic because of the G7 preparations, she reports, and half to encourage social distancing in urban areas. Their hospitality customers are struggling, not because they can't fill the tables but because they can't get the staff. That's Brexit of course, she says, but also a consequence of people realising during lockdown that there's easier money to be made than in a kitchen. I nod, saying the same is true back home in London; restaurants are crying out for people, but no one's coming forward to fill the vacancies.

'You can't blame them either,' she says. 'If you're a bricklayer, you can be home in time to read your kids a story.' Even those places that can get staff have nowhere to house them thanks to inflated property prices in this holiday hotspot. 'It's just a perfect storm for the hospitality industry really.' We all

---

* Gemma may disagree.

shake our heads, tsk-ing over what can be done for a sector already on its knees after 15 months of lockdowns.

Fortunately, Sally and her husband Bill have other channels for the meat from their traditional-breed pigs (Large Blacks and Gloucester Old Spots here on the farm, Tamworths, Welsh and British Lops from neighbours), which go to an abattoir five miles away ('we're lucky' she acknowledges – I nod, explaining to Gemma and Caroline that a third of small abattoirs have closed in the last decade) and then come back to be butchered – and smoked in the case of the gammon and bacon – on site. 'First lockdown,' she sighs, 'our mail order went stupid.'

Must be good to be busy? I offer feebly. Sally snorts derisively in the manner of someone who could do with a day off once in a while.

Get her onto the subject of hog's pudding, however, and she perks up – 'It's our most popular product by far – and it's something you only get in Cornwall.' I glare at Caroline who looks about to open her mouth: Sally's not, it turns out, Cornish born, but I'm still worried we might be asked to leave if anyone mentions the word Devon. 'Clotted cream, pasties, you can find them anywhere, but hog's pudding . . . we have customers for it all over the country. People often say they remember eating it at their granny's.'

In the old days, she continues, warming to her theme, every village would have made their own version – 'Some were better than others, mind' – but modern food hygiene legislation made it harder for one-man bands to operate and 'a lot just gave up'. The Luggs got their recipe from a local butcher: when he died a couple of years ago, 'they actually announced at the funeral he'd given his recipe to us'.

What that recipe is, however, remains a closely guarded secret – Bill, returning from his delivery round and hearing me trying to prise the details out of his wife, calls, 'Oh yeah, you don't want to be giving that away!' across the farmyard. He strolls over, evading the embrace of an excited dog who shoots out of the house at his approach, and tells us about the best hog's pudding he ever tasted, from a butcher whose recipe died with him. 'I tell you, ours is pretty damn close though.'

They will disclose they make it with belly and shoulder, though originally of course, Sally says, it wouldn't have been such expensive cuts; it was just a way to use up all the odds and ends of a pig – 'It keeps quite well once it's cooked, so people probably took it out to work with them, I imagine.' Apart from this, I can only find out what they don't put in, viz. too many spices ('you want to appeal to the most people'), oat groats ('that's a very West Cornwall thing though') or garlic, like a man on the Lizard: 'not', she says censoriously, 'traditional in any way, shape or form'.

HOG'S PUDDING

White pudding is the easiest of all the breakfast puddings to make, which is fortunate as it can be hard to come by in much of England and Wales. As sausage casings are a faff, I've chosen to bake this English version in a loaf tin instead. It freezes well in slices; simply defrost and fry as required.

Such puddings tend to have quite a fine texture, which is why it's best to ask your butcher to mince the meat for you. If you don't have a butcher, you can use a food processor to at least coarsely grind it yourself; cut it into largish chunks and freeze, spread out on a tray for 20 minutes, along with the food processor blade itself – this will prevent too much heat building up in the next step – until the meat is just solid at the edges, then mince in batches, never filling the processor more than half full.

Makes 8 slices
75g fine oatmeal
75ml whole milk
250g boneless pork belly, finely minced (see above)
250g boneless pork shoulder, finely minced (see above)
1 tsp ground white pepper
½ tsp ground mace
½ tsp ground allspice
½ tsp ground ginger
½ tsp ground coriander
1 tsp fine salt

1 Soak the oatmeal in the milk for 30 minutes.
2 Grease a 450g loaf tin and line with parchment paper. Heat the oven to 160°C/140°C fan/gas 3, and find a deep heatproof dish large enough to hold the loaf pan to use as a bain-marie.
3 Mix together all the mince, soaked oatmeal, spices and two-thirds of the salt. Heat a small frying pan and cook a small blob of the mixture, flattened, until browned on both sides, to test the seasoning. Adjust if necessary, adding more salt or other spices to taste.
4 Pack into the loaf tin and smooth down the top. Cover with foil. Boil the kettle, put the tin in the bain-marie dish, then fill this dish with boiling water until it comes halfway up the sides of the loaf tin.
5 Bake for 90 minutes; the middle should be at least 71°C on a food thermometer.

6 Allow to cool, then cut into slices and fry, preferably in
  bacon fat, to serve.

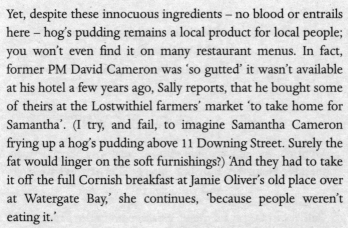

Yet, despite these innocuous ingredients – no blood or entrails
here – hog's pudding remains a local product for local people;
you won't even find it on many restaurant menus. In fact,
former PM David Cameron was 'so gutted' it wasn't available
at his hotel a few years ago, Sally reports, that he bought some
of theirs at the Lostwithiel farmers' market 'to take home for
Samantha'. (I try, and fail, to imagine Samantha Cameron
frying up a hog's pudding above 11 Downing Street. Surely the
fat would linger on the soft furnishings?) 'And they had to take
it off the full Cornish breakfast at Jamie Oliver's old place over
at Watergate Bay,' she continues, 'because people weren't
eating it.'

Perhaps, Caroline observes, they simply didn't know what it
was. Even Pam and John, who have been coming to Cornwall
for decades, aren't quite sure if they've tried hog's pudding
before – but as Pam says with some surprise when I cook some
of Sally's finest for breakfast the next morning, 'Oh, it's just
like a sausage!'

A sausage that needs our help. If it's going to thrive, rather
than just survive, it needs to break out of local butchers' shops
and farmers' markets, and be as recognised and celebrated as the
Cornish pasty, or clotted cream. Like haggis, or Stornoway black
pudding, you should be able to find it in fancy food halls and on
restaurant tasting menus, but it would be nice just to see it on
more breakfasts in the West Country. In France they'd probably
have a whole three-day festival devoted to it. 'Yeah, mate,
complete with special hog's pudding hats,' Caroline agrees.

Not that I want to give Sally any more work, but really Devon and Cornwall need to put aside their differences and stop keeping this treasure to themselves. It's just not fair on the rest of us.

Ridden: 94.69km
Climbed: 1,873m
Breakfasts eaten: 3 (malt loaf; beans on toast; full Cornish)

RED SAUCE OR BROWN?

Gemma: 'As I am a simple-minded creature I like red sauce, preferably Heinz ketchup, but cheaper alternatives have been known to delight.'

Sally: 'Just butter for me on a bacon sandwich: I can't stand either sauce!'

Pam: 'Red sauce and mayonnaise.'

John: 'Brown sauce.'

4
FALMOUTH TO GOWERTON
Cockles and Laverbread

Laver. This is a plant that grows on the rocks near the sea in the west . . . and is sent in pots prepared for eating . . . It is seldom liked at first, but people become extremely fond of it by habit.
– Maria Eliza Rundell, *A New System of Domestic Cookery; Formed upon Principles of Economy, and Adapted to the Use of Private Families* (1806)

It's so dismal the next morning that Caroline and I meet in the hall, swimsuits in hand, look out the window and wordlessly go back to bed. However firmly we bury our heads under the duvet, however, this holiday is definitely over – and we have borders to cross before we sleep.

The flesh is just about – give or take a few millimetres of tender tendon – willing to cycle from Falmouth to Wales but as usual the diary is not. It's now Wednesday, and I have an assignation with a shellfish and seaweed merchant on Friday morning on the other side of Swansea, so we're retracing our steps as far as Plymouth by rail and then getting another train to Bristol, from where we'll cycle triumphant across the

Severn Bridge, fuelled by a hearty breakfast of hog's pudding and bacon.

Annoyed by the constant overbalancing due to the weight behind me, and sceptical of how many opportunities there will be for camping in the weeks ahead, I've decided to leave my tent and rollmat in Pam and John's garage, keeping only the sleeping bag, which might come in handy in some remote Scottish bothy or, more likely, freezing bus shelter. Later I will feel a bit sad about this, but right now, I'm exultant at the extra room in my panniers.

Apart from a goodly amount of staring from fellow passengers, and the unexpected sight of a Confederate flag flying alongside St Piran's Cross just outside Par, the journey is uneventful in the way they so often are when you aren't actually cycling – though my baked-bean jersey amuses the staff at Plymouth station no end. 'You'll ride like the wind with that top on!' one chap shouts, creasing up with mirth as we come back through the barriers having failed to find anything to eat in the vicinity.

The damp weather sets in on the train to Bristol, and when the low clouds turn to drizzle and then to big splashy drops of rain, the 50km ride waiting for us at the other end looks less and less tempting by the minute. It's the only way we're going to get to Wales bar hopping on another train though, and that's not happening, first because it would mean giving up the thrill of cycling across the Severn Bridge, and second because it would be wimpy, and we are not wimps.

At least, I didn't think I was a wimp until the shower turns truly torrential coming down one of Bristol's many fine hills, we hit school-run traffic and someone shouts something out of their car window. What, perhaps fortunately, none of us catches, but I have the distinct feeling it wasn't an offer of a lift.

It's a relief to turn off the dual carriageway onto rural lanes in the direction of the Severn Bridge, leaving the car dealerships of Catbrain and the mall at Cribbs Causeway behind us: in fact, things are going so well that we think nothing of sailing through a closed cycle route sign, only to find it ends abruptly at the edge of the A403, a road that, from the safety of the rapidly dwindling pavement, looks terrifyingly fast and freight-heavy. It doesn't, however and crucially, look quite as bad as turning around and following the diversion – after all, how bad can it be? we decide, given the bridge itself is only a couple of kilometres away.

Gemma is typically gung-ho, and sets off across four lanes of traffic without hesitation. I'm less enthusiastic, but the idea of being responsible for Caroline's death is equally crushing, so I urge her to go first, reasoning my bright yellow panniers should provide fair warning to approaching vehicles. We soon lose our brave and noble pathfinder and I'm about to attempt to suggest over the roar of lorries that we try to catch up – safety in numbers – when I notice the rigid set of Caroline's back. When we eventually pull off towards the bridge, she lets out a loud noise, somewhere between a sob and a sigh. 'Mate, I was absolutely terrified.' (She now seems to be cycling in a pair of canary-yellow gardening gloves, but I decide this is not the time to mock them.)

Regrouped and relieved, we tackle the Severn Bridge, which, after the A403, feels like a positive pleasure ride despite the many warning signs to cyclists (one of which, I notice, expired in October 2006). Having driven it innumerable times, once, memorably, on the way home from a twenty-first birthday party after not quite enough sleep, when the suspension cables seemed to dance in front of my eyes, it's a treat to be able to stop and enjoy the view over the most voluminous river in

England and Wales. The Severn is a shining silver sea on this cloudy afternoon – we're lucky: later I read of cyclists who've had to hold onto the railings in strong winds just to make it across. Disappointingly there's no *Croeso i Gymru* sign on the other side, just some standard English graffiti: FUCK BORIS AND COVID 19.

Initially I'd planned for us to stay in Newport, handily located 30km west of the bridge, for the night, but Gemma, who spent her teenage years in South Wales – and has already called a merry *'bore da!'* to a gentleman cycling the other way in full waterproofs and an impressive handlebar moustache – has convinced me of the charms of the market town of Usk, some 25km north instead. I'm glad of the change of route; the roads up into the Monmouthshire hills wind through pretty woodlands and fields of green wheat, the humid air full of busy insects, and though we start climbing almost as soon as we leave Chepstow, it's beautiful enough for the views back across the hazy Severn estuary to take my mind off the nagging low-level pain in my hamstring.

After a thrilling 3km descent, we stop just outside Llanllowell for a pint of Welsh Pale in a pub decorated with pictures from the annual heaviest pumpkin competition (for those interested, the winner in 1983 was one Mr Tress Griffin, with a monster weighing 87¾lb – almost 40kg). Suddenly we notice the time – 7.20 p.m. If cycling in France is a constant rush for lunch, rural Britain is a race to dinner: turn up in most places much after 8 p.m. and you're risking a hungry night ahead, so we down drinks and crack on.

Our arrival causes a small amount of consternation at the New Court Inn, where locals nursing pints are briefly displaced to make room for our bikes in the snug before the landlord decrees they can go in a storeroom if we don't mind them being 'a bit squashed'. I speak for Eddy when I say I couldn't give a toss, shove him in there on top of the others, and firmly shut the door on them all.

Strolling around town after a substantial dinner (highlight: a golden-crumbed homemade chicken Kiev) I turn to Gemma and grudgingly concede she was right, Usk is quite lovely, with a Norman castle, the remains of a Roman fort, several medieval buildings and a handsome market square. She in turn confesses she had no idea any of this was here – it's just where they used to come for a spot of underage drinking. Passing one of its many pubs, buzzing even on a Wednesday evening, I suggest a snakebite and black for old times' sake, and am relieved when both she and Caroline say they'd rather go to sleep.

––●◆●––

As well as being handy with the garlic butter, the New Court Inn does very decent cooked breakfasts, where you can choose the elements you actually want, rather than picking your way around the mushrooms, or eating the hash brown because you feel bad about wasting it. When my order arrives, the bacon is thick-cut back, its fat a golden brown, the sausage a glossy chestnut, and there's a scattering of nicely charred cherry tomatoes next to an egg with the most delicate of brown lace on its creamy frill. I add a tentative swirl of ketchup, but it's hard to see it as an improvement. Ketchup is all well and good, I think – as long as you don't mind not being able to taste anything else on the plate.

Having dragged the bikes out from their hidey-hole, we're back in business. The route is initially more of the same prettiness – cow parsley, hedges, rolling hills, yada yada yada – but we soon find ourself heading into industrial South

Wales, roughly following the heads of the valleys through towns like Cwmbran, where I have to stop suddenly as a man in a Five Finger Death Punch T-shirt wanders into the road, and the old mining centre of Maesycwmmer, where we pass a sculpture made out of coal trucks on the huge railway viaduct, which closed in 1964.

A lot seems to be closed round here, in fact; we ride for miles through grey villages without seeing anywhere that might offer a hot drink and a sit down, just tanning salons and shuttered working men's clubs. The landscape is beautiful, the buildings handsome, but by the time we reach Treharris, 42km in and at the top of a punchy little climb, we're mentally prepared for disappointment, and maybe a Magnum from the shop if we're lucky.

Gemma goes over to investigate some tables and chairs outside the Navigation Hotel, named for the deep-mine colliery the town was built around, and comes back with good news. 'They're lovely . . . and they do frothy coffee!' Apparently we've hit the local jackpot, because they also offer apple turnovers, éclairs and custard slices from the local bakery, 'just like France!' Caroline says happily. The reading matter in the chilly loos – *Wales' 100 Greatest Tries* and a biography of Richard Burton – quickly brings her back down to earth, however.

By this point, almost every town we go through seems to have a memorial to its pit. More pertinently, coming through Aberaman, I spot a small plaque to Arthur Linton, an extraordinary Victorian endurance and speed cyclist who took victory in the 1896 Paris to Bordeaux race, covering an astonishing 560km in 21 hours 17 minutes. The English-born, Welsh-bred former coal hauler died shortly afterwards; had he lived, maybe he would have taken the inaugural Tour de France for the British, more than a century before Bradley Wiggins. I tip my helmet to him as we pass, though I suspect the great man would have been perplexed by the sight of three women bumbling along so slowly, and in such very eccentric dress.

We reach our highest point of the day shortly after a carb-heavy pub lunch (leek and potato soup, garlic bread, chips) and then begin our drop down into Swansea Bay, some of it ridden on the tranquil Neath Canal, with its mossy wooden lock gates and pot-bellied pigs grazing among the rushes, and some of it along the city's Ffordd Amazon, home to a distinctly less picturesque 74,000-square-metre fulfilment centre for the online behemoth.

I've booked a triple room in the centre, above Swansea market – squashed into the tiny lift with Eddy, I tread on a chip, and immediately think of Wilf, who I'm currently missing inordinately.

At 2 a.m., after a slap-up Sri Lankan supper to say goodbye to Caroline, who has to head back to London, and real life, in the morning, I'm woken up by loud voices just outside our window.

'You having a piss then, are you?'

'I'm desperate, mun!'

'Fair play to you, boy.'

━━━◆━━━

Breakfast is early – too early for the cafés in the market, but Caroline has a train to catch and Gemma and I have an appointment to find out more about the place of shellfish and seaweed on the Welsh breakfast plate, so we grab what we can at the café under the hotel. The other two go for bacon sand-wiches but – and I'm sure you won't believe it! – I'm very fussy about my bacon sandwiches. If they're any less than great (see page 313 for details) then I'd rather not bother, which is how I end up with a pot of the locally legendary Joe's strawberry ice cream instead. Like all ice cream, it proves particularly delicious at 8 a.m.

Leaving Gemma with the bikes, Caroline and I have a quick whisk round the market, where shutters are opening on piles of faggots and Welsh cakes and body-building meat packs, and, in the very centre, a magnificent display of cockles and laver-bread. Carol behind the counter, who recommends frying them up together in a pan of hot bacon fat, says trade is still good – 'We get people coming in to buy loads to take back home with them. Tourists, not just local people, mind.' Do you think they'd work in a spaghetti alle vongole? Caroline says, eyeing the pots of cockles. Carol looks perplexed.

And just like that, after 10 days together on the road, it's time to say goodbye. I hug her tightly, feeling quite teary – yes, she always orders salt and vinegar crisps in the pub even though I don't like them, but she also makes me laugh like a drain and swear like a trooper and I genuinely think she enjoyed the mustard factory even more than I did.* I'll even miss those ridiculous yellow gloves.

Caroline heads to the station and Gemma and I set off on yet another route that looks benign on the map but involves several short but steep little climbs to wake up the hamstring (13 per cent in a suburban street? Wales, you're spoiling us). After crossing the top of the gorgeous green Gower, we drop down between thick hedges into Penclawdd on the coast of the soft, grey Burry estuary, its sands teaming with plump cockles ready for the picking, and shelling, and serving with fried

---

* Plus, as she will no doubt point out, she definitely saved my life back in Exeter.

bacon and boiled seaweed. Much as I love such things, Gemma's face when I inform her of this traditional South Welsh breakfast perhaps explains why the Full English seems to be more popular in local cafés.

<hr />

Tea Break:
LAVERBREAD – 'WELSH CAVIAR' [RICHARD BURTON]

Nothing to do with bread, but a seaweed paste made from laver (aka sloke, or *Porphyria umbilicalis*), the same reddish plant used by the Japanese to wrap nori rolls: it only turns green once dried or cooked. Though in Britain laverbread is now seen as an almost exclusively Welsh speciality, usually served with cockles and bacon, it seems to have once been common fare on the west coast of both here and Ireland – the Cornish made a paste out of it known as black butter, often paired with hog's pudding, while Scottish sailors got their vitamins from sloke jelly spread on oatcakes.

Initially, like many freely available foodstuffs associated with the poor, 'fine potted laver', rich in iodine, vitamins and minerals, was, Dorothy Hartley claims, hawked to fashionable spa-goers on the streets of Bath in the eighteenth century as part of their cure. It was exported as far as London, where Victorian celebrity chef Alexis Soyer served it with roast mutton, and was particularly popular in the Peak District, where iodine deficiency was once so widespread that goitres were dubbed 'Derbyshire neck'. At the height of its fame, the Pembrokeshire coast was dotted with huts used to dry laver before it was sent to market at Swansea; indeed, you can visit a restored version at Freshwater West should you have a fancy to.

With a high protein content (as much as 47 per cent), laver is the treasure we now leave rotting on the beaches. Thankfully, businesses like Selwyn's, and the Pembrokeshire Beachfood Company further west, are doing their bit to bring it into the twenty-first century; Selwyn's sell their laverbread and crispy seaweed snacks online, while chef Jonathan Williams has developed a range of laver ketchups, butters and pestos for the latter's Café Môr van on Freshwater Beach car park, which laver lovers can order from their website.

◆◆◆

Selwyn's Seafood Shack sits in a pale blue wooden building on the shore, next to a much bigger-looking processing operation – our improbably glamorous host, Kate, married to founder Selwyn Jones's grandson Ashley, explains that Selwyn started in the seafood business in 1945, with compensation money from the American government after he and his mother were hit by a drunk GI while walking home from the cockle beds. His son and daughter-in-law sold the factory next door to a Spanish firm in 2004: 'Without them, I don't think we'd have a business, if I'm honest with you. They're a family operation too . . . just a multi-million pound one.'

Her husband now manages Selwyn's Seafoods for the Spanish; this new seafood shop and shack is a sideline. 'We started it last year because we lost all our industry customers overnight, and it's really exceeded our expectations. I like it; it's more sociable than being in the office, or on the factory floor.'

She's busy prepping some handsome-looking local lobsters for a telephone order when we arrive, so we have a wander round the shop while she talks, admiring the displays of seafood and seaweed products, as well as the gallery of old photos that adorns the walls. Kate sees me looking at a barefoot woman with a laden donkey on the sands – 'That's Selwyn's wife, my husband's grandmother . . . she kept digging cockles into her sixties. It always used to be women's work, because all the men were down the coal mines. Now there's just me and Kirsty, we're the only women here.'

(We've already met Kirsty on arrival: 'Kirsty Cockle, that's her actual name, can you believe it? That could only happen in Swansea. I mean, people call me Kate Cockles, but that's a Welsh thing, it's not my *actual name*.')

Cockle season, we learn, sitting outside with a coffee on a bed of bleached cockle shells, is in full swing this first week of June, though it's been a little late this year because of the cold weather – 'The Spanish don't like them too small,' Kate explains – and will run until early spring 2022, when the cockles begin spawning. Wales is one of the few places they are hand-gathered, rather than dredged; better, she says, for both the marine environment and the consumer, as this way they don't get so much sand and grit in them. It sounds like back-breaking work though, the pickers raking the mud of the estuary into round sieve-like riddles, ensuring anything under-sized falls back along with the sand and water.

Once harvested, the cockles are washed, graded for size, and then boiled for three minutes before the shells are shaken off and the meat can be cooled, washed and refrigerated – or sent off to be pickled or canned, mainly for export.

In fact, about 90 per cent of British cockles go to Spain in tins, I discover: 'The UK cockle industry would struggle if we didn't have the continental market,' Kate admits. 'It's very small.' That said, she adds, 'I've seen people come in and buy a kilo bag of cockles and they can't wait – they just open it there and then and tuck in with a bit of vinegar and white pepper!'

But people eat them for breakfast, right? I interrupt, suddenly anxious that I've brought Gemma, currently looking slightly nervous that someone will ask her to actually eat a cockle, on a wild goose chase. Oh yes, she says, with bacon and laverbread for breakfast, but cockles go with anything. Great with a drink.

Husband Ashley is currently away cockle-gathering up in the Dee estuary in North Wales – he'll be gone for a couple of months. Despite his illustrious lineage, he doesn't have a licence to gather in the Burry Inlet, where we're sitting. Licences used to be handed down from father to son – Selwyn gathered cockles in the Burry Inlet by Penclawdd, then his son did, 'and Ash, it's all he wanted to do, even when he was in school he was looking forward to getting the licence from his grandfather . . . and then they changed the rules. So he's still on the waiting list for a licence to pick there.' (According to the latest information I can find, the waiting list currently has 61 people on it, and has closed to new applications.)

She admits regulation has been good for the industry, however, and for the future of the cockle population it relies on: 'The Three Rivers beds [just up the coast] used to be open to anyone, but ultimately it is a dangerous job if you don't know what you're doing, so now if you have a cockling licence you have to go through training, really invest in it. It's better for the beds too.'

There's a beeping sound from inside and Kate jumps up to tend to her lobsters. As she comes back out, a van pulls up, and she introduces us to Jamie from the Three Cliffs café in nearby

Pennard – 'People come in and ask where the cockles are from, and if I say Selwyn's, they're happy,' he tells us.

Oh yes, Kate calls over her shoulder as she goes to fetch his order, ours are bigger, they're sweeter: 'Come to think of it, I reckon if you asked most people they'd say Penclawdd cockles were the best.' Her laugh recedes into the shop, and I ask Jamie if he has Selwyn's laverbread on the breakfast menu too. He hesitates. 'What we found was that English people – no offence – couldn't handle the laver straight, so we make it into little cakes with cheese and oats and bake them. Once you've got yourself used to it like that you're ready for laver just like my grandad used to do it . . . a big dollop on a spoon and straight into the frying pan with the bacon grease.' That's the way to eat it, Kate confirms as she hands him his boxes.

The laverbread is a much smaller market than the cockles, presumably because there's not much in the way of export trade, it being somewhat of an acquired taste. Kate describes laver as a tough sort of seaweed, 'gathered from the rocks by hand, then washed thoroughly to get all the sand and little shrimps and things out. Then we pop it in a big pot with a bit of salt – it doesn't need a lot – and boil it for a few hours until it's really soft. Mince it and it's good to go. That's all laverbread is, see.'

Another car arrives. 'Oh, it's Kath! She's got the King Arthur, big wedding venue, or it was before all this Covid. You're getting back into it now, are you?' she calls.

Kath sighs and sits down next to her. 'Well, I dunno about that. It depends what they say about lifting these rules.' There's a respectful pause as we shake our heads over the uncertainty of it all, and then I ask her about laverbread, a subject she feels more confident on. 'We put it in a pot on the breakfast, rather than straight on the plate, because it's a bit like Marmite, but nearly everyone who tries it likes it – it's nice on toast actually.' Cockles, though, are strictly offered on request: 'They're too expensive to just give out. They're a delicacy, they are.'

On their brunch menu, she says, they do cockles and laverbread a bit differently, cooked with bacon, and served topped with Welsh Cheddar. Kate nods vigorously. 'That's the tastiest way I've ever had laverbread. Ever.'

This innovative use of such a traditional foodstuff confirms to me that, just as with hog's pudding, these are ingredients that aren't, and have never been, just breakfast items, and which will probably disappear if we insist on pigeonholing them as such. Even the stoutest heart might find shellfish and seaweed a bit much on a morning fry, but that's no reason not to eat them for lunch or dinner. Especially if they come with cheese on top.

BACON, COCKLES AND LAVERCAKES

You can add cockles and lavercakes, or indeed laverbread, to a fry-up, but they also make a very decent breakfast (or lunch, or supper) with a rasher of bacon or two. Make sure you choose some with enough fat to baste the cockles and cook the cakes; this is no place for lean meat. If you can only find cockles in vinegar, give them a quick rinse before use. If you can only find them raw, then it's best to cook them in their shells, like mussels, before use. Outside Wales, laverbread is easily purchased online: Kate herself sells it through her Selwyn's Seafoods website.

Serves 4
200g laverbread
2 spring onions, finely sliced (optional)

Grating of nutmeg (optional)
75–100g oatmeal, preferably fine or medium
Salt, to taste
4 thick rashers of smoked streaky bacon, chopped into chunks
100g cooked and shelled cockles

1 Mix together the laverbread with the spring onions, nutmeg and just enough oatmeal to make it firm enough to shape into cakes (the less you use, the lighter the cakes, but the harder they will be to handle: I find 80g ideal). Season with a little salt, and shape into 4 even balls, then gently push down to flatten. Turn the oven on low.

2 Heat a frying pan over a medium flame and fry the bacon until it begins to turn golden and give up its fat. Add the cockles and cook, tossing, until warmed through (they're already cooked). Scoop out of the pan into a heatproof dish, keeping as much fat back as possible, then cover and put into the low oven to keep warm.

3 Put the pan back on a medium-high heat, and if there isn't much fat left in there, add a knob of butter, lard or a dash of oil, then cook the cakes for about 4 minutes on each side until golden and crisp.

4 Serve with the cockles and bacon – I like a fried egg cooked in the same pan as well.

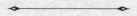

The two gossip about the cockle's celebrity fans – 'We had Michael Ball on the sands filming recently … he sang to me and I cried!' Kate laughs. 'We do get a lot of filming here because there's not many people doing what we do, but he's the biggest star we've ever had.'

Bonnie Tyler's a local girl, mind – 'and let me tell you, she looks great'. Given that neither of them look too bad either, I wonder if there might be something magical in this laver stuff.

Kath asks where we're heading next, and I tell them New Quay, 100km away on the west coast – we're getting the train as far as Carmarthen, I explain, 'so I hope it's not too hilly from there'. Kate, thrusting cockles, laverbread and seaweed snacks into our hands for the journey, laughs.

'We're renowned for hills in Wales. It's what we do!'

Ridden: 157.31km
Climbed: 1,793m
Breakfasts eaten: 3 (hog's pudding and bacon; fry-up;
strawberry ice cream)

RED SAUCE OR BROWN?

Kate: 'Am definitely a brown sauce kind of gal. And it has to be HP.'

Kath: 'Definitely brown sauce but only with a fry-up and sandwiches. If cockles and/or laverbread are present then it's malt vinegar.'

5

GOWERTON TO ABERDYFI

Honey

'I don't feel very much like Pooh today,' said Pooh. 'There there,'
said Piglet. 'I'll bring you tea and honey until you do.'
– A. A. Milne, *Winnie the Pooh* (1926)

Having pedalled like crazy from Selwyn's Seafoods to the station, Gemma and I find the train is running 25 minutes late. As we lower ourselves onto the sun-warmed tarmac to wait, I'm reminded of one of the most satisfying things about this nomadic way of life – when the journey is the destination, such minor hold-ups are a diversion rather than a delay.

I'm sorry for sounding like an inspirational cushion, but it's true – we have bags of time to get to New Quay so it's no particular hardship to sit on the platform eating Welsh cakes and discussing the route: a train to Carmarthen, where we run out of track in the right direction, then 50km to the coast, where we're meeting my friend Tess.

The view from the train, when it eventually arrives, is annoyingly flat – Gowerton to Carmarthen looks like it would be a lovely cycle, whereas from here on in, Komoot promises that things are going to get decidedly lumpy. Gemma is inexplicably down on the idea of eating the cockles and laverbread currently heating up nicely in my panniers, so we pause for lunch in Carmarthen. The café has run out of cheesy Glamorgan sausages, so I have to content myself with a faggot roll. She, meanwhile, has a hummus sandwich. I remember we are very different people.

Our route almost due north takes in some undeniably pretty if, as predicted by Kate Cockles, relentlessly spiky countryside, with narrow lanes and lots of sheep. The slate-roofed villages look like they've been drawn by a 2B pencil, and are just as silent – until we happen upon a chatty painter outside the village shop in Pontsian.

He's only moderately impressed by our story – 'We had some boys from Bristol ride through a few weeks ago, going to the coast. There and back, mind' – but does have sage advice on the route: we're going the wrong way. 'I've lived here all my life, that's 67 years girl, and I know.' Dismissing Our Graham's suggestion with a contemptuous wave of his brush, he instead directs us up a series of very complicated twisty-turny lanes. 'It's a short climb, this one, not like the way you were going.'

He downs tools to make sure we take the right turning – 'give my wife a wave as you pass, mind!' – which means we have no choice but to obey. Short is one word to describe the hill, but personally, wincing as my hamstring protests with every revolution of the pedals, I'd go with steep.

On the plus side, it does feel like we're on top of the world up here, or at least the top of Wales, bluebells tripping across the shadier verges, tractors silaging in the fields, faint outlines of distant peaks and a blank, flat horizon beckoning us towards the cyan sea.

The profound silence is broken by a call from Tess, who, though she and her husband Tor have vowed never to cycle again following the day of (inadvertent!) torture I put them through in the Loire Valley, has kindly offered to be my fixer in West Wales instead. She explains there's a road closed, and we might need guiding in, passing the phone to her brother Stefan, who is keen to come and meet us to help, and also clearly trying not to laugh at my Welsh pronunciation.

'So who are we staying with?' Gemma asks as I try to attempt to relay his directions. It all sounds quite complicated, I say, frowning . . . but I think it's a caravan in Tess's brother's wife's . . . parents' garden? The phrase conjures an image of something on bricks, the kind of damp box people live in for two winters in *Grand Designs* before getting divorced and selling their half-finished project, though I don't say so – it's very kind of them, and it's only for a night.

Ten minutes later, just as taking on a small but unexpectedly serious hill in the wrong gear prompts me to dismount for the first time (a good measure of progress in the injury department), I hear an engine behind, and Caroline's voice in my head: 'Always a car, mate.'

As I move to let it past, annoyed that the driver has caught me walking on this modest ascent, the window opens and Tess's blonde head sticks out. 'Hi!' My first thought is, thank God I didn't flick them the V. My second, given immediate plaintive voice: 'But this is the only time I've had to get off and push all day!'

Her brother doesn't hear my excuses, because he's busy unpacking an extremely fancy-looking bike from the boot. 'He's desperate to ride in with you,' Tess says, moving to the driver's seat. 'See you there!' She roars off, leaving me struggling to keep up with the other two so I can casually mention my handicap.

The 'caravan', it turns out, is actually a mobile home with cracking views across Cardigan Bay, and a tin of freshly baked Welsh cakes in the little kitchen. Tess and Tor's blue staffy puppy Jerry-Lee, anchored into the grass, is dancing with joy on the lawn, a canine swingball careering dangerously close to a table holding an ice bucket full of Gwd Thing! Celtic Lager. With the sun out, and the sky mirroring the blue of the sea, we could be on the Mediterranean.

It's so idyllic I'm almost in danger of forgetting why we're in West Wales in the first place, which is to meet a beekeeper and find out more about honey, a common breakfast item in this country since Roman times. Sales are on the rise – it's recently overtaken jam as the nation's most popular spread – and the UK is now the world's largest importer of Chinese honey. European beekeepers mutter darkly about adulteration with sugar syrup going on on the other side of the world, but whatever the truth of the matter, it seems an awful long way to bring something to drizzle on porridge, or spread on toast. I want to find out more about the homemade stuff.

Not now though, tomorrow, after local lobster and chips (and Kate's cockles, as plump and sweet as promised, and not apparently any the worse for a day in my panniers) in the garden. Tess's lovely mum, Faith, the *Guardian*'s biggest fan, has driven a FELICITY cake down from Aberystwyth to mark my arrival in Wales – lemon drizzle with lavender icing, though, she admits, she only has one tin for each letter, so the second I is actually a J with the end cut off – which we tear into after a modest few drinks down at the Blue Bell in town, where Tess is insistent it's cocktail time. Gemma pipes up, asking Simon the waiter, who also happens to be the owner, and Stefan's brother-in-law, whether they do anything blue.

'No . . . but give us five minutes,' he says over his shoulder, as Gemma explains my obsession with blue drinks to the slightly puzzled but enthusiastic table: in short, if you're on holiday, whether that's in the tropics or the Yorkshire Wolds, you have to celebrate by ordering something you'd never dream of drinking at home, i.e. a cocktail the colour of mouthwash.

Simon comes back bearing not one but two magnificently neon creations, one by him, one by the girl behind the bar. I get the Blue Bell Special, whose recipe I record here simply because it's so bloody nice that they need to put it on the menu in perpetuity – and let me tell you, that's not a given with blue drinks. The other is so punchy it makes Gemma's eyes water, so I'll leave that to your imagination.

BLUE BELL SPECIAL FROM THE BLUE BELL IN NEW QUAY, CEREDIGION

50ml Absolut Mandarin vodka
50ml cranberry juice
25ml blue curaçao
25ml sugar syrup
20ml lime juice
Orange peel, to garnish

1 Shake all the ingredients with ice. Serve in a tumbler of crushed ice with a curl of orange peel. Toast me in gratitude.

The next morning, a bad thing happens. Another bad thing, I mean, and I swear it isn't anything to do with those blue drinks. Having spent much of last night staring longingly at the sea, I'm determined to swim. We've been warned the cliff path can be quite treacherous, so I pick my way down at the pace of a careful snail . . . but apparently less stickily, because on a step slick with mud my right foot shoots away from me at such speed that I can feel my hamstring giving up the last pretence of solidarity as I hit the concrete.

'Are you all right?' asks Gemma as she takes a photo. To be fair to her, when we eventually make it back up to the top of the cliff I can't look at the image without hooting, even through snotty tears – I'm sprawled out in the mud in the attitude of someone who's been dead for some days – but right now it's all I can do to sit up. A pain that had been dull and fading is now acute and angry, and it takes me a good five minutes to cover the few hundred yards back to the caravan.

I cheer myself up by eating three slices of brown bread with two types of Welsh butter, a Welsh cake with more butter, some salty Carmarthen ham (a speciality locals claim gave the Romans the idea for Parma ham) and a piece of cake, while watching the video Gemma took of me hobbling up the steps. Even laughing hurts, I say miserably, wondering melodramatically if I'll ever ride again.

It's clear we're not going to be cycling to see my beekeeper Marion Dunn in Newcastle Emlyn anyway – I actually have to get Gemma to put my socks on, as I can't so much as bend down, let alone climb onto a bike – so Tess kindly agrees to drive us, though the car she's borrowed from Tor's sister Tia is so low that getting in and out leaves me momentarily winded.

Installed in a garden in rural Ceredigion, with a whippet by my side and a bowl of freshly picked strawberries in front of me, talking about honey with Marion and her husband Graham, I feel a bit better. They're not from the area originally – they moved up from Purley after taking early retirement from the corporate world. I ask what brought them here, though it's fairly obvious from the view. 'Space and quiet,' Graham replies. 'It's just heaven,' Marion confirms.

It's not her first foray into the honey business, however; she had bees down in Surrey too. 'I'd always wanted hives, I don't know why,' she says. 'I used to take a cup of coffee and just go and watch the bees before work, it was very calming.' The Purley bees, however, did not think Wales was heaven. 'They just dwindled ... it didn't suit them.' A swarm of feral bees moved in instead, and it seems they liked Marion's accommodation a lot better.

The agriculture here is all cows and sheep, and gardens are few and far between, so the flowers the bees feed on are mostly wild – hedgerow plants, blackthorn, hawthorn, fruit blossom. Very different from Purley, but not necessarily better – to my surprise she says they used to get 'fantastic honey down south. I think suburban honey is often more plentiful because people are growing such diverse things in their garden all year round.'

Tea Break:
HOW HONEY IS MADE

Unlike the awful wasp, or indeed the fuzzy bumblebee, honey bees overwinter, huddled together in their hives for warmth. They spend the spring and summer frantically laying in supplies to see them through these cold months: the art of the beekeeper is to give them the space to make more honey than they need, which can then be collected for human consumption – though the hive only requires about 10kg, it's capable of producing two or three times that amount.

Bees make honey by mixing the sticky, sugary nectar they collect from flowers with enzymes secreted from glands in their mouths, then store it in hexagonal wax combs until the water content has reduced to about 17 per cent – at which point they seal the comb to indicate the honey is ready.

It keeps indefinitely: the British Beekeepers Association informs interested parties that 'perfectly edible honey comb was found in the tombs of the pharaohs, over 3,000 years old'. They also make the impressive claim that bees fly around 55,000 miles to make 450g of honey – 2.2 times around the world for just one jar.

Both Marion and the BBKA warn me about adulterated honey, whether diluted with syrups, coloured or simply misla-belled, which is one good reason to buy direct from small producers – they tend to sell minimally processed, raw honey. The other, more compelling one is that their honey, whether that's Marion's hawthorn blossom, Lithuanian buckwheat or Greek pine tree stuff, tends to be more diverse and complex in flavour than the blandly pleasant big brands. Though we know it by just one name, honey is never just honey; it's the ultimate product of its environment.

<hr />

Marion pushes a bowl of limpid honey towards us to try while Graham goes and makes us a second breakfast, which, today of all days, I think I deserve. 'I've been waiting and waiting for this,' she says. It's the only honey she sells as a named variety, 'May Blossom', because in late spring, the sole food source for the bees is her hawthorn tree, which yields a distinctive malty, nutty flavour quite unlike anything I've ever tasted.

We also try the first honey of the year, made from dandelions, blackthorn and almond blossom and much more delicate and classically sweet. Both are fabulous on the homemade bread Graham brings out, along with plates of plump, peppery sausages with crisp brown skins from Mark Webb in Rhydlewis – 'he wins competitions with these' – Myrddin heritage bacon with a generous cap of fat, and scrambled eggs from a friend's hens, as yellow as a pat of butter. I have no regrets about finishing it all off, and then, discreetly, helping myself to Gemma's eggs too, because I can see her politely eating around them (an aversion to eggs is one of her few failings).

As we eat, I think about all the jars of honey in my local supermarket, and how the British stuff is always significantly more expensive than the squeezy bottles of unknown provenance. They both taste like honey. But the cheap stuff just tastes like honey. It's anonymous, unchallenging, almost bland – like white sugar in comparison to dark muscovado. Yes, there's a place for that, but it's not on my crumpets, dammit.

Support British bees! I say suddenly. Everyone looks at me a bit oddly, as if I might have fallen on my head. I'm happy enough though: pouring myself a shot of Marion's raspberry honey vinegar, I'm ready to settle in for a morning's chat – Graham is also a cyclist, and it's enjoyable swapping stories – but I spot Tess surreptitiously checking her watch, and remember we've got to go back and get our bags, to say nothing of Tor and little Jerry-Lee.

I'm determined to inspect the hives first though. Were we in London, I'd assume the ramshackle weathered wooden towers a few fields down from the house were some sort of challenging art installation. Admiring the shiny centrifuges and spotless preserving pans in Marion's work shed next door, it's clear nothing goes to waste; she makes the beeswax into candles and seals for her vinegar bottles, and the honey water into mead. Graham's even got her to do a chammy cream, the stuff cyclists smother on our undercarriages to prevent saddle sores. (I can confirm, after swapping my usual brand for her beeswax-based version for the rest of the tour, that it stays put, it works and, unusually for a cycling product, it also smells lovely. Not that anyone else is going to get close enough to notice.)

We walk, some of us faster than others, back up the hill, pausing at the top to look back at the hives, tucked away in the shelter of the slope. 'I am lucky here,' Marion says simply. 'I know I am.'

WELSH CAKES AND HONEY BUTTER

OK, I know most people don't eat Welsh cakes for breakfast, but they will serve you one if you ask nicely, and in a world where Pop Tarts exist, there's no shame in it. The honey butter is gilding the lily, but is also extremely good on pikelets (see page 265), porridge (page 206) and a warm soda farl (page 167). Lard will give your Welsh cakes a lighter texture but is not mandatory.

Makes 8–10
150g plain flour, plus extra to dust
1 tsp baking powder
¼ tsp salt
A pinch of nutmeg
30g butter, grated
30g lard (or use 60g butter), grated
40g currants
Finely grated zest of ½ a lemon (optional)

30g caster sugar, plus extra for serving
1 egg, beaten

For the honey butter
200g butter, at room temperature, diced
6 tbsp honey
A generous pinch of salt

1 Whisk together the flour, baking powder, salt and nutmeg in a mixing bowl. Add the fats, and rub in with your fingertips until the mixture resembles coarse sand.

2 Stir in the currants, zest if using, and sugar, then beat in just enough egg until you have a firm dough; you shouldn't need it all.

3 Roll out the dough on a lightly floured surface until about 5mm thick and cut out rounds about 6cm in diameter. Heat a heavy frying pan or griddle on a medium heat and cook the cakes for 3–4 minutes on each side until golden (a little less if you're not eating them immediately), then lift onto a cooling rack and sprinkle with sugar. Warm through if eating later, though really, they're best hot from the griddle.

4 Beat the butter with electric beaters, or a wooden spoon, until soft and smooth, then whip in the honey and salt. Taste, adjust if necessary, and eat with the Welsh cakes or as takes your fancy.

◆――――――――◆

It's sadly clear that I won't be riding anywhere today, so I'm grateful for having such good friends – despite having signed up for a cycling holiday, Gemma doesn't object when Tess agrees to drive us to Aberystwyth, bikes strapped onto the car as rattling badges of my ineptitude. There's a butcher she wants to introduce us to, she says. 'Unless you've had enough bacon for one day?'

Never, I say firmly. It's a shame; it would have been a pretty ride, through brightly painted fishing villages and up and down some gorgeous hills, which, it must be admitted, are probably better appreciated from the car right now, preferably while sitting as still as possible.

As we park, Tor informs us that, when Next opened here in Aber, 'must have been about 10, 15 years ago it was so exciting that people went in just to ride on the escalator. We'd never had one before.' Tess claims they even came and did the Radio One breakfast show from here to mark the occasion. (I'm sceptical, but Gemma quickly finds the footage on YouTube. It really happened.)

It's also Tess's home town, which means she knows exactly where to buy tomorrow's breakfast: butcher Rob Rattray used to coach her brother's rugby team, but also, she says, knows his way around a pig as well as the sheep he keeps himself, this being Wales. Having presented Tess with her order, two alarmingly big bags of breakfast meats, the boy serving from the door goes off to fetch Rob, who's having his lunch out back. He appears still wiping his mouth, a big smiling man in a striped apron who breaks off periodically to greet passers-by in Welsh as we discuss the important matter of breakfast.

He looks in Tess's bag to check what she's ordered. 'Oh, you've got to have some of my treacle bacon too. I was talking to this guy in the pub – ages ago it was! – and he was telling me how they used to cure hams and such in treacle, so I got in touch with an old boy from the company that did the cures, and he told me what to do. Must be 10, 12 years I've been at it and it's really popular.' There's a tray of it in the window, thick cut and well fatted, with a rich, dark outer bark.

The black pudding, he says, nodding approvingly, uses the back fat from their own Welsh pigs, and we must have some of the pork and leek sausages too – 'You have to have a sausage with a breakfast, know what I mean?' He goes back in and puts a packet in the bag, waving away extra payment. 'You enjoy them now!' he says, going back to his lunch.

Handily, another of Tess's brothers is part owner of a boatyard on the southernmost border of the Snowdonia National Park; well, part boatyard, part tourist accommodation – Gemma and I are staying the night on a wooden fishing vessel that's in the process of being done up, and thus sits somewhere in between. Resting on the shingle banks of the River Dyfi, *Hannah* has had a door cut cleverly in her side to allow access into the neat galley where I'll be cooking up breakfast tomorrow, if I survive the night – unfortunately the pain in my bum is still considerable.

Tess, as ever, has come equipped with more wine and beer than we could possibly drink even if we weren't going out to dinner in Machynlleth, where I finally get my extremely cheesy Glamorgan sausage, plus enough booze to partially anaesthetise me to the pain of getting into my bunk. I'm glad I've kept my sleeping bag, but that's the only thing I'm thankful for this evening; it's impossible to get comfortable, both because of the injury, and my worries about how long it will take to heal. By 2 a.m. it's clear to me I'll never be able to cycle again and I may as well give up this whole hopeless endeavour now. If I wasn't so dehydrated from the local Dyfi Distillery gin, I'd cry.

Frankly it's only the thought of Rob Rattray's treacle bacon that gets me up the next morning. I can hear lucky swimmers splashing about outside as I fry rashers as thick as a piece of toast, plump leek sausages and a delicious lump of softly fatty coal-black pudding on *Hannah*'s little stove, while Gemma and Tor make a fire on the shore to finish them off.

When I emerge with the food, I see the estuary is dead calm, drifts of high, wispy cloud perfectly mirrored in the water, the hills on the other side just visible in the early mist – perfect bathing conditions, I think miserably. Still wincing from the short walk to the picnic table, I have to content myself with a sausage instead, wrapped in a duvet of white bread with a big wodge of Shirgar butter (no relation to the horse, I'm assured).

Even through the fog of anxiety about my hamstring, I can appreciate this is all very good stuff: as rich and savoury as you could hope for, the treacle bacon mildly sweet and emphatically porky, the leek-flecked sausages charred by the campfire. I even feel momentarily excited about all the other breakfasts that lie ahead – it's only when I start to clear up that I realise I've forgotten to cook the eggs.

Washing up, I ponder this. Oddly, it's the first time I've considered how weird the concept of so many cuts of cured pork on one plate is, even diluted with an egg or two, and maybe a tomato for window dressing, and it seems an especially bizarre thing to eat when you've just got out of bed. Is the fry-up actually a bit gross? I worry, as we set off in the car back to England.

Tor looks at me in the rear-view mirror, concerned, then looks at Gemma. 'How many painkillers is she actually on?'

Ridden: 77.89km
Climbed: 1,248m
Breakfasts eaten: 3 (Welsh ham and Welsh cakes;
fry-up and honey and strawberries; eggless fry-up)

RED SAUCE OR BROWN?

Tess: 'I like ketchup on my bacon sandwich and mustard on sausage and with a fry-up. Tor has no sauce at all!

Stefan: 'Neither. English mustard (and, goes without saying, obviously butter) and if I want to pimp it, mustard, iceberg and Hellmann's Mayo. And never in between toast.'

Marion and Graham: 'We're generally not big fans of sauce but the exception is with a bacon or sausage sandwich when it has to be brown sauce.'

Rob: 'It'd have to be ketchup.'

6
PORT TALBOT
Baked Beans

I just love them. I could eat beans any time of day or night. Hot or cold. On toast or not. Just so long as I can eat beans.
– Nigel Slater, *Guardian*, 9 April 2000

Here I must yank you forward a couple of months, from early June to early August, when, having been home three weeks, I find myself heading back to South Wales to tick off the baked bean element of the British breakfast. I'm not a big fan of beans on a fry-up,* as you may have gathered, but a YouGov survey back in 2017 found that 71 per cent of respondents expect them as part of a Full English, so it would be churlish of me to leave them out of this book altogether. After all, they're very nice on Marmite toast.

I'd hoped, of course, to visit the world's largest baked bean factory in Wigan, Greater Manchester, which turns out several

---

* Who wants them lapping at the snowy skirts of their fried egg, or worse, spilling over onto a tattie scone?

million turquoise tins of Heinz a day. I slightly prefer Branston*
myself, but I keep quiet about this fact in my correspondence
with Nigel from Kraft-Heinz,† who tells me in early spring that
though he can't make any promises as regards a tour, if I let
them know when I'm passing, he'll see what he can do.

Unfortunately, when the Delta variant hits the North West
hard a few months later, when I'm already on the road, it's a no
from Nigel – which puts the dampeners on my hopes of seeing
the eighth wonder of the world in action. Prevented from even
visiting the outside of the factory by regional travel restrictions, I brood on the matter the rest of the way round Britain,
hoping that things will calm down on the Covid front, and
Nigel will change his mind.

By late summer this hope is running as thin as cheap
bacon, so when Twitter tips me off about the existence of a
Baked Bean Museum in Port Talbot, I'm straight on to
Tripadvisor. By all accounts, it's a corker – in fact, the site
claims it as the town's number-one tourist attraction with
more five-star reviews than there are beans in a tin – 'you've
gotta see it to believe it', the most recent claims. More importantly, unlike the world's biggest bean factory, it's still
welcoming visitors.

Having read up a little on its curator, a former computer
operator called Barry Kirk who changed his name by deed poll
to Captain Beany back in 1991, I decide there's only one choice
of companion for this particular expedition; my friend Martha,
who has never knowingly been daunted by anything, even a
grown man dressed as a giant baked bean.

---

* The beans feel smaller but the sauce is thicker and tastier. No need to
reduce a tin of Branston before serving.
† His namesake Nigel Slater is also a fan, writing back in 2000 that 'there
is perfection in a can of Heinz baked beans'.

As Barry hosts the museum in his council flat, entry is by appointment only, which makes the experience feel pleasingly exclusive, like booking into a couture show at Paris Fashion Week. Admittedly the similarities end when he picks up the phone and shouts, 'IT'S CAPTAIN BEANY BEANING IN FROM THE PLANET BEANUS!' but still, it's hard not to smile, even when I later discover a piece in the *Sun* headlined 'TEENY-WEENY BEANIE! Baked bean fanatic, 65, opens up about his 4.5in penis after 10 years without sex'. (I decide not to tell Martha about this bit, in case she changes her mind.)

❖❖❖

Tea Break:
BAKED BEANS AND OTHER VEGETABLES

An American creation that may pre-date the Pilgrim Fathers – the story goes that settlers adopted the Indigenous custom of slow-cooking beans in maple syrup and bear fat for the Sabbath, when food preparation was frowned upon – baked beans arrived in the UK in 1886, and have since gone thoroughly native. Indeed, to those familiar with sweet, porky Boston beans, or the tangy Southern barbecue variety, the simple tomato sort may seem to have strayed so far from the family fold as to be thoroughly estranged.

The internet is full of videos of Americans trying 'beans on toast', standard fare in Britain, Ireland and the Antipodes, as if it's the weirdest thing ever. As one blogger put it, 'Beans on toast in America is decidedly NOT a thing. And I don't mean "not a thing", like "some people eat it, but most of us don't". I mean "not a thing", like "WHO IN THE WORLD WOULD EAT BEANS ON A PIECE OF TOAST?"' Their loss. Heinz don't even sell baked beans in the US market these days – hungry expats have to import them, currently at a cost of £2.10 a can.

Despite almost three-quarters of the English (I can only hope other home nations are more sensible) choosing them for our ideal cooked breakfast, beans are a relatively recent addition to the plate, popping up in the post-war years as a thrifty filler. Their progress was helped by an early-Sixties partnership with Danish Bacon, offering housewives the chance to win £20,000 of prizes, including electric sewing machines and 'movie cameras' in return for penning a sentence about why beans and bacon go so well together.

Personally, I object to the way they encroach on everything else – one approach, as Alan Partridge famously told Sonja in the static caravan, is to put 'distance between the eggs and the beans. I may want to mix them, but I want that to be my decision. Use a sausage as a breakwater.' Another is to put them in a fussy little ramekin. I'd suggest the simplest of all: leaving them out altogether.

❖❖❖

When I meet Martha by the ticket machines at Paddington at 7.15 a.m., she's rooting in an M&S carrier bag wedged in her bike basket. 'What's that smell?' I ask. Just some ham I found, she says casually – want a coffee? I'm left to hope she found it in M&S rather than on the floor, but frankly, knowing Martha, anything's possible.

On the train, I bring out my contribution, a breakfast frittata, made with black pudding, chipolatas, bacon and, of course, baked beans, cut into thick wedges and served in two

buttered rolls. Martha immediately puts away her ham. I have
earned her respect.

BREAKFAST FRITTATA

*I'm not going to give a recipe for black pudding because I haven't
found a source of high-welfare pig's blood. Instead, buy a decent one
and make it into this rather excellent frittata; a whole breakfast in
your hand, and perfect picnic fare. Cook it the night before, stuff it in
your jersey pocket, and enjoy it by the side of the road, or on a train
to visit Captain Beany if you prefer. I have, you will note, allowed
both chips and beans in this breakfast, because I am nothing if not
contrary.*

Serves 4
60g bacon lardons, or thick-cut streaky bacon, cut into strips
2 chipolatas, cut in half lengthways
80g black pudding
*100g oven chips, defrosted, or boiled potatoes, sliced, or leftover
    cooked chips*
½ 400g tin of baked beans
4 eggs, beaten and seasoned
4 cherry tomatoes, cut in half

1 Heat a frying pan about 20cm in diameter on a medium-high
   heat and add the bacon and sausages, cut-side down. Cook
   until the bacon starts to release its fat, then crumble in the
   black pudding. Fry until the pudding is beginning to crisp,
   and the bacon and sausages are golden, then scoop out of
   the pan with a slotted spoon, leaving as much fat in there as
   possible, and set aside.

2 Fry the oven chips or potatoes in the pan until lightly golden. Take the pan off the heat, take out the chips and make sure the base and sides are well greased (add oil if necessary) before returning half the chips, bacon and black pudding. Drain the sauce from the beans before adding half of them too.

3 Put the pan back on a medium heat and pour in half the egg. Add the remaining chips, bacon, black pudding and beans, followed by the remaining egg, and arrange the chipolatas, cut-side down, and tomatoes, cut-side up, on top. Cover the pan with a lid, heatproof plate or foil and cook until set around the edges and underneath. Heat the grill.

4 Put the frittata under the grill until the sausages are well browned and the top completely set. Allow to cool slightly before cutting into four to serve.

◆————————◆

A lifelong Londoner, Martha was genuinely astonished when I assured her we could travel to Wales and back in a single day, and still seems mildly suspicious when we disembark at a station where the signs are in two languages and the air smells faintly of sulphur. Isn't it weird being somewhere where they actually still make stuff? I say, gesturing at the steel plant chimneys belching steam into the distance. I make sourdough actually, Martha retorts huffily, putting on her helmet.

This is nice, we say, pedalling down Station Road in the sun. A handsome Victorian parade, a mixture of beauty salons (Big Chopper Hair Co. is our favourite), takeaways and an ancient angling shop, all painted in cheery colours, gives way to retail parks, and then to pebbledash blocks. Magnificent hills loom over the grey estates – imagine living with a view like that, I shout back to Martha as we pass a place advertising pigeon corn and horse feed. She doesn't hear me, she's still laughing at Big Chopper.

Barry, or Beany, lives on the Sandfields estate, a low-rise post-war development built for steelworkers, with wide roads and profligate levels of green space by London standards, all weirdly deserted this fine Tuesday morning. Maybe everyone's off making things. We lock the bikes to a lamppost and head off in search of Flint House. 'Are you nervous?' Martha says. 'I'm nervous.'

Nonsense, I say, feeling nervous.

I ring the doorbell. There's a long silence, and then something unintelligible crackles over the intercom. Martha and I look at each other. 'Captain Beany?' I say, feeling foolish. There's a slightly manic cackle as the door clicks open. 'Come in and I shall bean you up to number six, my love!'

———•◆•———

We bean ourselves up the concrete stairs to the third floor. On the top landing is a very ordinary black front door ('I thought it would be orange!' Martha whispers) decorated with a Tripadvisor sticker declaring the flat RECOMMENDED. A voice from within asks for a password. I panic and there's a long moment of silence before it swings open, just as I squeak BAKED BEANS?

Both of us are momentarily stunned by the apparition before us: a small, wiry man, dressed in baked-bean-print T-shirt and shorts, baked-bean-print socks and mask, and a bean-print beanie hat sporting an orange rosette that declares, I JUST LOVE BAKED BEANS! His sunglasses and trainers are merely extremely orange. 'Ooh, I like your top,' he says, gesturing at my Heinz Beanz jersey. 'Where did you get that from then?' I feel oddly proud to have a bean accessory he's not got.

'You can take your masks off if you like,' he says as he leads us down the hall, 'I'm double jabbed. And I'm immune to diseases on this planet anyway.'

We decide to keep them on; it's very warm in here with the windows closed, and I'm not sure I like the optics of us putting a local charity legend in hospital. Beany bustles off in a swish of polyester to make a pot of tea as we sit dumbfounded on the orange vinyl sofa on the orange shagpile carpet in front of the glossy orange coffee table. Perhaps predictably, the walls are painted orange too; the shelves (also orange) bow under the weight of bean memorabilia.

Martha's eyes are popping above her mask as I nose about, noting a picture of Beany, resplendent in an orange suit, meeting the Duchess of Cornwall, next to one of him, apparently naked apart from orange make up, leaning out of the window of a custom bean-painted Ford Escort (subsequently, we learn, towed away by the council). On the opposite wall is a large painting of our man in full superhero garb canvassing for sponsorship for some charitable endeavour in Aberafan Shopping Centre, and two framed pages from the *Sunday Sport*. In one, Beany peers out from the front page submerged in a bath of beans under the headline BAKED BEAN FREAK'S BUM EXPLODES. The other claims, no less startlingly, MY NUTS FROZE BATHING IN BEANS.

How long do we have to stay? Martha asks quietly as I sit back down. I think he said he's got another booking at 12.30 p.m., I say as I check my watch – 10.55 a.m. – but we won't be here that long, surely.

Once Beany gets talking, however, it's difficult to stop him. Born in Port Talbot in 1954, a 'very shy, introverted child', the young Barry Kirk nevertheless always had, he says rather grandly, 'a passion for drama'. Or to put it another way, he loved the attention of an audience, but found it impossible to learn any lines. Instead, armed with five O Levels, he went to work for the DVLA down the road in Swansea, finally landing up operating computers at the BP chemical works at Baglan Bay, where he stayed for 14 years.

While at BP, he began doing 'crazy stuff for charity – I love a cause and I love dressing up!' Photos show the Artist Formerly Known as Barry selling 'knickers for a nicker' (£1) to jolly ladies at a Tom Jones concert – 'saved them the bother of taking their knickers off to throw at him, see' – and pushing a supermarket trolley while dressed, for reasons unclear, as the Angel of Mercy, but it wasn't until 1986 that he hit upon the role that was to define him.

'I came across this album' – he passes us an LP of *The Who Sell Out*. On the cover, Roger Daltrey stares up balefully from a bath of baked beans above the tagline, Get Saucy. 'Well, that got me thinking, see. If it's good enough for him, you know? So I did some research to find out how long people had laid in various substances, custard and so on, and found there wasn't a record for baked beans. If it wasn't for that album cover I don't know where I'd be today.'

We contemplate this astonishing prospect in silence as Barry turns to his computer to cue up a slightly shaky video of the day, 35 years ago, when his life changed forever. The camera pans around a self-conscious crowd in suits and Eighties perms in the bar of the Aberavon Hotel. The bath, donated by a local businessman, sits in front of a hand-painted fundraising thermometer of the type you used to see outside churches, tracking the progress of their roof appeal. The beans themselves, donated by a cash and carry, stand in serried rows to the side like a wobbly Warhol installation.

Our hero, a young-ish Beany, or Barry as he was back then, appears in a pair of boxer shorts. 'That's me,' he explains, somewhat unnecessarily, 'but the majority of people in this are dead. There's my ex-girlfriend, you'll see my mother in a minute' – he slaps the desk in excited anticipation – 'see, this is a YouTube moment!' On screen, Young Barry gets into the bath, skids and falls, hitting his head on the side: 'I slipped on the beans and fell on my bloody arse. Split the bath.'

The action mercilessly moves on to giggling kids in matching tracksuits pouring beans over his head. 'No ring pulls in those days,' he notes, as if that was the worst bit about spending four days and four nights in a bath of cold beans. (As no record existed to beat, he'd decided to set the bar high with a nice round 100 hours.)

I can't say Barry looks particularly happy in the film. He agrees it was harder than he'd imagined. 'Why I did it in September I don't know; I got hypothermia. I went in there, beans poured over me and I started shaking, I thought I'm not going to last 100 seconds, let alone 100 hours. I didn't think it through. I suffered from sleep deprivation, I put on weight. But the body adjusts. Mind, when I got out I started shaking again. You can't test drive these things.'

He fast-forwards several days to Barry, still in his bath, now wearing a rather dazed expression, being ambushed by a kissagram (nothing in this film is more Eighties than this detail) before being hauled shakily to his feet by two elderly men whose gold chains glint in the lights – 'Two mayors we had there,' he says proudly. 'Two.'

'You look like you've just been removed from a war zone,' Martha says censoriously.

The stunt raised £1,500 for the Gateway Club for disabled children, but, though Guinness sent Barry a certificate, he didn't make it into the book, he says, clearly still resentful, because they hadn't supplied anyone to certify the record.

How long did it put you off beans for? I ask, hoping to take his mind off it – I still can't drink peach schnapps and it's over half a lifetime since I overdid it on that.

'I'll be honest with you, it was about a year and a half. The smell sticks in your psychic ... ' he laughs, 'I might say psycho mind.' (I hear Martha shift uneasily beside me, possibly working out the nearest usable exit.) 'I could have slept for a week after too.'

It can't have been all that traumatic, because five years later he decided to legally change his name to Captain Beany – who wouldn't prefer to be a superhero, he says, than plain old Barry Howard Kirk? 'The lawyer thought it was so funny he didn't charge me a bean,' he recalls proudly, passing across the official records in a buff-coloured envelope, 'but then I went to the bank and the first thing they asked me was, but what's your first name then? Captain, I said. And that was that.'

Not content with this gesture, he also paid to name a distant star the Planet Beanus ('Lucky I didn't lay in a bath of peas, eh?' he winks at Martha), and designed a flag for it based, he explains, on the UN one. I read later he even landed himself in court in 1990 claiming he was exempt from the poll tax on the basis that 'I am not a human being so the tax does not apply to me ... Everyone knows I am from Beanus. You just have to look at me to see that.' The magistrate was unsympathetic and brought him back down to earth with a bill for £247 plus £15 costs to Port Talbot District Council.

Beany does not mention this particular political battle. He does, however, show us his collection of campaign memorabilia, having stood for election at every level, from local to European seats – he even challenged First Minister Mark Drakeford for his seat earlier this year, though Beany was hoping to be elected President of Wales instead: 'It has a nice ring to it,

don't you think?' Though he lost his deposit every time, he
beat UKIP in Neath 2010 by more than 60 votes, which must
have felt good.

He's run several marathons with a plate of heavily varnished
beans on toast in his hand, and did the Cardiff Half in 2013
pushing a vacuum cleaner on behalf of Keep Wales Tidy. He
even completed a virtual Land's End to John O'Groats during
lockdown. 'I was averaging 50 miles every other day,' he tuts. 'I
got obsessed, I lost a stone in weight. I look back now and
think, what was I doing?'

You must be a bit of a local celebrity, I say. He beams. Oh, I
am, he says. The neighbours don't take a blind bit of notice to be
honest, I'm still Barry to them, but when I go into town, people
stop me and say, my name's on your head (to mark his sixtieth
back in 2014, Beany had 60 initialled baked beans tattooed on his
scalp to raise funds for a local girl with cerebral palsy).

It's fair to say he keeps himself busy, despite having been
unable to find work since he was made redundant from BP
almost three decades ago. (Port Talbot has among the highest
unemployment rates in Wales.) He devoted himself to
looking after his mother until her death in 1997, and then,
finding himself on his own in the flat, decided to cheer
himself up (his words) by turning the living room into a
baked bean museum.

'I bought all the stuff on eBay, painted everything orange,'
he says, leading us into the Heinz Kitchen ('like in New York,
you know, Hell's Kitchen?') with its Heinz green washing-up
bowl, soap dish and drainer, though when he briefly opens the
fridge to put the milk back I'm sad to see it's full of ready
meals. (To be fair, as Martha points out later, you don't keep
beans in the fridge.) We move on to the Branston bathroom
with its orange walls, orange loo brush and orange shower

curtain. A big sign declares NO FARTING ALLOWED. The kids love a photo with the loo brush, he says hopefully. I pretend not to hear: I have my limits.

Replacing it reverently in its orange holder, he tells Martha she looks a lot like his girlfriend, Tina Beans – 'You've got that look.' The look of a tin of beans, I say delightedly. Why, I've always thought that too!

Beany and I are still laughing as he opens the museum door, at which point I stop abruptly. I'm not sure what I expected from a museum in someone's living room, but it wasn't anything this . . . slick.

The curtains are drawn against the light and the room is filled with shelves and professional glass display cases of packaging and memorabilia, plus clocks, paintings and archive advertising material. New England bean crocks compete for my attention with Heinz-branded mugs, keyrings and recipe books. As I'm looking at a photo of a polar explorer posing with a tin of beans in the snow of Antarctica – Scott's ill-fated expedition was sponsored by a number of companies, including Heinz – Beany bounds over to show off a set of bean-shaped cufflinks he's concerned that I missed, presented to some poor sod in recognition of 20 years of faithful service at the HP factory in Wisbech.

Greedy to the last, we're particularly fascinated by the collection of baked beans from around the world – including an ill-fated Asda chocolate-flavoured spin-off – but Beany confesses he's never tried any of them. I sense his interest is more obsessive than gastronomic.

He didn't win Great British Eccentric of the Year 2009 for nothing though; the spotless displays are guarded by an inflatable alien in a Heinz cap and apron, holding a Heinz shopping bag, standing on a Heinz rug between two Heinz bins, and gazing expressionlessly at a life-sized cut-out of Beany in full superhero spandex and gold pants on the back of the door. I can feel Martha shoving me towards it as we admire the selection of Mr Bean memorabilia. 'I got there with the whole bean thing before him,' Beany says, with some bitterness. 'I asked him to be a patron of the museum but I never heard back.'

Though it seems clear from the branding on the loo brush, I ask him the million dollar question; is he a Heinz or a Branston man? Ooh, I can't be partial like, now I'm big in beans, he says; a true politician's answer.

Outside in the hall, he tells us he's recently applied for *Come Dine With Me:* 'I don't even care if I win,' he says with commendable candour, 'it's all another five minutes of fame.' This reminds him of the story of when the Olympic Torch came to Port Talbot back in 2012. 'I waited to get the call and it didn't come, so I went to B&M and made one' (I peer at the photo, trying to work out if another loo brush is involved) 'then took it for a couple of bevvies. When the torch was about half a mile down the road I started running. I went to the nearest Wetherspoons pub and everyone wanted their photos taken with me. What a buzz!' He sounds genuinely happy in the memory. 'If it wasn't for charity, I think I'd be locked up by now. When I'm dead, I hope some people will remember me for it.'

At this tender moment, there's an actual buzz – 'That'll be the next lot!' He bounds off along the corridor and I realise 90 minutes have flown by on a puff of leguminous wind. Genuinely Beany is one of life's good guys, I think, as we hurry giggling down the stairs and into the fresh air. A bit complicated, perhaps – but who hasn't wanted to run away from reality occasionally? He's done it, in gold pants and orange high heels, and he's helped a fair few people in the process. Good on him.

That said, I suspect his interest is less in beans specifically, and more in anything that offers a brief escape from the sheer ordinariness of existence – had he looked at a different side of that LP sleeve, he could equally have found himself condemned to 40 years dressed in leopard print and clutching a teddy bear like John Entwistle. But I suspect he wouldn't have got so much attention, because beans occupy a cultural niche somewhere between foodstuff and national treasure. They're the stuff of childhood teas, and school dinners, that you eat when you're feeling a bit ill, or sad, or too tired to cook. They're reliably, comfortingly consistent; easy to prepare and even easier to consume. There's a reason I could buy a baked-bean jersey for this trip, and Beany has been able to amass such a collection of memorabilia; like it or not, they've become part of the UK's collective identity. Which I'm fine with, as long as they don't come on a plate with eggs.

My God, it was hot in there, Martha groans. Did you see there were two toothbrushes by the sink?

One of them is for you, I say. Do you think he lives with all that stuff out all the time? I couldn't see anywhere else for it to go.

Definitely, she says, unlocking her bike. I bet he only wears orange pants too.

BAKED BEANS

These are baked beans as I wish they were; less saucy, richer and more savoury, with a kick of spice. Altogether better on a breakfast. I haven't added any pork, because I'm assuming you're serving it with quite a lot already, or perhaps don't eat it, but if you're pairing this with no more than some well-buttered toast, then you might want to add four chunky slices of streaky bacon, sliced into lardons, in step 2. Note – if you don't have any kombu (strips of dried kelp used in Japanese cookery, and easily obtainable online), you can simply soak the beans the day before in cold water with plenty of salt. Kombu is well worth the small investment, however; not only does it improve the texture and flavour of the cooked beans, but it also helps to neutralise some of the elements in them that seem to cause the human digestive system so much noisy trouble.

Serves 6
450g dried haricot beans
1 strip of kombu (see above)
2 tbsp oil, lard or bacon drippings
1 onion, finely sliced
2 garlic cloves, crushed
1 tsp hot smoked paprika (or you can use sweet if you'd prefer)
4 tbsp tomato purée
2 tbsp wholegrain mustard
2 tbsp dark brown sugar
500ml chicken or vegetable stock
Worcestershire sauce or vegetarian alternative
Salt, to taste
Knob of butter or a glug of oil

1 Heat the oven to 200°C/180°C fan/gas 6. Put the (yes, unsoaked!) beans into a large ovenproof pot along with the kombu and cover with about 5cm of cold water. Bring to the boil, cover with a lid and put into the oven. Cook for 60–90 minutes or until tender, checking on the water occasionally and topping up the pot if the beans start to look dry.

2 Meanwhile, make the sauce. Heat the fat in a medium pan over a moderate heat and cook the onion until soft and golden. Stir in the garlic and paprika, fry for a couple of minutes, then add the tomato purée, mustard and sugar, followed by the stock. Set aside.

3 Once the beans are just tender, turn the oven down to 170°C/150°C fan/gas 3. Stir the sauce into the beans – it should come just above the top – and bake, covered, for about 2 hours, or until the beans are soft. Remove the lid and bake for an hour or so until the sauce has reduced; how long this takes depends on the width of your dish.

4 Add a few dashes of Worcestershire sauce and season to taste. Just before serving, stir in a knob of butter (or a glug of olive oil if you're keeping it plant-based).

Job done, we cycle into Swansea, feeling, on this sunny day, like birds released from our urban cage, enjoying the sea breeze, the first blackberries by the side of the cycle track, and, in Mumbles, the contented buzz of a seaside resort at play. We're too late for the breakfast menus at the caffs, but we do find some cockle popcorn and whitebait from a stall on the promenade. Save me some, I say to Martha, I'll just be a minute. I jog through the park towards the chippie as best I can, given that three months after the accident, my hamstring no longer hurts but is now merely on strike. 'Do you do beans?'

We do, says the man behind the counter. Not got any on at the moment though. Mushy peas?

Ridden: 55.19km
Climbed: 148m
Breakfasts eaten: 1 (breakfast frittata – which at least
contained beans)

RED SAUCE OR BROWN?

Martha: 'Ketchup.'

Captain Beany: 'As for red or brown sauce, well, it has to be the former as you do so well know: you have to ketch-up with me with all my half-baked antics!'

7

BIRMINGHAM TO LIVERPOOL
Marmite and Staffordshire Oatcakes

It is a well-known fact that English people never know anything.
They only think. The only exception they know and they are sure
about in the whole world is Marmite. 'Love it or hate it.' There are
no other options; there is no space for grey space.
– Angela Kiss, *How to Be an Alien in England: A Guide to the*
English (2016)

That's quite enough about bloody beans: instead, let us backpedal two months to my first departure from Wales in the company of Tess, Tor, Gemma and Jerry-Lee the dog, stuffed full of Rob Rattray's sausages and treacle bacon, with a jar of Marion Dunn's Wenallt Hive honey in my panniers and a tear in my hamstring so sharp it brings tears to my eyes. Unsurprisingly, I'm not cycling across the border on this occasion, and I'm not even going by train – those dread three words, rail replacement service* have put paid to that notion – but by car, the two bikes rattling behind the five of us all the way to Shrewsbury station.

After bidding farewell to our chauffeurs, whose generosity has made the last couple of days considerably less painful, Gemma and I board a train to Wolverhampton. Thanks to yet more weekend engineering works, this is the closest we can get to her hometown of Birmingham today. I'd planned to spend the night with her anyway before heading north, so, unsure how long this new injury will take to heal, I've decided to stay a bit longer to lick my wounds and consider my options.

Having seen worse cases get back up and finish a hockey match, my hostess is blasé, suggesting it might well sort itself out; following a worrying hour on the train with Dr Google, I'm not so sure, but I so desperately want to believe her that I pooh-pooh her suggestion that Eddy and I might get a cab for the final leg of this afternoon's journey – after all, Wolverhampton is but an ostensibly flat 22km from Brum along the canal.

That said, as I'm not sure if I can lift my leg over Eddy's crossbar, and am too scared to find out on a platform full of people, it's entirely possible I'm going to have to walk the whole way.

Outside the station, I can defer the awful moment of truth no longer. To make life easier, Gemma holds Eddy still as I wince my foot upwards, then stop abruptly, swearing in frustration. In the end I have to remove the panniers in order to get my leg over the back wheel, as I can't lift it high enough to get on any other way, and my faithful domestique/slave then has to replace them before I gingerly attempt motion. It's fine pushing down, and

---

*   In France, of course, the driver just slung Eddy underneath the bus without even stopping to stub out his cigarette.

painful coming back up, but I think it's just about bearable, I report, riding slowly back towards the taxi rank.

Three minutes later, I've changed my mind. Too stubborn to say so, I spend the entire journey bathed in bitter regret at the no doubt permanent damage I'm causing with every revolution of the pedals, fully expecting to hear the sickening snap of a tendon at any moment. In my mind's eye, my hamstring is now hanging on to my pelvis by the most frayed of threads.

That my mind is elsewhere is a shame, because this is a side of the West Midlands I haven't seen before, the canal alternately grittily industrial and surprisingly green and bucolic, with the usual scattering of old boys and Eastern Europeans fishing along its length – though, focused on the idea of Gemma's sofa, for once I can't summon the enthusiasm to enquire what for. Even the sight of Tipton's intriguingly branded ISLAMABAD UK SHOP WARSZAWA WARSAW emporium fails to rouse my interest – I couldn't get off for a look if I wanted to.

I feel somewhat better once I'm propped up in her kitchen, eating Indian takeaway in the company of local friends Harry and Jay – Harry may be the world's worst camper, as anyone who read the Tatin section of *One More Croissant for the Road* will recall, but she makes a mean chocolate brownie, and Jay, a keen cyclist, is gratifyingly sympathetic to my injury . . . though the first thing he actually says is, 'Christ, you look tired.'

—•◆•—

It seems to me that short of doing something grown-up like booking in to see a physio, there's nothing for it but to continue on foot for the next few days and hope a miracle occurs in my buttock in the meantime.

The thing that would really lift my spirits, of course, is a trip to the Marmite factory. As I'm a true savoury-yeast-based-spread fanatic, the first pin that went into my big map last year was Burton-upon-Trent – finally, I thought, an excuse to see where the magic happens. As someone who sits firmly in the savoury camp at breakfast time, I've loved Marmite for as long as I can remember – half my childhood was spent arguing with my mum about whether a jar was empty enough to replace (to this day I find it difficult to give up on even the tiniest scraping*). At boarding school, where food took on outsize importance, one's taste in toast was held to be an extension of one's personality; I favoured mine barely kissed by heat, then loaded up with the fruits of the EU butter mountain and spread black with Marmite from a vast, sticky, much-fought-over tub. Even now, I almost always take a jar on holiday with me.

So yes, I like Marmite. (And not just at breakfast time: it's an excellent addition to cheese on toast, adds savoury oomph to everything from French onion soup (sssh) to sticky ribs, is divine with pasta – just ask Nigella – and surprisingly delicious in caramels. Miso is great, but for me, Marmite is better.)

I'm not alone; Statistica figures from last year show Marmite to be the single most popular brand of spread in the UK, ahead of both Hartley's jam and Nutella. Perhaps because it is so peculiarly British, and divisive in flavour, Marmite is at once a condiment and a tribal marker. There is, as far as I can tell, no real export market: a British tourist held hostage in Kashmir in the mid-Nineties told newspapers the first thing he did on getting home after his release was to eat some Marmite on toast: 'It's just one of those things – you get out of the country and it's all you can think about.' Similarly the *Guardian*

---

* Top tip: wash them out with hot water to add flavour to a stew or soup.

explained to overseas readers puzzled by panic over Marmite shortages in 2016 that people are upset 'because Marmite, like the Queen, the stiffer upper lip, and getting really drunk, is something that is seen as uniquely British'.

Although some may think Yahoo's US food team were too kind when they decided that 'on the Gross Scale (0 being the most palatable, 5 being the grossest), we give it a 4.5', everyone has an opinion on the stuff. At least half my readers are going to love this, I think triumphantly in early spring, as I arrange my visit with Unilever's PR company. It might even prove the centrepiece of the book.

By now, you've probably guessed what happens next. They're keen as their Colman's mustard on the idea, until whispers of the Delta variant cause a severe downgrade in keenness. Whatever I have to offer in terms of vaccination certificates, PCR tests and medical-grade masks – I even briefly consider purchasing a hazmat suit, so desperate am I to see those bubbling vats of tasty tar – aren't enough. As an adult, I have to concede they have a point. My inner child, however, threatens to throw a tantrum at the unfairness of it all.*

I'll show them, I think crossly as I stand in Gemma's kitchen, liberally buttering two bread rolls. After yesterday's painful experience on the way from Wolverhampton, it seems wise to leave Eddy here to recuperate for a few days, so I've managed to persuade Tess, who I only said goodbye to 22 hours ago in Shrewsbury station car park, but who happens, handily, to be in the Midlands today for a meeting, to drive me to Burton-upon-Trent instead. (I have a faint, slightly unhinged hope that, by proving my love with a pilgrimage, the powers that be will

---

* Yes, I know this really is the very least of the inequities exacted by Covid-19. Inner children, like outer ones, are not rational.

relent and let me in for a look-see.) In return, I'm keeping her company tonight at a spa hotel she's working with in Staffordshire; which puts me in pole position for one of the county's famous oatcakes tomorrow morning.

Applying an equally generous coating of Marmite, I sandwich the rolls together and wrap them back up. I have no idea whether Tess likes Marmite (there are some things too sensitive to jeopardise a friendship with) but if she doesn't I'm happy to eat two while quietly calling a cab and never calling her again.

There's a hoot outside. I blow Eddy a kiss, tell Gemma I'll be back for him some day, and hobble out to meet Tess and my salty, yeasty destiny.

• •

Tea Break:
TEN DREAMY FACTS ABOUT YOUR MATE MARMITE

1. Marmite owes much to the nineteenth-century German chemist Justus von Liebig, who created the OXO cube. He also discovered, by chance, that spent brewer's yeast could be turned into a tasty paste – but it wasn't until 1902 that the idea was commercialised.

2. The name comes from the French word (pronounced mar-meet) for the pot on the label, a *marmite* – and was certainly in use in this country by the sixteenth century. By the early nineteenth century, marmite was military slang for a pot-shaped bomb.

3. Marmite cubes were issued to British and Commonwealth forces in the First World War – in August 1916 5,000lb of Marmite rations were distributed to soldiers serving at Basra, and it was routinely given to troops in the region to ward off beriberi, or thiamin deficiency. Marmite was also included in Red Cross parcels sent to British prisoners in both world wars, and the Scott Polar Research Institute in Cambridge holds a jar sent to Antarctic surveyors in the 1950s, though sadly it's empty.

4. Marmite was sold in earthenware pots up until the 1920s, when the current glass jar was adopted with a metal lid, which was replaced by the plastic version in 1984, causing no small outcry. A shortage of raw materials in 1974 briefly meant it was sold in ordinary clear jars, which are no doubt now worth a fortune.

5. The Love It/Hate It campaign launched in October 1996, and the phrase 'a bit Marmite' has since been used to describe such divisive subjects as flavoured condoms and former education secretary Gavin Williamson.

6. Marmite special editions, most of which I have, some of which I regret finishing and recycling: Guinness, Marsden's Pedigree, XO, Marmite Gold (with gold flakes), Summers of Love and Hate (with lager yeast), Chilli and Trick or Treat.

7. Marmite spin-off products, most of which I have eaten: cheese and Marmite spread, Marmite sausages, Marmite ale, Marmite rice cakes, Marmite breadsticks, Marmite pasties, Marmite cheese, Marmite cereal bars, Marmite crisps, Marmite cashews (big fan), Marmite milk chocolate, Marmite Easter eggs, Marmite hot cross buns, Marmite savoury biscuits, Marmite breakfast biscuits (recommended), Marmite Brussels sprouts, Marmite peanut butter, Marmite body wash and deodorant (didn't eat those), Marmite

butter, Marmite hummus ... and none of them better than simple Marmite on toast.

8. In 2003, it was revealed that 14 per cent of Britons took Marmite on holiday with them, and in 2017, that it was the most seized item at airport security. I always pack a small travel jar, because as I may have mentioned, I take my Marmite seriously. Also, I don't want to be caught short if I'm ever kidnapped abroad.

9. The Marmarati, an officially sponsored cult of Marmite superfans which I have never been asked to join, must pledge the following: I hereby and hereon solemnly swear on celery, yeast extract, riboflavin and vitamin B12 to keep the following oath and agreement; I promise to do my duty to Queen, Country and Marmite; I swear to be faithful and bear true allegiance to the Marmarati; I will defend the ebony elixir against all conspiracies, protect its distinctive flavour and honour its orb-like jar; I will reject any second-rate pretenders; I promise to spread my dark and sticky mistress throughout the land, as well as on toast [bit weird that one]; And finally I swear never, ever to consort with members of the Marmaladi [well, that would be me out].

10. The closure of pubs during the March 2020 lockdown led to a reduction in beer production – which in turn led to a shortage of raw materials for Marmite. Production of all sizes bar the 250g jars briefly ceased, causing panic among those fools who did not have emergency rations stashed at home.

❖❖❖

Burton-upon-Trent has long been known as the brewing capital of the UK thanks to the specific mineral content and hardness of its water, ideal for the manufacture of pale ale in particular, and its canal and river transport links, which, in pre-motorway and -railway days made it easy to get the beer out to market.

This also made it the obvious choice for a product dependent on the surplus yeast produced during the brewing process, though the Marmite Food Extract Company once had factories in London, Britain's second-biggest brewing hub, too; a short-lived venture in Camberwell, and another in Vauxhall, which was in operation until 1967.

These days, the one and only Marmite factory can be found in an industrial estate on the outskirts of town, a series of low, grey corrugated buildings bearing a large painting of a familiar yellow-and-brown jar – further down, I spy the cheery red of Bovril, the savoury beef extract I've never quite warmed to thanks to the school rumour that it tasted 'of hooves'.

'Over there!' I say to Tess, opening the window and breathing deeply, though in truth all I can smell is the toasty cereal of the malting plant up the road. We abandon the car outside an electricity substation and walk back towards the factory, me in my Marmite cycling jersey and feeling quite self-conscious in front of a huddle of staff on their fag break.

'Ask one of them, go on,' Tess urges. 'Just say you want to know how it's made.'

I squirm slightly.

'Do you want me to do it?' she says.

My pride is pricked. No, I say indignantly over my shoulder – I just want one of them to agree to swap clothes with me so I can sneak inside. I limp towards the group, which looks alarmed, and then I see one of them is a security guard, which makes me alarmed . . . but it's too late now.

'Is it . . .' I squeak . . . 'I'm here because I really love Marmite. Like, I'm its biggest fan.' The guard looks like he's about to start laughing, so I press on quickly, before Tess can come up behind me and take charge. 'It's not . . . I don't suppose it's possible to go inside? Just for a quick look?'

No, he says, quite gently. Not without an appointment, love.

They troop back through the gate, though I swear I hear one woman mutter something over her shoulder about me being welcome to swap with her if I'm that keen.

That was a no, right? Tess says, giggling. I think so, I sigh, unwrapping the Marmite rolls. Looks like we're stuck out here. I can see the guard looking at us from the booth as we tuck in (and I must say they're very good; the soft blandness of fluffy white bread proving the perfect foil for 'the devil' condiment, as Liam Gallagher once dubbed it). Now, I say sadly, I'll never get to the bottom of whether the recipe really has actually changed in recent years, or if it's simply nostalgia that makes it taste stronger in my memories.

Marmite's 'quality specialist', St John Skelton, was tight-lipped on this point back in 2015, when I spoke to him on the phone for a *Guardian* article on my favourite spread. Clearly interrogation trained, he would only concede that 'owing to changes in the availability of materials, and improvement of manufacturing methods, we have been forced to adapt [the recipe]' while insisting Marmite's character 'has been rigorously retained'. Not rigorously enough for this superfan, St John. Why, these days, instead of treating it with the respect usually accorded to chilli sauces advertised with skulls and crossbones and unexploded Second World War ordnance, you can practically ladle it onto your crumpets. Is nothing sacred?

It's all I can do to stop myself charging the barriers, tracking old St John down and dangling him over a bubbling vat of yeast until I get to the truth of the matter . . . though I'd settle for a mere guided tour. Instead, I have to content myself with reading out the Microbiology Society's account of what's going on on the other side of that fence:

'Once the raw material, in the form of a beige sludge of spent yeast, arrives at the factory from breweries around the UK –'

'Sounds lovely!' Tess giggles.

I give her a stern look – this is no joking matter – before going on: '... it's pumped into heated tanks to encourage autolysis, which apparently is the breakdown of its proteins, carbohydrates and so on into liquid amino acids. They then filter it to remove any solid stuff, which goes for fertiliser, and reduce it – they should spend a bit longer on that bit in my opinion – flavour it with salt, vegetable, spice and celery extracts, and pack it into little jars of joy to spread on toast and dip in boiled eggs and bake into pastries and all the other wonderful things you can do with Marmite. And one day, I swear I will see it all for myself.'

I shake my fist at the factory in a vaguely threatening way, just as a man approaches the perimeter fence in high-vis, muttering into a walkie-talkie. 'Shall we go?' Tess suggests brightly. Glumly, I follow her back to the car, still sniffing the air in the vain hope of catching a whiff of Marmite.

It's a disappointment, if I'm honest, but I try to put on a brave face as we leave Burton behind: 'They do say you should never meet your heroes.'

'Exactly,' Tess says briskly. 'It's for the best.' She shivers theatrically. 'Some mysteries are better left unsolved.'

MARTHA DE LACEY'S SOURDOUGH 'MARMITE'

I challenged my friend Martha, who preaches the gospel of sourdough via her online cookery school the Muff Kitchen,* and truly believes everything is better fermented, to magic me up a Marmite substitute from the stuff you scoop off your sourdough starter when you feed the beast. Over to her:

Full disclosure: this is nowhere near as good as the real thing, which can never be beaten or even matched. But it's salty and sticky and black and quite fun to try if you have a spare old loaf of sourdough floating around.

Makes about 350g
1 loaf of sourdough (700–800g), sliced and extremely well toasted/liberally charred, please
500g sourdough discard
30g soft brown sugar
22g salt
10g MSG

1 Put the toasted bread, sourdough discard and sugar into a very large saucepan with 4 litres of water, mix well, cover and leave for 5 days, stirring occasionally.
2 Strain through a sieve into another large saucepan, squeezing as much liquid out of the bread as possible.
3 Discard the solids and bring the liquids to the boil, then lower the heat and simmer slowly for hours and hours and hours, descumming regularly, until you have a large-jar-sized amount of thick black tarry gloop.

* Yes, she knows.

4 Scrape out of the pan and into a jar, season with salt and MSG and leave to cool before eating on more sourdough.

———◆————————◆———

Hoar Cross Hall (Staffordshire's biggest spa, according to Google) is a nineteenth-century pile in an architectural style I think of as Boarding School Elizabethan and, even on a Monday morning in late May, absolutely rammed. When we go to check in at the hotel it seems half of Staffordshire has congregated in reception in their towelling dressing gowns, or robes as I believe they're now styled. (I have a peculiar aversion to the things – you never quite know what's underneath – and find them particularly unnerving in this High Victorian setting. As we queue, I fancy I see a crinolined ghost fade back into the wood panelling, a look of pure horror on its face.)

Tess has clearly pulled a few strings to get me a room as big as my flat, with a free-standing bath complete with seaweed soak, and some complimentary dog treats that I shove into my bag for Wilf, who, according to video evidence, is currently pining for me on Kaj's heated floor, following a bath in something optimistically named 'perfect puppy' shampoo.

Apparently I have to put on a 'robe' for my spa experience. A suit of armour on the stairs gazes impassively at me as I slowly limp past in my oversized slippers. Sorry, I whisper, I know. What has this country come to?

Having located Tess with some difficulty in the steam, we float lazily in the 'hydro pool', which sounds pleasingly like the kind of place you'd exercise injured racehorses, and watch a photoshoot in the hot tub, a girl draping herself over the side while her friend diligently snaps her from every conceivable angle. On our way out, I spot a button reading 'Press to

Activate Volcano' above a sign beseeching those inclined to do so to inform other pool users first. Who could resist? – it's the best laugh I've had for weeks.

I'm back in the same robe the next morning: Tess has kindly booked me in for a relaxing massage before I leave. This is an oxymoron as far as I'm concerned given the paper pants involved, but after 30 minutes of polite, if stressful, pummelling, I pluck up the courage to ask my assailant a question.

Have you ever had a Staffordshire oatcake? I say, face squashed against the bed.

The pummelling stops abruptly. I explain that I've heard great things about the local delicacy, and was hoping to try one while I was here.

'Ooh, no, I've never heard of them, sorry. Could you relax your shoulders a bit for me?'

I leave with the feeling I am quite the weirdest client she's had for a while.

———◆◆———

Having slid greasily back into my clothes, I call a cab to take me to Stoke-on-Trent, where they've definitely heard of oatcakes – and not just the hard, biscuity kind favoured north of the border. Round here, an oatcake is a thin, floppy wrap more like a crêpe, once more widely consumed in the region than ordinary bread. The scientist Sir Humphry Davy even observed of Derbyshire miners in 1813 that 'this kind of nourishment enables them to support their strength and perform their labour better', though I suspect higher wages would have seen an even greater improvement.

In urban areas oatcakes were often sold from the front window of terraced houses as breakfast for workers on their way to clock in. The last of these 'holes in the wall', in the Stoke suburb of Hanley, was forced to close in 2012, after the terrace was earmarked for development (Google Street View suggests it's been replaced by a row of vaguely faux-Georgian semi-detached boxes), though you can still find dedicated oatcake shops going strong to this day, and most local bakers* sell them for mere pennies.

As with many beloved regional foods, devotees can pick up on minute differences in styles: Buxton's Georgia Wild told the town's website that 'Leek and Buxton have the most substantial of oatcakes, thick with oatmeal. The Potteries towns of Tunstall and Longton have the finest, with oatcakes as lacy and delicate as edible brown doilies.' She claims that her brother could tell where an oatcake had come from, even blindfolded, just from the texture.

Me, I just want a good one so I do what served me so well in France, and Google 'best Staffordshire oatcake competition winner'. Ding dong – 6 Towns Radio, based in Stoke-on-Trent, has designated 8 August Oatcake Day, an idea conceived after several drinks, their website informs me, and still going strong over a decade later.

The Oatcake Day website features pictures of several confused-looking celebrities, including Ricky Gervais and Slash from Guns n' Roses, holding photocopied signs declaring their support for the festival, as well as, somewhat improbably, the rapper Coolio wearing an Oatcake Day T-shirt on stage at Stoke's Liquid nightclub. Below, Oatcake Day founder Terry Bossons recounts how he gave the 'Gangsta's Paradise' star a lift

---

* Necessity has forced me to learn how to make my own, as they're only rarely spotted in the bread aisle of my local Sainsbury's alongside entire shelves of bland, pappy white 'wraps' – that said, you can buy them online, or from Neal's Yard Dairy shops should you be in London.

to Tesco after the gig so he could try the local delicacy. (There is nothing I can say about this story that does it justice. I urge you to go online to the 6 Towns Radio website and read it for yourself.)

As part of the celebrations, the station runs an Oatcake Shop of the Year competition, and the latest winner I can find is one Six Towns Oatcakes in Birches Head, which is where I'm now heading. (Lest you think I'm the kind of person who casually takes a taxi 50km across the country, even with a dodgy leg, Six Towns keeps traditional oatcake shop hours, opening at 7 a.m. for breakfast and closing at 1 p.m., which makes this an official emergency.)

I ask Muhammad, my driver, if he's ever tried an oatcake. 'No, I live in Burton,' he tells me. 'Stoke is a long, long way. If it's not Burton, I will not know.' Having cleared that up, we have a lovely chat, only a third of which I catch due to the combination of masks, an open window and the remarkable speed of his speech, touching on the beauty of his home region in the mountains of northern Pakistan (he's delighted I've heard of their famously sweet apricots), his strong views on the corruption of its government and his equally strong disappointment at the British government's handling of the pandemic, as well as the complex iniquities of local taxi licensing. He and his family were back in Pakistan visiting relatives last spring and had to return home on a special plane chartered by the British embassy in Karachi – 'They were very good people.' At least, I think that's what he says; the conversation moves so fast it's hard to know how to arrange my face appropriately. Thank God, I think, for masks. They have their uses.

'Are you sure this is where you want to go?' he says, concerned, as we pull up in a suburban street some way outside the centre of Stoke. I've already spotted the banner: 'Oatcake Shop of the Year for Two Years Running!' and am proffering a handful of banknotes: I've made it with half an hour to spare, but who knows how long it will take me to hobble across the road?

Thanks to Covid, Six Towns, which scooped its first award only nine months after reopening under the ownership of Kinga and Matt Lofore in 2018, is currently serving through the window, old-school style. This gives me ample time to peruse the menu, which is mostly devoted to the oatcake, with a brief mention of sandwiches and pikelets as an afterthought. They offer 13 different filling options, including the Belly Buster Breakfast Box containing two oatcakes, rashers of bacon, sausages and eggs with mushrooms, tomatoes, beans and a tea or coffee for £5.50. I hesitate. It's very warm for a belly buster, especially when I haven't done any exercise for four days. I ask the girl at the window for advice, explaining I'm an oatcake novice – I did once have one from a van at Glastonbury, but that hardly seems very authentic, so I don't mention it.

Like Kinga, she's Polish – 'I'd never had one before I moved here either, but they're really nice!' she assures me. 'My first one, I had just cheese and red sauce.' OK, I'll have that then, I say. 'Most people here have them with bacon though,' she adds. As the most expensive menu items clock in at £2.20, I tell her I'll have a cheese and bacon version too, with brown sauce to make it fair. Two filled oatcakes and a 'can of pop' (Diet Coke, I'm an athlete) come in at a whopping £3.80.

A notice warns customers that 'all our oatcakes are hand poured in the traditional way, this takes longer than the automated process'. Indeed, craning my neck I can see her expertly using the bottom of a ladle to smooth the batter into a circle before flipping it for topping. They're delivered through the window in warm, gratifyingly greasy rolls of paper and I almost get run over in my haste to get to the park and eat them

– 'Please enjoy!' the girl calls after me, a note of alarm in her voice as I wave an apologetic oatcake at the bus driver. I keep forgetting I can no longer move at pace.

I unwrap the first – cheese and ketchup – crisp and slightly chewy at the top, deliciously soft and savoury in the middle, and oozing with warm Cheddar and sweet, vinegary tomato. It doesn't last a minute, and, reasoning they'll be nicer hot, I turn my attention to the bacon and brown sauce version, the pudding, one might say, which is even better – more substantial, more breakfast appropriate – then lie back, wiping my oily fingers on the grass, and have a nap.

STAFFORDSHIRE OATCAKES

Like any pancake, once you get the knack of these they're so easy to knock out – and so much nicer than the vast majority of commercially produced 'wraps' – that you might want to make extra to keep in the freezer (layer them between squares of greaseproof paper so they don't stick together). You can use all white flour if you prefer, but wholemeal will give them a more interesting flavour.

Makes 10 large oatcakes
4g dried yeast
250g fine oatmeal (or whizz rolled or other grades of oatmeal into a flour in a food processor)
100g strong white flour
100g strong wholemeal flour (see above)
1 tsp fine salt
Fat of your choice, to cook (lard, bacon drippings, clarified butter, vegetable oil)
Toppings, e.g. cooked bacon, cooked and sliced sausage, grated cheese, fried eggs

1 Measure out 900ml of warm water, stir a little into the yeast and leave until frothy on top. Meanwhile, mix the oats, flours and salt in a large bowl.
2 Stir the yeast mixture into the dry ingredients, then whisk in the remaining water until you have a smooth batter. Cover and leave in a warm place until bubbly – probably about an hour, but judge by eye.
3 Grease a large frying pan (nothing too heavy) with a little fat and put on a medium heat. If a drop of batter sizzles as it hits the pan, then it's ready.
4 Give the batter a quick whisk, then add a ladleful to the pan and quickly tilt it to spread it out evenly. Cook until dry on top, then loosen the edges and carefully turn it over.
5 Add any toppings you would like to melt or heat through and cook until golden on the bottom. Fold over and eat, or allow to cool, then cover and store in the fridge or freezer, reheating in a dry pan before use.

◆———————◆

It takes me an hour and 20 minutes, rather than the advertised 48, to get to the railway station to catch a train back to Birmingham. My left hip has begun to grumble at the extra work involved in hoisting my right leg around, and I can barely muster the will to cross the road for a closer look at a café advertising 36 sorts of naan, let alone go in for one. Tomorrow, I think: right now I just need to find a sofa.

Tea Break:
THE DESI BREAKFAST

Desi is a term used by those of Indian, Bengali and Pakistani heritage to refer to one of their own. In breakfast terms, this means anything from South Indian rice and dal dumplings to Bengali mutton parathas, Dishoom's Parsi power breakfasts to the 50p puris at Glasgow's Namak Mandi. It's not always easy to find a desi breakfast outside areas with a high concentration of people with links to the Indian subcontinent, but with just over a fifth of Birmingham's population identifying as such, compared to just 5 per cent nationally, it feels like a good place to try.

Spoiled for choice in the city, I pick Chaiiwala, a rapidly expanding chain set up by the great-grandchildren of a Delhi tea seller, which has been described as 'the Indian Starbucks', though thankfully without the Iced Matcha Green Tea Lattes. Instead I have a milky, warmly spiced glass of karak chai, and a green chilli and cheese omelette with a bowl of dal and a neat triangle of buttery paratha. Flecked with green slices of searing herbaceous heat, the omelette does a better job at waking me up for the day than any British eggs, beans and toast combo could ever hope to. I could certainly adopt this into my breakfast routine if someone else were cooking, I think, wondering if any of the four Pret a Mangers on my local high street might be up for a swap.

After two very profitable, if rather slow, days in the Midlands – days Eddy has spent lazing around in a shed with Gemma's bike

Phil,* it's time for me and Eddy to say goodbye and head north ... although not quite in the direction I'd hoped. Thanks to soaring infection rates in the region, there will be no congee in Manchester's Chinatown, black pudding in Bury, or even ceremonial ride past the world's biggest baked bean factory in Wigan. Instead, I'll be taking the train straight to Liverpool where I can flee Britain for Belfast, which is perhaps for the best given that I haven't been on a bike in three days, and have no idea whether I can actually get on one without Gemma's help anyway.

As I struggle to keep Eddy upright through the ticket barriers at New Street station, I realise that this is the first time I've been on my own this trip. It's not for long, as Lucinda, the school friend who came to see me off at Paddington, is joining me at the ferry terminal in Birkenhead tomorrow for the Northern Ireland leg, but nevertheless it feels significant, the sudden rush of freedom both nerve-racking, given current injuries, and undeniably exhilarating.

Eddy and I will be spending our solitary night in the north west at the Adelphi, a vast art-deco palace from the heyday of the transatlantic liner. Having hosted everyone from Winston Churchill to Bob Dylan, it's now reduced to offering cheapskates like me a bed for £28 a pop. Not only does it suit my penchant for decayed grandeur (it once had Turkish baths, and heated tanks in the basement to ensure a supply of fresh turtle soup for the dining room) but it's close enough to the station that I can push Eddy between the two, thus deftly putting off the awful moment of truth until tomorrow.

The hotel's beautiful mahogany revolving doors are still in action, to my considerable inconvenience (two men smoking outside kindly give me a shove), and the lobby still lit by chandeliers and faced with marble, but the American Bar is firmly

---

* Collins. He's a Genesis Tour de Fer 30 Touring Bike.

shuttered, and the man in front of me in the reception queue is insisting, in a voice emotional with drink, that it's not his fault he's lost three key cards in two days.

I prop Eddy up against a large bronze deer, and check in – the friendly chap behind the desk regrets they're unable to look after the bike, 'due to Covid, you see'. I don't really, but he's happy for me to take Eddy up to the room, so I don't quibble.

The wide empty corridors upstairs remind me uncomfortably of *The Shining*, and my room is a very odd shape, suggesting a recent past as a storage cupboard, but there's just about room for both of us, the TV works as long as you keep the curtains open, and most compellingly, it's half the price of the taxi I took yesterday just to eat a couple of oatcakes.

On the way out to forage for food, I sneak into the Adelphi's empty function rooms, marvelling at the proportions of the grand lounge, with its palm trees and elegant arched booths – I can almost hear a phantom pianist playing over the tinkle of tea cups and the murmur of gossip. I'm pleased when the receptionist tells me it's a popular wedding venue in normal times: it deserves a bit of love.

———◆◆◆———

Normal times these are not, however, and I'm so surprised to find the city outside buzzing that I momentarily check my watch to reassure myself it's Wednesday, rather than Friday night. People are spilling out of every pub dressed to impress and there's a merry air of revelry which makes it feel more like Bar Street in the Balearics than Liverpool in partial lockdown.

Heading home after a quiet bowl of Scouse,* dawdling for the pure pleasure of watching other people's fun, the general

---

* Liverpool's famous meat, potato and onion stew.

energy is summed up by a woman I hear shouting at the bouncer outside the Blarney Castle to let her in: 'WE'VE BEEN SHUT UP FOR YEARS – ALL WE WANT IS A DRINK!'

I realise belatedly, when I'm woken at 2 a.m. by loud voices in the corridor outside my door, that the Adelphi feels quite like the kind of place you might get murdered. Fortunately, I survive long enough to be woken again by my alarm, set early to comply with Lucinda's strict orders to meet her in the ferry terminal car park no later than 9 a.m.

As I'm not sure how cycling is going to work out, I leave the hotel safely behind before I gingerly hoist myself into the saddle (progress!) and roll very slowly down to the Mersey shore, and the ferry to Birkenhead. Passing the booth for the Isle of Man Steam Packet Company, blank and empty except for a scrolling message informing the world that the island is currently closed to non-residents, I think sadly how much I'd like a kipper right now, instead of a Marmite oatcake on the Mersey ferry.

Ridden: 25.79km
Climbed: 149m
Breakfasts eaten: 4 (Marmite roll; avocado and poached eggs on toast at the spa; cheese and ketchup and bacon and brown sauce oatcakes; desi breakfast)

RED SAUCE OR BROWN?

Lady at Six Towns Oatcakes: 'Red sauce, that's what I like with bacon.'

8
THE ISLE OF MAN
Kippers

*In the herring we have the most plebeian and common of fish, a fish
of endless resource and sovereign merit. The love of good red
herring is in our island blood ... Wherever the Briton settles, his
home-sick appetite for herrings remains unabated . . . the impartial
herring gives us of itself not only in vast profusion, fried, boiled,
broiled, grilled and baked, with mustard sauce or no sauce at all,
but subtly transforms itself by smoking into the glorious kipper . . .*
– P. Morton Shand, *A Book of Food* (1927)

I have to wait quite a while to get that kipper. As I pootle
around Northern Ireland, and then pass it again on my way
to Scotland, the Isle of Man stays resolutely shut. My friend
Marie, my official Manx Correspondent, continues to have no
good news to impart in her regular bulletins from Ramsey. But
after 17 months of splendid isolation in the middle of the Irish
Sea, the island finally reopens in late June, just as I draw level
with it again on my way back down the opposite coast . . . by
which point I have other fish to fry.

Once back in London a few weeks later, I'm straight online to book flights – sadly Eddy will not be of the party as my new best friend the physio, who has diagnosed me with a 'grade 2–3 hamstring tear', is firmly of the opinion I'd be better off not riding up any hills for a while, and Lucinda, my companion on this leg, says she won't stick around if mine falls off. From what I remember of the roads (mountainous, with no upper speed limit), I'm not entirely sorry – frankly I'm no Mark Cavendish* right now.

Marie's magnificent cheese toasties were a significant part of the reason I used to go over to the island several times a year with my ex. Having lost access to these superlative sandwiches when I parted ways with her son, there didn't seem much reason to return, and my memories of the place – a happy cross, to my mind, between the purple moors of Lancashire and the rolling fields of Northern Ireland – receded to a general impression of a damp rock full of bikers and bungalows and not much else, bar a lot of scenery and some tail-free cats. In fact it's been years since I had a Manx kipper – they're not that easy to get hold of down south – and as Lucinda and I board the plane, I'm looking forward to making their reacquaintance.

Looking at the little patchwork quilt of greens and yellows from above, with – rather unusually it must be said – hardly a cloud in sight, I'm surprised to feel a deep tug of affection for the place. There's even the faintest flutter of nostalgia as we sit in the shed of an airport; the 40-minute wait for our rental car on an island that's only a third of the size of Hertfordshire immediately confirms that time still operates differently here.

---

* The island's most famous sporting son, who recently shot back into the spotlight by taking the green jersey at the 2021 Tour de France at a stage in his career when even he'd hinted at possible retirement.

I have an appointment with Paul Desmond of Moore's Traditional Curers in Peel, on the island's west coast; wary of infection from Across, as Great Britain is known here, he's not doing his usual guided tours, but he's agreed to have a chat in the open air. Having had no response to my final email confirming timings, I'm relieved when a familiar, ancient smell seeps through the car window as we approach Peel harbour. 'Clearly someone's smoking today,' I say, sniffing the air appreciatively. 'Let's hope it's him.' Lucinda, who strongly dislikes all forms of fish, already looks rather green about the gills.

⁘⁘⁘

Tea Break:
BLOATERS, KIPPERS AND FINE FINNAN HADDIE

One is always perfectly safe in providing some kind of dried fish for the first breakfast for the man on leave who has just returned from service abroad ... for until one has been deprived of what so many home-stayers regard as the most ordinary of viands one does not realise how great and universal is the liking for dried fish by all Britishers.

– Blanche St Clair in The Quiver

Though I haven't been able to find out exactly when Blanche was writing (context suggests the 1940s), it's striking how much our tastes have changed in a couple of generations, in keeping with a more general narrowing of breakfast menus in the same time. The only fish found even occasionally on most British and Irish tables before noon these days is smoked salmon.

In contrast, Georgiana Hill's 1865 *Breakfast Book* claims that 'no comestible is more deservedly popular for the breakfast table than fish', and F. Marian McNeill includes an entire chapter on fish in her 1932 *Book of Breakfasts*, with over 40 recipes, from things which might still whet appetites today, such as potted trout and devilled salmon to the less immediately appetising likes of cod liver balls, windblown whitings and 'crappit heid' – boiled fish heads stuffed with oats, or barley and fish offal.

Next time you're reaching for the smoked bacon to go with eggs, consider the similarly rich and salty smoked mackerel or kipper instead. Brown crab meat or buttery potted shrimps on hot toast or crumpets make an especially fine start to the day, as do salted anchovies on a slice of bread spread thick with cold, unsalted butter. On weekends, a bowl of kedgeree (page 156), an omelette Arnold Bennett (page 351), or a plate of bubble and squeak (page 365) with salt cod and a fried egg on top all hit the spot for me. As for those boiled fish heads, well, I'm working up to them.

❖❖❖

Right, I say. Let's go talk kippers. We stroll back down the harbour, admiring the cheerfully painted boats, the old sail lofts and the Sailors Shelter, the red-and-white buildings of the smokehouse at the end somewhat dwarfed by the power station behind. You can't miss it though; MANX KIPPERS the sign reads in foot-high letters. Moore's Still Smoking in the Same Way as 1882. TRADITIONALLY OAK-SMOKED BACON. Factory Shop Inside. A blackboard leaning against the wall promises a crab or kipper bap and a drink for £4.99.

Lucinda puckers her nose. My father used to have a kipper and a pot of coffee for breakfast every single day, she says. I cannot stand the smell, even now. You're noble to come, I say, squeezing her arm gratefully and poking my nose round the door of the little shop. More signs. KIPPERS POSTED FROM HERE. Please Ring Bell for Attention.

'Is Paul around?' I ask the woman behind the counter. 'My name's Felicity, I've come to talk about kippers?' She looks momentarily thrown. 'He's out in the smokehouse,' she says. 'Wait here a minute.'

She's gone rather a long time; long enough for me to peruse an article from the July/August 1973 edition of *Manx Life* jauntily entitled KIPPERS! It describes a world in which Peel boasts five kippering houses – down from the 17 Mr Percy Moore, interviewed in the piece, claims there were when he started out just before the Great War. In 2021, there are but two remaining, and honestly, this one feels pretty quiet.

'He's just outside,' says a voice from behind me.

A man stands in the doorway opposite, tendrils of smoke creeping out around him. 'Hi!' I say jauntily. 'I'm Felicity and this is my friend Lucinda. Thanks so much for making time to see us.'

Did you not get my message then? he says, taking off his cap to scratch his head.

No . . . I say, puzzled, I'm pretty sure I haven't had anything from you since last week.

There's a silence. The thing is, he says, I changed my mind. I decided it was too risky and I wouldn't do it after all. I did send you a message.

I hear Lucinda shifting awkwardly from foot to foot behind me.

'Oh,' I say, feeling inexplicably guilty. 'I didn't get that message, no.' There's a pause, then he shrugs and starts talking.

And Paul Desmond can talk – he gives us almost 90 minutes of a working day that started at 4.30 a.m. and isn't likely to finish until 7 this evening, give or take the odd break to check on his fires.

Though kippering – in which fish are split, gutted, salted and then smoked – is a preserving process that probably started with salmon (the word comes from the old English *cypera*: male salmon), it's come to refer almost exclusively to smoked herring, a product first developed in Northumbria in the mid nineteenth century.

Unlike some rival kippers, Manx ones aren't dyed, but change has come to the industry nonetheless. Paul is the last one on the island smoking the fish the old way, over oak fires, rather than in the more modern, and efficient, electric kilns used by his only remaining competition. The kilns can turn out a batch of kippers in a consistent three hours, rather than the four to 14 required when you have to rely on the vagaries of smouldering sawdust. I ask him how this affects the finished kipper.

'Well . . .' he pauses, chewing over his words. 'I don't want to slag anyone off but it's like with a mass-produced loaf of bread and an artisan loaf; you can taste the difference.'

It's hard work though. When Paul started coming to the yard in the late 1960s to buy stock for his dad's fishmongers, he estimates there were 25–30 people working here 'around the clock'. Moore's always had the reputation of having the best kippers, he says, 'it was the Rolls-Royce of the trade', but Peel had loads of yards back then – they'd be throwing the boxes of fish out the back door onto locomotives to take them straight to the capital, Douglas, from where they could be shipped to Liverpool and beyond.

Mind you, he says, there were 50-odd shops selling kippers in Douglas too at the height of the tourist trade – 'We used to have all the top bands on back then – they'd have a thousand people queuing to get in. People had kippers for breakfast, they took kippers home with them, they were cheap!' He shakes his head. 'Now the people who ate the kippers are all dead. The trade is maybe 10 per cent of what it was in the 1970s, when they'd be doing 120 tons a week in the summer. These days it's just people coming in wanting a few pairs.'

Surely, I say, the restaurants must take them; if I ran one here I'd certainly want to shout about the Manx kipper: they're almost as famous, really, as your Bee Gees.* He shakes his head; those electric kilns mean the other producer can sell at a price that wouldn't even cover the cost of his fish. 'I've never even tried to compete. People come in and say, your kippers are dear, aren't they? Well, if they don't like it, they can go to him.'

Whether he admits it or not, however, I sense a gently simmering rivalry between the two kipper houses. At one point he suggests that certain individuals were not happy when he took on the business, letting it be known that 'if anyone else bought the yard, they'd not be able to get the herring.' Intimidating phone calls are hinted at. 'They all wanted to be King Kipper, see. They didn't like it when people wanted to talk to me.' Fortunately, he says with some satisfaction, he had deep enough pockets not to be intimidated; 'because it's a cut-throat business, kippers'.

Supply of herring is, of course, a big deal for a kipper producer, especially here. In the 1600s, I learn later, there were 600 boats fishing out of Peel Harbour; 'Even when I started coming,' Paul says, 'there were 30 or 40.' But unreliable herring numbers, and the problems it was causing the kipper industry, were already being discussed in Tynwald, the island's parliament, as early as the 1950s.

* The three Gibb brothers were born in Douglas, Isle of Man, in the late 1940s. There's a new statue of them on Douglas seafront, though they moved away in the mid-1950s, and the family emigrated to Australia when Robin and Maurice were eight.

There was a brief moment of glory in the late 1970s and early Eighties, when the North Sea fisheries were closed in a panicked attempt to rebuild stocks. 'Suddenly you couldn't get herring from anywhere else, so people came to the Isle of Man. Big boxes went from £20 to £70. Officially there were quotas, but you know . . .' he tails off tactfully. It may not be squeaky clean now, he says, but back then, corruption was rife; 'They were flying money over on planes, all sorts.'

Unfortunately, the cash vanished as quickly as it had arrived – 'Fishermen never think they're going to be poor,' he sighs. 'One man said to me, I made a grand in a week. I asked what he was going to do with it, he said, oh, it's gone now, we went on the drink. Then the North Sea opened up and all the buyers disappeared. The Manx boats were small boats, they didn't have the equipment to make the big hauls, see. Three years of boom, and it ruined the whole industry.'

Quotas were sold off, and now two huge boats own the rights to all the herring available for commercial harvesting in the Irish Sea, or at least so Paul says. He tells us about Norman, the last Manxman to fish herring. 'I remember asking him for fresh fish and it took him three weeks to find them. He'd been fishing them for 50 years. When he brought them to me they were so small, I had to sell some of them for bait.' There's a mournful pause. 'He had an immaculate boat, you could eat your dinner off it. He was in his seventies by then, and he wasn't fishing for money, he was fishing because he loved it.'

Now the fish comes from the port of Fraserburgh, 420 miles away on the east coast of Scotland. 'The agent I deal with there likes me because we can talk about the old days together and there's not a lot of people who can still do that. We get the best herring because we pay a lot for them,' he says with satisfaction. 'Poor-quality fish doesn't always go through the machine, and I wouldn't be happy with the result anyway. I never even ask the price, I just tell him how much I want.'

The machine in question is a 1950s device that splits 55 herrings a minute. The process is otherwise exactly the same as when the yard opened in 1882: the fish are briefly brined for flavour and colour, then impaled on nail-studded 'tenter sticks'* in the upper storey of the 40-foot-high smoke-house and left to drip dry. (Light the fires straight away, and the herring will steam and fall off their hooks.) Paul then sets six fires on the floor of the smokehouse; white pine chips for heat, oak for flavour. On a windy day, he might dampen the oak to stop the fires becoming so hot they cook the kippers rather than smoking them.

'It's all about air flow, and the weather makes a massive diffrence,' he says. 'On a good day you could smoke them as well as me, but you might only get one of those out of 10; a bad day, that's when the smoker earns his money, and herrings are so dear now you can't afford to get it wrong.'

From there, it's a waiting game – checking the fires (each lasts about an hour, and needs to be reset before it goes out, an eye-stingingly smoky business), checking the wind,† opening doors and hatches to adjust the draught and 'physically climb-ing up like a crab' to test the fish. He can tell they're done by looking at the drops of oil that gather on the tails, though look up at the wrong time, he warns, and you'll get it in the eyes instead. A smokehouse is a dangerous place altogether it seems: 'I've never had a rack fall on my head, but I have had one hit me on the shoulder, and I can tell you it hurts.'

---

* The phrase 'on tenter hooks' comes from the use of similar sticks to stretch out wet cloth in the textile industry.
† Fun fact: a stationary seagull always faces into the wind.

Once upon a time this was a 24-hour operation; the day's catch split and salted fresh from the 8 a.m. fish auction, then left to drain until the smokers arrived in the late afternoon to work through the night. 'In the old days they'd work in pairs; you'd have a small fella that could run in and do little jobs and a tall fella who could reach the high ones and they'd get £100 a night, which was good money.' Now it's just Paul, a medium fella, doing it all himself.

For how much longer is unclear; 'It's only me and the wife, and we're getting older,' he admits. 'We've just got one lad and he's a chartered accountant . . . I was going to pack it in a few years ago, then my son said, I'll go into business with you. He took a six-month leave of absence from work, did five weeks and that was enough; he told me, Dad, it'd need two men to replace you!'

So the problem remains – Paul is past retirement age, 'doing 80 hours a week probably', and he desperately needs to train someone to help, and eventually replace him. In the early days, he employed assistants, but they'd sometimes rush the job by whacking the heat up so they could go home earlier. He needs someone he can trust, he says.

'If I had two or three sons, or daughters, it would be easy; I could do less of the heavy work, but you just don't fall as well in your sixties. I'm fit, but if I put a stone on,' he pats his wiry stomach, 'I couldn't work here. I have to climb around, jump down, it keeps you fit.' Plus the business needs someone internet savvy, he observes: the last 18 months have at least been good for online sales, but that's no good if there's no one to produce the kippers in the first place.

The problem is, Paul thinks, the island has changed. Back in the 1960s, most of his grammar school friends went away to university and never returned. He himself only stayed because he was running his dad's shop from the age of 15, catering for the 'Dover sole tastes' of the wealthy tax exiles who arrived here in the 1970s and Eighties. He talks of driving around the island with hundreds of pounds of cash to buy fish: 'playing lots of sport, meeting lots of girls – but I've committed my whole life to this. I've enjoyed it, but anyone in the fishing industry, they all know how hard I work, it's bloody hard work – anything in the trade is.'

Nowadays, although the offshore banking industry may not be what it was before the financial crash, e-gaming is huge, and the island has full employment – and kippers are hard, physical, smelly work, clambering about with heavy planks of fish in smoke so thick you can hardly see through it. As I'll hear time and time again on my travels, whether it's hospitality, fruit picking or kippering, people aren't exactly falling over themselves to learn the trade.

Business is slowly picking up again: 'perhaps 30 to 40 per cent of what it was' pre-Covid, but he says the pandemic has taught him a few things about life. 'I haven't been doing the same hours; I left the shop open with an honesty box, and I could spend time with my grandchildren. Now we're back, I'm struggling to cope, my wife can't work as much and I'm two years older. Next year it'll nearly kill me. I want to see my grandchildren . . . yet I don't want to let my customers down. It's a young man's job.'

The idea of Moore's closing, the end of an era for the island, seems like wanton vandalism of an already fragile culinary heritage, and I tell him so. He gives me a tired look. 'It's hard to know what to do; if somebody came along and offered the right money, I'd give them three months of my time and that's it. You're either in it or you're out of it. It's like the fish shop; I gave it up four or five years ago, and haven't filleted a fish since.' He looks me straight in the eye: 'If you offered me £10, £15 to fillet a fish now, I wouldn't do it.'

As he opens the bottom half of the doors to shovel some more sawdust on the fires, I crane my neck for a glimpse of the ghostly rows of herring suspended above, slowly communing with the smoke. If this place were in East London, I think, he'd be beating off interested parties with a tenter stick.

————◆————

Even Lucinda concedes the kipper business has more to it than she'd imagined, 'Despite the smell, ugh,' she whispers, sitting carefully upwind of my lunch, purchased from Mrs Desmond in the shop. The kipper, freshly cooked and swaddled in fluffy white bread, is deliciously oily – rich and almost creamy with salty, smoky fat. Healthy fat, as Paul would no doubt point out. As we take our leave, I promise him I'll buy a few pairs to take home later in our trip. 'You can get them on the way to the airport,' Lucinda says sternly. 'I'm not having them in the car for two days in this weather.'

VICTORIAN KIPPER KEDGEREE

I've written recipes for this colonial favourite before, usually nodding vigorously to its sub-continental origins. Kitchuri (also known as khichri, or khichdi), a dish of rice and pulses, is beloved in countless iterations from Bangladesh to Sri Lanka, and can be sweet or savoury, vegetarian or studded with chunks of meat, hot and tangy or comfortingly simple – and yes, it can even contain fish, an addition that took the fancy of British imperialists. They dropped the suspiciously foreign lentils and most of the spices to turn it into a big bland buttery pile of rice which pairs beautifully with salty, smoky fish.

This version is based on Eliza Acton's 'kedgeree or kedgeree, an Indian breakfast dish' from 1845, with its fiery red cayenne pepper and chopped hard-boiled eggs, and does indeed make a fine, if not very Indian, breakfast. You can use any smoked fish you like, though partial as I am, I'd particularly recommend a Manx kipper or an Arbroath smokie.

Serves 2, easily doubled
180g long-grain rice, preferably basmati
Salt, to taste
2 eggs
1 kipper
2 tbsp butter, plus extra to serve
2 shallots or 1 small onion, finely chopped
¼–½ tsp cayenne pepper, or to taste
A small bunch of watercress, chopped
½ lemon, to serve

1 Put the rice into a small saucepan and cover with cold water – if you rest your finger on top of the rice the water should come to the first joint. Add salt, bring to the boil, cover, reduce the heat to as low as possible and leave to cook for about 25 minutes, or until it stops steaming – don't open the lid until you need to check the rice at the end. Fluff up with a fork, and leave covered until you need it.

2 Put the eggs into a small pan of boiling water and simmer for 10 minutes, then drain and run under cold water.

3 Meanwhile, put the kipper in a large, shallow dish, pan or jug and cover with boiling water. Leave for about 7 minutes, or until the flesh pulls away easily from the bone. Drain and flake the flesh.

4 Peel the eggs, tapping the blunt end on a hard surface and starting from there. Scoop out the yolks and set aside for now, then roughly chop the whites.

5 Melt the butter in a frying pan over a medium heat and add the shallots. Fry until soft, then stir in the cayenne pepper.

6 Add the rice to the pan, and stir to coat with butter. Increase the heat slightly, and once the rice is hot, add the flaked fish and chopped egg whites and a little more butter. Mix well, check the seasoning and transfer to a serving dish.

7 Crumble the egg yolks on top and finish with the chopped watercress. Eat immediately, with a squeeze of lemon juice.

◆———————◇

I bathe the next morning in the satiny waters of Douglas Bay under the surprised gaze of dog walkers and people on their way to work, who all seem to regard this as the height of eccentricity. It's still chilly enough to give me a serious appetite for breakfast at the Devonian, a B&B I picked specifically for the seriousness with which it seemed to take the latter part of the arrangement. Hosts Gillian and Kevin could not be more welcoming, and the cooking does not disappoint; I have a grilled kipper and a poached egg, though I can't help noticing everyone else is tucking into a fry-up.

I'm sad to learn from Gillian, a Lancashire native who moved to the island 17 years ago, that kippers aren't terribly popular these days, even among the B&B crowd who, I think it's fair to say, are probably older than the population as a whole – 'We maybe go through 10 a week in season,' she reports. Personally, she's as sceptical about them as she is about the overrunning promenade refurbishment outside, telling me she only does them in summer, 'when we can have the door open to get rid of the smell. I can't stand the things myself.' In winter, she tells disappointed guests, the kippers migrate to Florida: 'They believe me as well, it's awful!'

Usually the couple buy boxes of kippers direct from Devereau's on the seafront – Paul's rivals! I think, feeling quite indignant – but business is so quiet right now that Kevin picks them up from the supermarket with everything else. They're just happy to be open though.

I tell her how delighted I am to be here, and assure her I won't leave it so long next time. Apart from anything else, it sounds like the kipper business needs me. I can't do it alone though. You don't have to fancy them for breakfast, although I must point out that cooked in a jug of hot water they're no smellier than salmon, as well as lower in both calories and fat, and higher in EPA omega 3, vitamins A, D and B6, folates, calcium, iron and iodine . . . the list goes on, but I shan't bore you.

More importantly, they're similarly delicious wherever you might want something salty and smoky and a little bit rich and fatty (think warm salads, or omelettes, fish pies or fishcakes, risotto or pasta) and they come filleted too, if you're squeamish about bones. I must add that the sustainability situation with herring is complex, so the Marine Stewardship Council recommends checking their Good Fish Guide online for the most up-to-date information. This can be particularly difficult to come by when it comes to cured fish, like kippers . . . but it's worth pursuing if we're going to save the silver darlings for the next generation.

Ridden: 0km
Climbed: 0m
Breakfasts eaten: 2 (Pret a Manger airport croissant
(squashed, disappointingly doughy);
kipper and poached eggs (excellent))

RED SAUCE OR BROWN?

Marie: 'Under no circumstances would I put ketchup
anywhere near a fry-up, my ancestors would spin in their
graves. It has to be brown sauce every time, preferably HP. I
don't use much ketchup at all.'

Paul: 'I like brown sauce on my bacon!'

Gillian: 'Brown!'

9

LIVERPOOL TO BELFAST
Soda Farls and Potato Bread

*Beans in a fry is an anglicised 6 counties version of the traditional
Ulster fry with dippped [sic] farls, black & white pudding, eggs,
bacon & ispiní [sausage]. Fried spuds in a fry is [an] Americanised
addition. If you're gonna eat a fry eat an authentic indigenous fry.*
– Tweet from former Sinn Féin leader Gerry Adams,
28 March 2021

Rewind to Liverpool and early June where, having paused
at the Isle of Man Steam Packet Company's deserted ticket
office in respectful homage to the forbidden kipper, I'm boarding the Mersey ferry. In contrast to those floating Cornish
sardine tins, here I'm the only person in sight. Getting off the
other side, I push Eddy through a ticket hall stacked with piles
of old wooden benches taken from the boats in the service of
'social distancing'. I find both these facts strangely melancholy.

My mood is cheered by Lucinda's visible surprise when I rap
sharply on her car window in the Birkenhead ferry terminal
car park 15 minutes later – she's so amazed that I'm early for

once in my life that I decide not to mention the fact that, after almost a week out of the saddle after accident number two in Wales, I wasn't sure if I'd make it at all. She's not brought a bike, reasoning that she can be my support vehicle instead, though as I tell my tale of woe, she interrupts me to sharply ask whether I should be cycling either. I've made it almost 5km this morning, I say proudly: one has to start somewhere. She raises a sceptical eyebrow. 'Well, at least you can have a lie down on the ferry.'

She's not wrong: overexcited, perhaps, after a year stuck at home, Lucinda has booked us into both the Stena Plus lounge and a private cabin, though we'll be in Belfast long before bedtime. Possibly she thinks this boat is going to be like *Titanic* before it all went stern up, except with unlimited tea and Tunnock's Caramel Wafers instead of champagne and caviar. Not that I'm complaining, I love a Caramel Wafer, and so, apparently, does everyone else in the lounge: 45 minutes into the sailing there are just two left, one of which I quickly pocket.

Coincidentally, my Armagh-born friend Fionnuala rings just as we're waiting to drive off. As soon as I can get a word in edgeways, I tell her where we are. 'Oh God,' she says, 'it's horrible there. Get out as quick as you can.'

Though I can't tell if she's talking about the port or Belfast in general, this local recommendation doesn't fill me with great confidence, but once we've negotiated Belfast's fiendish flyovers and checked into the hotel (and my companion, an inveterate accumulator of total tat, has tucked her new Stena Line teddy into bed), we take a stroll and find the city very pleasant indeed this June evening. There are an awful lot of union flags around though, as Lucinda points out on the way back from dinner.* Looking across the road, I clock a JESUS HAVE MERCY ON ME sign taped to a lamppost opposite the Royal Bar, outside which smokers are congregated around a barrel painted with the red hand of Ulster. By the time we pass the marching band supply shop and reach the banner wishing the Queen a happy diamond jubilee, I realise, slightly belatedly, that we've stumbled upon a loyalist stronghold – some months later, when I describe Sandy Row as being 'quite intense', my friend Orla laughs her head off.

Thankfully it's quiet tonight, apart from some boys who run up to us with a red, white and blue sticker that says something about Ulster being (you guessed it) British. 'WADDAYOUSE THINKA THAT THEN?' one shouts, shoving it in my face. I'm so shocked I bat the sticker away like an insect, a reaction that clearly surprises him too, because they watch us walk away, mouths hanging open with disbelief. Oops, Lucinda, says quietly beside me, giggling slightly. That could have been worse.

—•◆•—

I'm here for something far more important than politics though: the Ulster Fry. Traditionally this includes not one but two breads, potato and soda, and sometimes it also comes with toast on the side, and occasionally with pancakes too. The Ulster Fry is thus hands down my favourite fry – though, as with everything in this small country, it's not without its controversies. Gerry Adams thinks baked beans are an English abomination, and my friend Joe swears blind that Gerry's white

---

* Potato soup, potato pancakes, and, only because there were no potato-based desserts on offer, a Guinness ice cream sundae.

pudding has no place on his plate. Reddit users, meanwhile, seem very keen on something called vegetable roll that Orla assures me has nothing to do with vegetables.

••

Tea Break:
POSSIBLE COMPONENTS OF THE ULSTER FRY

Bacon, sausage, egg, white pudding, black pudding, vegetable roll (vegetarians beware: the 'vegetable' roll is actually made from minced beef, mixed with herbs and onions or leeks – all vegetables – and sold in large sausages. And yes, you can get them battered at the chippy), fried soda farl (flatbread), fried potato bread, fried bread, buttered bread, pancakes, baked beans, tomatoes, mushrooms, hash browns, chips.

••

It's the two breads that I'm really interested in here – the double carbs that set the Ulster Fry apart from its rivals – so when, several months ago, I'd asked the Northern Irish tourist board for breakfast recommendations, and they'd offered to book me on a baking course with a lady called Tracey in rural County Down I'd jumped at the chance. Secretly I'm very much looking forward to being better at something than chronic over-achiever Lucinda.

Still full from last night's potato party, I decide to test my leg by cycling there, a distance of some 30km, while Lucinda follows by car – as ever, she has some Very Important Emails to attend to first. Despite an unnerving proliferation of flags and signs which alternate between loyalist and religious slogans (IT IS TIME TO SEEK THE LORD, one outside Killinchy reads, making me feel a bit bad that all I'm seeking is bread), the countryside is beautiful, lush and green, with only the most benign of hills once I'm outside the city.

A narrow lane runs along the reedy shores of Strangford Lough to Tracey's whitewashed farmhouse, where my fellow students, minus the painfully punctual Lucinda, are already halfway down their cups of tea. After a quick wash in the cloakroom, I join them, apologising for Lucinda's lateness (such a sweet feeling!), as I reach for a slice of generously buttered fruit loaf. Tracey tells me that American and Canadian visitors can't get enough of Irish butter: 'I tell you, they'd eat it with a spoon!' I laugh, half wondering where she keeps her spoons.

By the time my companion arrives, fresh from an altercation with a local farmer and flustered because I've beaten her to it, Tracey is passing round another favourite snack, a bag of dried red dulse seaweed, as crisp as an autumn leaf in contrast to the gelatinous laver purée of South Wales. The others, all locals, tell me how much dulse they ate during their childhoods: 'My daddy would take us down to the shore where we'd gather it up and he'd hang it on the washing line to dry – my granny would just eat it like a pack of crisps,' a lady called Sue recalls.

Big Sammy in the armchair agrees: 'When I was a kid you'd get thruppence for a wee sweetie bag of dulse.' Now, Tracey says, bringing things smartly back to breakfast, you can buy dulse butter, which is great on potato bread, 'though in an

Ulster Fry I usually cook it in the bacon pan. Sure, it's a heart attack on a plate!' she adds cheerfully.

Talk turns to the fry; there are the breads of course, but what else makes it different from across the water? 'We never have beans,' Hilary says firmly. There are murmurs of agreement from around the table, but Sammy shakes his head: 'See, I wouldn't have a fry without them.' Clearly, as with the one true cassoulet, matters are never quite as neat as some would like to claim.

We move into the kitchen, where tables are set up for us to learn the secrets of Tracey's family recipes, complete with bowls of local flour and bottles of buttermilk – which gives me the opportunity to launch into my well-practised rant about the difficulty of finding real buttermilk in Great Britain. (In fact, it's something I discussed with Mary Quicke back in Devon; having tried and failed to find a market, they have to chuck most of theirs away.) The artificially soured stuff, we agree, is just not the same; it's thick like yoghurt, and unpleasantly astringent rather than fresh and tangy. Sue shakes her head pityingly; 'My daddy's 95 and he still drinks buttermilk – he loves a glass with his champ.' He wouldn't love our stuff, I say ruefully; even the dog won't touch it.

Tracey proves an excellent teacher: patient, encouraging, and infectiously laid-back – I hear her at one point reassuring someone it doesn't matter that they've dropped one of their half-cooked farls on the floor – 'Sure, the hens will have it!'

Following her lead, we make three breads, potato, soda and a deliciously nubbly wheaten loaf (excellent toasted on the side, should you require a third bread on your fry) in little more than an hour so one is totally doable at breakfast time.

SODA FARLS

This is based on Tracey's recipe, but with a couple of tweaks to account for the difference in ingredients between Northern Ireland and Great Britain. If you're using Northern Irish soda bread flour, omit the bicarb, and if you're using real buttermilk, as opposed to the thick, artificially soured stuff, you can use 120ml of it and omit the milk. Tracey also recommends adding a tablespoon of treacle or molasses to the mix in place of the honey.

Makes 4
145g plain flour
½ tsp bicarbonate of soda
⅓–½ tsp salt
100ml buttermilk
1 tbsp honey (optional)
20ml milk (see above)

1 Mix together the flour, bicarb and salt on a clean surface (Tracey's preference) or in a large bowl. Make a well in the middle, and add half the buttermilk.

2 Whisk the honey, if using, into the rest of the buttermilk and add that too, along with the milk. Mix with your hands, just until you have a thick, porridgey dough then shape into a circle the size of a small plate. (Don't worry, it's meant to be sticky – floury hands will help!)

3 Flour a knife and cut into four farls. Heat a greased, heavy-based griddle or frying pan (if you have a crêpe maker, they're great here too) over a medium-low flame and cook the farls for about 5 minutes on each side until golden, then stand them on their non-pointed ends to brown the sides too ('harning', as Tracy would call it).

4 Eat split and covered in butter, with a fry or as is.

POTATO BREAD

If you're making this from scratch, rather than from leftover mash, use floury potatoes like Rooster, Kerr's Pink or Maris Pipers: you'll need to start with about 350g of raw potatoes, give or take, and make sure you mash them well, or you'll have lumpy bread. I've added dulse flakes – which can be bought online, or from health food shops if you're not in Ireland – as a nod to Tracey's favourite dulse butter, but they're more traditional without.

Makes 4
250g cold mashed potato
60g plain flour, plus extra to dust
½ tsp crumbled dulse (optional, but delicious)
Salt, to taste

1 Put the mash, flour and any seasoning (including dulse if using) into a bowl and mix until well combined – it's easiest to use your hands for this.
2 Turn out onto a lightly floured surface and shape with floured hands into a circle about the size of a side plate. Cut into quarters. Prick with a fork in a few places.
3 Heat a griddle or heavy-based frying or crêpe pan over a medium heat, cook the bread for about 4 minutes until golden, then flip and repeat. Tracey likes to spread one side with butter, then cook it for about 10 seconds before eating, preferably on an Ulster Fry.

◆――――――◆

Having confirmed my hunch that this is her first foray into the dark art of breadmaking, Lucinda nevertheless proves a typically diligent student and, frowning with concentration, manages to turn out three very respectable loaves (which I make her pose with so I can reassure her mother that she's not yet beyond redemption domestically). Once they're cooling on their racks, we sit down for another round of tea.

In fact, I must have drunk at least five pints of the stuff before I decide I've drained poor Tracey dry of as much information as she can impart on the subject of breakfast. Sloshing slightly, we take our leave, Eddy in the boot, parcels of warm bread on my lap; I eat half the potato one before we even reach the end of the lane.

✦✦✦

Tea Break:
ON BREADS AND BREAKFASTS

All the national fries contain a bread of some sort – usually wheat bread fried, or toasted, for the Full English and Welsh, with tattie scones (similar to Ulster potato bread) north of the Scottish border. But bread is also, of course, the backbone of a breakfast sandwich, a diverse grouping which includes the noble Staffordshire oatcake (Chapter 7) and the Geordie stottie (Chapter 12). I like it best, though, when it's allowed to be the star turn. Here I present some of my many thoughts on the perfect piece of toast, my ultimate comfort food:

1. Choose your fighter – for me there are two broad options here. The first is the simplest and most pleasurable: a soft white bloomer. I'd recommend this for the very young, the very old, the hungover, infirm or sad, because it puts up minimal resistance. In fact, it basically rolls over and begs you to eat it. Option two, sourdough, is more robust and, once

toasted, liable to cause injuries to the roof of the mouth if consumed without due respect. Its superior structural integrity, however, makes it a good choice for weightier toppings (avocado, smoked fish, etc.), while the open structure allows butter to collect in pools on the surface.

2. Cut it quite thickly, so the inside remains fluffy (bloomer) or damp and elastic (sourdough) while the outer skin crisps in the heat of the toaster. Sliced bread is acceptable, but always cut too thinly for my taste – thin bread is good for pâté later in the day but you don't want it for breakfast.

3. Preheat the toaster. If you've cut the bread really thick, you can pretend you're in a hipster brunch joint and use a lightly oiled griddle pan, but though the stripes look cool, you'll never get it as crisp as you'd like. If you happen to have an AGA or similar, you must make it on the hotplate, because that, my friends, is always the best toast. Sadly I don't.

4. Toast the bread to your liking. Personally I favour it quite well done, except if I'm feeling very sorry for myself, when I like it just warm enough to melt the butter. Arrange your mise en place, butter ready on the knife.

5. If you're buttering your toast, do so IMMEDIATELY. If you're not – perhaps you want a crisp base for some avocado, or ... well, I can't think of many other scenarios in which you don't want buttered toast, but I'm sure there must be some – stand the toast up. A dedicated rack is ideal, but not mandatory: I use my draining rack as it's handy for the toaster. This keeps it crisp as it cools.

6. Coda: If you're serving your toast with something wet, like scrambled eggs or baked beans, I'd strongly advise only covering half of the toast with it, or serving the toast on the side, if you're immune to mockery about being uptight. Soggy bread is an offence against nature.

7. I asked my friend Martha de Lacey, of Captain Beany fame, maker of some of the best sourdough in London, for her opinions on toast. As usual, she had a few: 'I like two slices of very well-toasted thick-cut (at least 2cm) seedy white, malted wholemeal and rye sourdough (at least two days old) bread, featuring at least some light black speckled surface charring; a thickish scraping of Marmite (ideally a pre-2000 jar, or the Guinness or XO stuff); plump, pillowy white waves of full-fat Philadelphia (approx. half a tub); inch-thick slices of some superbly ripe and juicy tomatoes (ideally Italian or Spanish, because ideally we are in Italy or Spain, now and always); smoked salt (Cornish or Halen Môn); freshly ground white pepper, lots; a drizzle of super grassy olive oil to make it just that little bit extra. Chilli flakes optional.'

8. Me, I like butter and Marmite.

✦ ✦

We spend the rest of the day doing Lucinda-type things: driving to look at a ruined abbey (which is closed because windy ruins are a notorious source of disease transmission) and poking around a lot of antique shops, some of which appear, to my untrained eye, to deal primarily in junk. She is delighted and buys several items,* while I spend a lot of time on the phone to

---

* During the four days we're away she amasses 'postcards of Dunluce Castle, the dark hedges and the *Titanic*; a *Titanic* Third Class cabin mug; a *Titanic* snow globe; a Belfast snow globe; a Giant's Causeway snow globe; a *Titanic* medallion coin; a Giant's Causeway commemorative coin; a pendant made of rock from near the Giant's Causeway; three different brooches by local artists (felt, crochet and ceramic); a sculpture of a small bronze mouse sleeping in a horse chestnut; a colourful Art Deco jug and an 1850s carnelian cameo ring depicting Ajax ... you know – just the usual holiday treasure haul, and not

ScotRail trying to game their bike booking system ('I can only see the same information on screen as you can, hen, sorry,' the man on the phone reports mournfully) before eventually retiring to a pub for a half of Guinness in the restful company of a large hairy dog.

———•◆•———

The next morning, I get to experience another big bread moment at St George's Market in the form of a Belfast bap* stuffed with sausage, black pudding, bacon, egg and potato scones, a combination aptly dubbed 'the Titanic', given that it completely sinks me.

If I'm going to be picky, I'd say that the black pudding could have been cooked a bit more, so it formed less of a claggy alliance with the potato, and the egg a little less, so it provided more in the way of lubrication (though brown sauce, which somehow feels right with sausage and black pudding, helps in that department) but it's satisfactory. Personally, though, I prefer a more pared-down breakfast sandwich – one meat (salty), one egg (rich) and one carb (stodgy) feels like the perfect balance.

---

everything was for me ... some were presents for friends and family and post lockdown it's v. important to stimulate local economies ... oh and how could I forget the phone attachment and charger cable for the car from Belfast market? That actually has revolutionised my driving experience!!!'

* The Belfast bap is a large, crusty bread roll created by Armagh-born bakery and milling magnate Barney Hughes as an affordable loaf for families during the Famine, and a popular choice as a vehicle for breakfast items such as egg and bacon, or indeed later in the day with a pastie, which isn't a pastry at all, but a deep-fried battered sausagemeat and potato burger.

The market itself, a handsome wrought-iron affair, is, thanks to Covid restrictions, almost the only local attraction currently open. Even the tourist information chap tells us, 'Look, I wouldn't knock yourself out looking for the little hidden nooks and crannies of Belfast; we're a post-industrial city where people enjoy killing their neighbours' – before suggesting we visit the Ulster Folk Museum, a plan which neatly combines Lucinda's interest in old stuff and mine in old kitchens.

In a little farmhouse there – just a couple of rooms, dark and chokingly smoky – we find a costumed volunteer making boxty over the fire. The recipe, she says, pleased to have found someone to talk to among the lurkers awaiting their free sample, came from a farm about 10 miles away. Mashed and grated raw potato, mixed to a dough with a little flour, butter-milk, scallions and seasoning, shaped into cakes, boiled for half an hour and then fried in bacon fat. The effect, when we take the hot, greasy wedges in our hands, is bouncy and glutinous, rather like gnocchi, and definitely substantial: 'They needed to be hefty,' she agrees, 'because they'd take them to the fields when they went out to work.'

Would they have been eaten for breakfast? I ask.

Oh, I'm sure, she says, they're lovely with rashers, why not?

A boxty pancake, topped with crisp bacon and a fried egg, I think, now that would be a way to start the day.

—•◆•—

Knowing Lucinda's mania for the grander moments of history, however, I've booked us into a Georgian guest house just outside Ballymoney for the night. O'Harabrook, hidden at the end of a long, tree-lined drive that puts me in mind of Daphne du Maurier's Mandalay, proves very much to her refined tastes, and she and the French owner, Karine, whose husband Rupert inherited the place from his parents, sit and natter over tea in the hall while I make a fuss of border terrier Dash, who fairly bristles with a very familiar small-dog energy.

Our room is country-house perfection: lamp lit, with stately twin beds and 1980s bonkbusters on the mantelpiece, the kind of place one could happily settle into for the evening, though I make Lucinda get back in the car for fish and chips instead. As she doesn't really like fish, this makes her a very kind person, and I tell her so while stealing her chips.

The pressure is on for Rupert with the next morning's fry – I sit magisterially at the end of the long dining table, overlooked by portraits of gloomy ancestors, a small stuffed owl and a collection of hunting trophies, and appraise his efforts.

As he and Lucinda chat away, I silently award points for the presence of both black and white puddings, nicely crisped, alongside the usual sausage and bacon, plus a slice of potato bread underneath a competently fried egg. I'm neutral on the matter of tomatoes and mushrooms, but, if I were to nitpick, which of course I never would, I'd observe that, with the accompanying toast, the breakfast only contains two carbs, three if you count baked beans (Sammy would approve). I magnanimously decide to cut Rupert some slack, however, given that I've finished everything on the plate.

They're now talking antiques and treasure; he starts unrolling ancestral military commissions in spidery handwriting, and I make my excuses and go and put on my cycling shoes for the first time since swapping them for trainers in Somerset. Walking may still be painful, but it's a beautiful morning, and after the success of yesterday's ride I feel the siren call of Eddy's pedals.

Indeed, once I've negotiated the even longer and less well surfaced back drive, it proves a truly beautiful ride up to the Giant's Causeway, where I'm meeting Lucinda once she's ticked off several castles and a road that has something to do with *Game of Thrones*. For the next hour or so, however, it's just me, Eddy and a surprising number of roadside goats. The countryside is bursting into full summer fig, the trees overhead an almost painfully bright green, the verges rampant with knee-high cow parsley.

In short, it's the kind of morning that makes you want to sing out to everyone you pass, WHAT A DAY TO BE ALIVE! though I confine my chat to a man in a van who kindly pulls over, seeing me looking at the map, to ask if I'm lost.

'You don't sound like a Ballybogey girl,' he says as soon as I open my mouth.

I say no, I'm from London, but if it's always like this here I'm seriously considering relocating. He laughs and tells me his son is at agricultural college over in England, 'but he'll come back right enough. I know he'll come back.' And why wouldn't he, I think, to a place like this?

Satisfyingly, I beat Lucinda to the Causeway. It's a privilege to cycle into this extraordinary ancient tessellated landscape – and my hamstring rises to the occasion. I make it back up without a single squeak, which puts me in high spirits as we head back towards Belfast, to round off our visit at the unfortunately named Titanic Experience.

Having sat on the steps of the cinema for the entire three hours 14 minutes of the James Cameron epic back in 1997, I can confirm this is more enjoyable – if one can say that about a tragedy which claimed 1,500 lives. Breakfast never far from my mind, I learn that *Titanic*'s galleys were equipped with 'the best up-to-date gadgets available'. With 3,000 people to feed, she set off with 40,000 eggs in the cold stores: indeed, a frying pan was found in the debris field around the wreck, though try as I might I can't locate it in the interactive tour of the silty remains.

The First Class dining saloon, we discover, was kitted out in 'early seventeenth-century Jacobean style, with detailed ceiling plasterwork, oak furniture and a piano . . . and extravagantly lit using 404 lightbulbs as well as benefiting from natural light', lest anyone miss you tucking into your morning tea and toast. The Second Class equivalent was in the Early English fashion, while the Third Class is described as 'basic . . . the white walls were partially panelled and partially exposed steel and were used to hang advertising posters'. Single men travelling steerage, like Leonardo DiCaprio's character Jack, were segregated from the women and families for meals.

* *

Tea Break:
BREAKFAST ON BOARD

Annoyingly there's little information on the breakfast menus, though I sneak a peek in one of the books in the gift shop and find that Rose in First Class might have started the day with baked apples, grilled mutton or lamb collops in addition to 'standard breakfast fare' such as Quaker Oats, kidneys, bacon or omelettes cooked to order. Jam was from Wilkin & Sons in Essex, and marmalade from Oxford.

Further down the ship Jack might have had porridge, ham and eggs, herring or, intriguingly, ling fish with egg sauce.

(Tea, the book notes, was served with every meal in Third, though in my recollection it doesn't seem to have been what fuelled the Irish dancing in the film.)

First Class breakfast menu, RMS *Titanic*, 14 April 1912

Baked apples
Fresh fruit
Stewed prunes
Quaker Oats
Boiled hominy
Puffed rice
Fresh herrings
Finnan haddock
Smoked salmon
Grilled mutton
Kidneys and bacon
Grilled ham
Grilled sausage
Lamb collops
Vegetable stew
Fried, shirred, poached and
   boiled eggs

Plain and tomato omelettes
   to order
Sirloin steak and mutton
   chops to order
Mashed, sauté and jacket
   potatoes
Cold meat
Vienna and Graham rolls
Soda and sultana scones
Corn bread
Buckwheat cakes
Black currant conserve
Narbonne honey
Oxford marmalade
Watercress

Third Class breakfast menu, RMS *Titanic*, 14 April 1912

Oatmeal porridge and milk
Smoked herrings [kippers!]
   and jacket potatoes
Ham and eggs
Fresh bread and butter

Marmalade
Swedish bread
Tea
Coffee

Lucinda has been very cagey about our accommodation for this final night, though I have a suspicion given her gleeful expression that we're not going very far. This is confirmed when I follow her into the Titanic Hotel, which thankfully is in the former shipyard drawing offices rather than on the open seas. They've missed a trick with the decor – not a porthole in sight – but the view of the city's famous yellow cranes, Samson and Goliath, is a cheerful one as, in true steerage fashion, I take advantage of the heated towel rail to do a spot of washing.

There's even a baked potato restaurant over the road, but, determined to tick off everything *Titanic*-themed short of actually drowning, we eat in the restaurant downstairs – I start with a frothy, citrussy Punch Romaine, which claims to be one of the last cocktails offered to First Class passengers, though when I look it up I discover it was actually a palate cleanser between the roast meats and the savouries, served just a couple of hours before that fateful encounter with the iceberg. 'Is this all a bit sick?' I ask Lucinda, then remember she's ordered the Jack and Rose, a revolting-sounding concoction of honey-flavoured whiskey, banana liqueur, lime and sugar with a shot of rose liqueur on the side, and thus isn't to be trusted on anything.

Exploring the old slipways after dinner, I find myself similarly disconcerted – away from the bright lights and merry chatter of the dining room, this place feels eerie. Illuminated to show the position of the *Titanic* and its sister ship the *Olympic*, built side by side, even the modern benches are positioned exactly where they would have been on deck. Shivering suddenly, I decide to lighten the mood. 'Did you know a

Pekingese dog called Sun Yat Sen survived?' I ask Lucinda. 'And that one woman apparently stayed on board because they wouldn't let her bring her dog on the lifeboat?'

'That would have been you.'

That night I dream that Wilf pushes me off a lifeboat.

Ridden: 57.04km
Climbed: 602m
Breakfasts eaten: 3 (Tunnock's Caramel Wafers; Belfast breakfast bap; Rupert's Ulster Fry)

RED SAUCE OR BROWN?

Lucinda: 'Neither – though butter in a bacon roll, please.'

Tracey: 'My preference would always be brown sauce with a fry or a bacon and egg soda [sandwich]. I don't take brown sauce with anything else, but on a fry I definitely would!'

Karine: 'I am not the type of person to have brown or red sauce – I am more of a croissant type of person. To be honest I had never heard of brown sauce until I came to England!'

Rupert: 'If I have anything it would be a small amount of tomato ketchup on a bacon sarnie but nothing on my breakfast! Karine is French. She doesn't understand cultural British subtleties. Dash will take whatever is going but normally gets spared the sauces.'

10
BELFAST TO CARRBRIDGE
Porridge

Porridge is a primeval dish . . . one of Scotland's two great gifts to the world's breakfast table – the other being orange marmalade.
– F. Marian McNeill, *The Book of Breakfasts* (1932)

5.15 a.m. is not a time I like to be up. It's certainly not a time I like to be up on my own, pulling on damp Lycra in the dark (having severely overestimated the power of the hotel hairdryer) and gingerly pedalling a laden bike through a deserted underground car park.

It is, however, a great time to explore a strange city on two wheels. Though my route from the Titanic Quarter to the ferry terminal is not the most obviously scenic, it offers a fascinating glimpse of waterside Belfast. I slink silently through the sleek developments that have replaced the old docklands, past abandoned pubs and a church, marooned now by dual carriageways, bearing a plaque to two children killed in the Troubles, and into the twenty-first-century industrial zone of Chinese cash and carrys, nutrition supplement manufacturers and the inevitable branch of Screwfix.

I'm solo – Lucinda is driving back to England with her car full of souvenirs later, but I'm booked on the first ferry to Scotland, hoping to make it as far as Glasgow this evening. It seems Belfast to Cairnryan, 150km across the North Channel,* is not a route much used by cycle tourists – they don't seem to know what to do with me, eventually deciding to stow Eddy against a desk in the office.

By the time I make it up to the seating area, most of it is occupied by men in high-vis and work boots, stretched out full length and already snoring. I find a corner spot underneath a sticker reading FOR GOD AND ULSTER, bend myself uncomfortably around it, and drift off next to someone's socked feet, only to be woken every quarter of an hour by an urgent call about timber or cavity walls or drainage.

I'm first down to the deck as soon as the doors open: as I can find no one foolish enough to recommend cycling the route from the ferry up to Glasgow (the freight-heavy A77, one local reports, 'definitely comes under "rather you than me!"'), I've decided to take a train from nearby Stranraer as far as Troon, where other, smaller roads offer more attractive alternatives. There are only four trains a day on this line, however, and one has already departed, which means I'm particularly anxious to get going as soon as possible – if I miss the mid-morning service then I'll have to wait until 3 p.m., which, even with these long summer evenings, doesn't leave me much time for the 90 or so kilometres into the city by the time it gets in at half four.

---

* Rupert informs us, to my surprise, that people regularly swim between the two countries – the shorter Mull of Kintyre route is only (!) 17km, though subject to the vagaries of the tide, and of course the whims of passing jellyfish.

The eleven kilometres from the port to Stranraer have rarely felt such a long bloody way, and the last 10 minutes, in sight of the station, the end of the line, sticking out on a pier into the water as I force myself south through the headwind, is positively painful.

But when I make it on to the train, everyone's in festive mood: Scotland's Euros campaign kicks off later with a match against the Czech Republic, and as I ride north into the wind from Troon, having executed a clumsy outfit change in the train loo, I spot saltires and lions rampant hanging from almost every house.

The weather could be better, but there's no denying the thrill of freedom that comes from being back in the saddle with nothing to do but pedal, passing kite surfers on the beach before snaking inland through country parks and past timber mills, hearing the roar of football fans in Kilwhinnie as I pause to take a picture of the Susan Fraser School of Dancing (motto: 'we can't all be stars but we can all twinkle'). Lochs and follies give way to the outskirts of Paisley (sample graffiti, the usual FUCK THE TORIES and the more niche FUCK THE POPE) and at last the tangle of Glasgow itself, where I cross the Clyde and head up the beautifully named Hope Street to the National Piping Centre, where I'm staying the night. (Piping as in bagpiping. I'm not kipping down in Plumbase.)

The centre, its website informs me, 'exists to promote the study of the music and history of the Highland Bagpipe', and the rather institutional, tartan-themed accommodation upstairs is clearly designed for students of that noble instrument. Sadly the attached museum is closed for the night.

En route to chana chat and methi keema mutter at the much recommended Mother India, I spot a stirring banner hanging from one of the city's striking red sandstone terraces: 'Glasgow Endures'. By the state of the football fans rolling around in the bike lane on Sauchiehall Street it can endure everything but disappointment. The score: 2–0.

———◆ ◆———

My first full day on my own, a prospect ripe with possibility of all flavours ... but mostly pork, as I have a date with one of Scotland's best-known butchers. I leave Eddy slumbering in the room, and grab a breakfast menu from underneath an Eat Drink Pipe poster downstairs. Reluctantly dismissing the pipe major's special (Ayrshire bacon, Stornoway black pudding, Ramsay of Carluke's haggis, eggs, tattie scone, Lorne sausage, mushrooms, potatoes, baked beans and grilled tomato) in case I'm offered some of these things at the very same Ramsay of Carluke later, I order a bowl of porridge with Glenfiddich whisky and double cream. 'Och, and why not?' the girl says. 'You're on your holidays after all.'

I immediately feel guilty, but the porridge is good: nubbly and textured, suggesting it's been made with oatmeal rather than pappy rolled oats, with just a pinch of salt: a pleasingly bland foil for the yellow, fiercely alcoholic cream which I pour over the top with gay abandon. Had I spent less time drinking whisky cream from a spoon, however, and more time looking at my watch I would have saved myself the indignity, shortly afterwards, of hobble-jogging through Glasgow Central station to the Carluke train with Eddy in tow. Cycling may now be doable, but running certainly is not.

———◆ ◆———

From small beginnings on the family farm back in 1857, Ramsay's is now a substantial butchery business, known to me from the sheer number of awards they seem to win for their meat, and particularly their black pudding. So giant are they in my mind that I'm quite surprised to find myself standing, some 50 minutes later, outside an ordinary village butcher's shop, albeit one with a lot going on out back.

Andrew Ramsay, the lady behind the counter informs me, is busy with a pig – 'he'll just get changed and be right out'. I inspect the displays: 'half-time packs' for football fans, hot dogs, Scotch pies and sausage rolls displayed on a tartan backdrop next to serried ranks of black, white and fruit pudding slices guarded by two square lines of lorne sausage, one bright red, the other a more muted pink.

Not only are they an unusual shape for a sausage, but the crimson ones are made from beef, a rare ingredient on our break-fast plate these days. Traditionally Ramsay's was known as a pork butcher, Andrew tells me when he emerges in a clean white coat: the family started as bacon curers back in the nineteenth century so they still sell more pork lorne because people come to them especially for it – 'Most butchers round here just do beef.'

I tell him the 'Scottish pork taboo' has always intrigued me – the idea that Scots alone among Northern European peoples have a general aversion to the consumption of pig. James VI (or I, depending which side of the border you're on) is said to have 'hated pork in all its varieties', while one of Sir Walter Scott's Highland heroes curses his English enemy as a swine eater who knows 'neither decency nor civility'.

Andrew scoffs at my notions, saying the truth is that cows were just more widely kept up here, but whatever the explana-tion, we agree Scotland lacks the wealth of pork products one might expect. 'If Scotland excels in the curing of fish,' wrote Florence Marian McNeill, an early-twentieth-century cookery writer and folk historian, 'England excels in the curing of bacon.' Indeed, the Orcadian-born author, who went on to help found the SNP, called this culinary blind spot the 'national disability', confessing 'it was not until I tasted Wiltshire [cure] that I realised how delicious bacon could be'. Ayrshire alone, she says, has the art of it.

Though Ramsay's is in Lanarkshire, their bacon is indeed Ayrshire cure. Described by Tom Parker Bowles as 'pure bacon bliss', it's made from boneless, skinless pork, always from female pigs (boars tend to be a bit 'teuch',* Andrew tells me), pickled in a vat of the family's own brine, about which he is tight-lipped. He's keener to tell me what they don't do – inject the brine into the meat, or add polyphosphates to encourage water retention, thus keeping the weight up. Both are common, often justified on the basis that they make the meat juicy. In practice, this moisture leaks out during cooking, with the unfortunate knock-on effect that the rashers poach rather than fry. (Phosphates should be listed in the ingredients, but a tell-tale sign is an iridescent sheen on the surface of the pork, and an unpleasant white goo in the pan.)

Strangely enough, if you've ever tucked into a bacon naan from Indian café chain Dishoom you've already tried Andrew's handiwork – 'We did think it was odd, an Indian restaurant wanting to talk to us about bacon,' he admits, 'but when we went to see them, we got it.' They send Dishoom a ton of streaky a week, but Ramsay's meat travels a lot further than London; they have a contract with the Ministry of Defence to supply the troops, once sold some lorne sausage to Michael Flatley, and dispatch a regular standing order to a member of the royal family. Who, I promise Andrew I won't say. It's a good one though.

---

* Tough.

Moving down the counter to other breakfast items, he tells me their white pudding is based on his grandmother's recipe – 'she was from just below Aberdeen and used to make it for the family. It's like . . . a warm oatcake with a bit of smoky bacon and onion' – but it's the black stuff that's the star of the show, winning countless awards since, Andrew says, they explained to the organisers how to cook it, in a dry frying pan, so it crisps in its own fat.

I ask about the difference with the Bury black pudding I had to leave untasted in the North West, and he admits that for a long time they didn't sell theirs south of the border, because they thought the English taste was for a pudding with large chunks of fat. Then one year they decided to take some to the BBC Good Food Show in Birmingham (a terrifying scrummage of polite greed – I speak from traumatised experience) and shifted almost two tons in five days.

Such is Ramsay's reputation for black pudding that brands now approach them for what is known in social media circles as 'collabs' – including, intriguingly, with my personal 'wreck the hoose juice' of choice, Jägermeister. 'They came to us saying, we've heard you're the people to speak to about black pudding,' Andrew recalls. 'I said, well, we can do it, but I can't promise you it will be good. But actually, with all the herbs they have in there, and the sweetness . . . it gave it almost a Christmas pudding flavour. It wasn't bad at all.'

—•◆•—

After leaving Carluke without any pudding at all, Jäger-flavoured or not, thanks to the difficulties of refrigerating things on a bike, I indulge myself with a lunch of macaroni cheese and chips, washed down with sugary Irn-Bru, back at

Glasgow's much-loved University Café – which doesn't seem to have let starring in an episode of Anthony Bourdain's *Parts Unknown* go to its 103-year-old head.

The interior is a magnificent riot of flock wallpaper, bevelled mirrors and wood panelling, crammed with old photos, sweetie jars and ice-cream paraphernalia, a legacy of Italian immigration to Scotland in the early twentieth century. Pasquale Verrecchia and his wife came from Cassino, midway between Rome and Naples, to open up this business in 1918; today it's run by their grandsons, and the etched glass booths are full of workmen tucking into the 'high-vis offers'.

I sit outside, where I can keep an eye on the bike, and work my way through about half the plate of starch before admitting defeat and getting an espresso and a bag of sugary tablet* for the road – and then, before the caffeine can wear off, hoist myself back onto Eddy and point him in the direction of the bonnie bonnie banks of Loch Lomond.

My route takes in the cranes of Clydebank, the House of Muscle gym and the garage that sold me a secondhand car last summer without sticking the new windscreen on properly† before climbing onto an old railway line, which is succeeded by a canal towpath. It winds though Dumbarton – the cycle route briefly blocked by a Covid test tent – across a field of cows and on to the River Leven, where a lone fly fisherman stands waist-deep in peaty water. Eventually this leads me to the famous loch, which, it must be said, looks rather underwhelming from this angle.

---

* Grainy, snappy Scottish fudge. Knocks soft English stuff into a cocked casquette.
† It's all very well buying a bargain 550km away from home, but it feels like less of a bargain the first time it rains and you realise you've purchased a humidor on wheels.

I take a picture of Eddy enjoying the view from the castle to send to my friend Suse, who used to work the tourist boats here as a teenager, and am just trying to work out where the bike path goes next when a man walking a large black Labrador stops and introduces himself as the local Sustrans* volunteer. He asks where I'm headed. Callander, I say, watching his face carefully for signs that he thinks this over-ambitious.

Thankfully, he just nods and warns me against continuing on the NCN7 route after Aberfoyle: 'It's all forest tracks, it's really steep, and you won't do it with those tyres. The road is fine, I've done it a couple of times.' He pauses. 'Mind you, if you do get run over by a bus on there, we've never met.'

I have cause to thank God for this chance encounter many times over in the hours that follow because the beginning of the NCN7 is bad enough, up over a moor where rain falls in cold, drenching sheets, reducing my visibility to zero though I don't need to see the devastating potholes to know they're there. In the end, summoning what little I know about skiing in whiteouts, I loosen my grip on the handlebars, shut my eyes and hope for the best. (NB: This is not official advice. Should you ever find yourself skiing in a whiteout, we've never met.)

I'm less grateful to the driver I meet shortly before this on a single-track road outside Drymen, who purses his mouth in the unmistakable international symbol for 'rather you than me' as I pass on my way up a brisk ascent into the mist, immediately sending my morale into free fall. When the rain finally stops and I chance pausing for a piece of tablet, I'm immediately pounced on by midges, and though I spot a red squirrel by the side of the road shortly afterwards, to say my

---

* The charity for sustainable travel, Sustrans looks after the NCN, or national cycle network.

mood is low by the time I make it into Callander is to put it mildly. I spend 20 minutes just lying on the Highland coo cushions and tartan throws in the Highland Guest House watching *Poirot* with dead eyes before I can even muster the energy for a shower.

Callander is a nice little place, but not oversupplied with dining options on a Tuesday evening so I end up eating venison stew in the pub in the company of a holidaying couple from Yorkshire, celebrating their fiftieth wedding anniversary with an impressive number of drinks. They persuade me to join them in a last dram on the basis that you should always take a shot of spirits before bed because 'they open your arteries so you're less likely to have a heart attack in your sleep'. Or perhaps, I think, less likely to notice it if you do.

———◆◆———

Having survived the night thanks to that final whisky, I opt for a vegetarian fry-up the next morning: always an intriguing prospect given that 75 per cent of the average cooked breakfast is meat. Here landlady Jan has chosen to replace the bacon and sausage with a heap of stir-fried peppers and onions, alongside the usual egg, mushrooms, nicely grilled tomatoes, baked beans and a buttered tatty scone. I like all of these things, so I'm happy, but it could do with something more savoury on the plate too; maybe, I muse, finishing my tea, a mashed root veg and oatmeal cake flavoured with Marmite and fried in copious amounts of butter or oil. You could even make it square to replicate the lorne sausage. I briefly wonder if this idea might make my fortune, and then remember actual vegetarian sausages already exist.

I pick up a Scotch pie for the road, enjoy a brief but satisfying visit to the deliciously eccentric Rob Roy Story on the high street, and then set off into the drizzle. I'm meeting up with Harry and Jay, who comforted me with curry in Birmingham back when I could barely walk up Gemma's stairs, this evening – Jay will be riding with me to St Andrews tomorrow; Harry, who has sworn off cycling as well as camping after her experience on the trail of the tarte Tatin, will be in charge of driving the bags. Today, however, I have a fairly leisurely ride east across central Scotland, with a brief pause to eat pie in the grounds of Doune Castle* and a coffee date at Gleneagles, the five-star resort much favoured by the organisers of political summits and professional golf tournaments.†

My friend James, who started his career in hospitality at the hotel and still lives nearby, gives me a discreet guided tour, one-year-old Rory on his back. Neither of them are able to tell me much about breakfast service, but James does show me the swagged and colonnaded dining room where it's taken, which allows me to nose at the menus. I'm interested to see that their full breakfast includes haggis (very Scottish) and hash browns (not very Scottish, and arguably tautologous on the same plate as a tattie scone), black but no white pudding, a chipolata but no lorne sausage. Passing swiftly over the grain bowl and the egg-white omelette (an abomination unless you are on a low-fat diet for medical reasons, in which case you have my sincere sympathy), my attention is also caught by smoked salmon with fresh crowdie – an ancient Scottish cheese made

---

* As featured in *Monty Python and the Holy Grail:* coconut shells are available in the keep for fans eager to recreate the film.
† I discover later that in the 1920s the Gleneagles house band would spend the winter months playing the Adelphi, where I stayed in Liverpool last week for £28. The rates here tonight start at £585.

from raw milk, gently warmed until it sours, then heated until it splits into curds – served in a croissant bun, an edible tribute to the Auld Alliance.

Before we part ways, as well as suggesting I return for breakfast the next day, James also introduces me to the resident gun dogs, one of whom pushes us a soggy tennis ball through the fence of the enclosure with a wet nose so we can throw it for her. Even though Wilf would no sooner return a ball than he would play a round of golf, I feel a pang imagining him there, in his ancestral homeland, begging for crumbs of croissant bun.

Tea Break:
THINGS FOR SALE BY THE ROADSIDE FROM CALLANDER TO AUCHTERMUCHTY. 16 JUNE 2021

Honey
Strawberries
An old microwave full of eggs (the microwave wasn't for sale, but is, I discovered, commonly repurposed in this way)
Potatoes
Bedding plants

I return to Gleneagles the next morning in the company of Harry and Jay, to discover the grand dining room is currently closed to non-residents thanks to Covid. Instead we join the men in neatly pressed polo shirts and comical visors in the golf club bar, which has deep tartan carpets and a full fire going at 10 a.m. on this fine June day.

Spotting the excellent-looking morning rolls the table next to us are tucking into with knives and forks, Donald Trump style, I decide it's time to show them how it's done. Ignoring what I learnt in Belfast about such rolls – best confined to one meat product, one carb product and one egg – in my greed to try as much as possible, I order mine with lorne sausage, Stornoway black pudding and a fried egg. It arrives with two of both, which really throws down the gauntlet in the consumption department. Undaunted, I open my mouth like a python, and take a bite, eyeing the men next door with undisguised triumph. They look horrified. I feel the warm caress of egg yolk on my top – but I have no regrets.

The lorne sausage is interesting – salty, like a pork sausage, yet distinctly beefy too, like a fatty, finely ground burger – the Stornoway black pudding crisp, rich and sweet, and the egg perfect. My only complaint is the bun, which I suspect to be a brioche. Brioche is too soft and sweet to contain anything wet, whether it's a burger with sauce or an egg yolk, and this is a cause I am prepared to die for (if really pressed).

After I've rinsed the yolk from my jersey in the loos in the company of a disapproving lady golfer reapplying her lipstick, Harry drops us off in Perth, a mere 60 or so kilometres from St Andrews, taking our bags with her in the car. Apart from a big climb at the beginning to put Jay – who claims not to have been out much over the winter, but then starts talking about running and cold-water swimming in a way that suggests he's got triathlons in his sights – through his paces, it's a pleasantly flat but rarely dull ride, mostly along the shores of the Dee.

Crossing the 2.2km-long Tay Bridge, a strangely unsettling experience, we find ourselves in the Kingdom of Fife, as my brother-in-law insists on referring to it, where the sun is out, the hedges high and the skies big in the way you only find on the east coast. I see a kestrel, hanging still above us, suddenly plummet into a field of whispering barley. It's all perfectly lovely, but hot work, and by the time we reach our Airbnb in St Andrews, I'm ready for a cold pint. Five hours later, I fall into a bunker on the Old Course on the way back from a lively dinner with some university pals of Harry's, plastic tumbler of wine still in hand. Luckily this time nothing goes pop.

I must say that I find my haggis Benedict the next morning more restorative than I'd expected – having ordered it simply because the combination of rich, offaly pudding and rich, buttery hollandaise sounds too revolting to pass up, I end up finishing the lot. Somehow the buttery acidity of the sauce works with the earthy, savoury haggis, cloaking a rough diamond in silky French elegance . . . well, either that or I'm just hungover.

Jay is too, so Harry insists we get a bloody Mary. I'd forgotten what a bad influence these two are on me. Feeling brighter and bushier of tail, we set off on a remarkably comprehensive guided tour of her old student hangouts, taking in the 'pier walk', which I decide belatedly, once I've clambered up the iron ladder, isn't a good idea for someone still slightly disabled, Kate and William's old halls, where I sit for a photo in my best princess pose, and most importantly, Fisher & Donaldson's bakery where I pick up a rhubarb pie for immediate consumption, and a round of oatmeal shortbread for my panniers.

Lunch is with Harry's old friend and local restaurateur Tim Butler who tells me, as I tuck into my steamed halibut, about the time he bought a 100kg example – 'it was 6 foot 3; we had to take the back door off the kitchen to get it in!' I didn't even know a fish could get that big, I say, forgetting my manners as I sit open-mouthed, trying to imagine such a thing.

Afterwards, I convince Jay we should run into the North Sea (a balmy 12°C as midsummer day approaches) to wake ourselves up – Scotland is playing England this evening, and I'm keen to watch this ancient grudge match unfold, though sadly the deep-fried haggis I order at the pub turns out to be more interesting than the actual football. The game ends 0–0, and is followed by a rousing chorus of 'Flower of Scotland' from the assembled company.

As we quietly depart I hear a woman shout, IT'S AS GOOD AS A WIN AGAINST THAT LOT.

━━◆━━

The next morning we all wake early – I have a meeting about porridge in a couple of days' time up in the Highlands, and Harry has to head back south for work. Jay, who is clearly keen to get in as much cycling as possible, has volunteered to stay on a day and drive me some of the way north as long as we can get the bikes out en route. Given the state of the weather, I jump at the chance of a warm, dry car – as well as Jay's sparkling company, naturally.

After dropping Harry at Leuchars station, the two of us head towards the Cairngorms National Park, which seems as likely a place as any for a bike ride, stopping at a café in Blairgowrie for breakfast. I watch a solemn huddle of kilted men and bikers by the war memorial in the rain (something to do with the Falklands according to a man in leathers by the till) as we linger over our breakfast rolls, waiting for it to clear. This time, I make myself keep it simple, just a lorne sausage and a fried egg with a liberal saucing of ketchup, which feels more fitting than brown sauce on what is basically a beef burger. Though I can't knock the quality of the Gleneagles produce, this floury white bap is just as enjoyable, and quite a lot cheaper too – though if I'm honest it tastes mainly of ketchup. 'No subtlety,' I say to Jay, mopping up sauce with my finger.

He turns his attention from the silver-haired table next to us, already raucous over their tea at 11 a.m. – 'I've got myself in a lot of trouble over the years with my quick tongue!' one sweet-faced lady is happily bellowing, 'Och, Moira will know that. That time we were up at the loch with Joyce and Margaret . . . ' – to the gloomy view from the window, and abruptly pushes back his chair.

'It's not going to get better, is it. Let's just go.'

Regretting my ambitious choice of shorts (in Scotland, in June! What was I thinking?), I follow him back into the car, interrupting a tartan-clad marching band member practising his drumming on the bonnet, and we continue up into the mist.

I have no firm plan for our Cairngorms ride until I see a sign for a ski station, at which point I tell Jay that's where we're going, excited by the idea of revisiting my Alpine triumph of 2018. Queen Victoria took this route, I tell him, googling it in the hope of discovering a source of tartiflette at the top. She called it 'completely wild Highland scenery, with barren rocky hills' and 'a very bad, and at night, positively dangerous road'.

They've probably resurfaced it since then, Jay points out mildly.

As the only place to park in the Spittal of Glenshee – a desultory settlement even Victoria was hard-pushed to describe as a hamlet – appears to be guarded by a man with an air rifle, we abandon the car by the side of the road instead.

Slotting Eddy's front wheel on, I feel the first flutters of the fear that always comes before a big climb. The A93, also known as 'the snow road', is the highest public road in Great Britain, bookended by gates to close it off in bad weather, and though we're only tackling a short part of it, I have vivid enough memories of that morning on a French mountain to not be particularly looking forward to the experience. Or at least not in the short term – these things generally fall into the category of Type B fun, to be regretted in the moment and relished in retrospect.

This isn't quite the Alps of course: the road yawns ahead in a dispiriting false flat, the valley falling away to our right, the slope rearing up to our left – it's an ascent, but one that's dully gradual enough to leave me enough time to worry about what's around the corner. Jay, ahead of me, is firmly in the zone, focused entirely on the tarmac in front. I fix my gaze on a neon-clad cyclist in the distance, trying to assess the gradient ahead from his speed – he seems to be taking ages on the bend. My legs wobble in trepidation.

Before long, however, we're round the corner ourselves, and I can see a huddle of buildings up ahead. They can't be the ski station, I tell myself: while this is certainly a hill I'm climbing, it doesn't feel like the 15 per cent my Strava thinks it is, or the 12 per cent promised by the warning sign, even on this steep final section – but apparently it is. As on my first ascent of Box Hill years ago, the mountain was merely in my mind: the reality is a slightly, if gratifyingly anticlimactic, hill.

Cursing ourselves for not bringing locks so we can have a go on the ski lift, we duck into the café for a fruit scone and a milky coffee (no raclette on offer, sadly), smug among the car drivers, none of whom look particularly impressed by our amazing feat. I have one quietly gratifying additional victory under my belt though; chasing Jay up the last few metres, I managed to stand up on the pedals for the first time since falling into the stream back in the West Country. My hamstring, still so stiff and unresponsive off the bike, is almost back to normal on it, which is, right now, considerably more useful than the other way around.

Needless to say, I enjoy the descent a lot more, particularly cheerily calling 'not long now!' to those still on the way up, some of whom do seem to be genuinely suffering. I'm clearly fitter than I thought after almost a month away, even if I've barely managed three weeks in the saddle.

'Lots of corpses up there, weren't there?' Jay says cheerfully as I pull into the layby, my fingers so cold I can barely operate the brakes. What? I squawk, alarmed. I didn't see anything. 'What, not the rabbits or the hare, or the sheep, or that lamb? Not the pine marten thingummybob?' I shake my head, looking anxiously at my tyres, and am relieved to see them clear of fur given I've apparently been in a world of my own for the last 10 minutes.

The sky is so low now it's debatable when cloud becomes fog, which feels like an excuse to head straight for the nearest hotel for dinner, whisky and a shamefully early night – but, we reassure each other, it's not that we're old, it's just tomorrow is going to be a long day on the road for both of us. Jay is driving back to Birmingham, and I'm tackling the Highlands, alone. Listening to the wind howling around my turret bedroom, the prospect is not an attractive one.

━━━◆◆━━━

A full fry feels in order before we leave: as at Gleneagles, Dalmunzie Castle's efforts include a compact disc of haggis the size of a slice of black or white pudding, fried to a delicious crisp. I didn't expect to be eating so much haggis for breakfast (do tourists expect it, I wonder?) but I'm certainly not complaining. It shares the plate with two rashers of back bacon, a link sausage (as opposed to a lorne sausage), a slice of black pudding, a fried egg, a field mushroom and a tomato that could have done with a bit longer under the grill but is still preferable to baked beans. Having learnt my lesson yesterday, I stick with brown sauce, which, as I keep forgetting to put my jar of mustard in my jersey pocket, is fast becoming my condiment of choice in such situations.

After putting away a second round of toast (the lack of tattie scone on the breakfast has not gone unnoticed), Jay drives me to Pitlochry. As we head towards the Highlands the landscape becomes noticeably wilder – or perhaps it's just because I'm going to be on my own again that it suddenly seems more desolate.

I jam the wheel back on Eddy in the shadow of a wicker stag sculpture, already feeling jittery about crossing the Pass of Drumochter, familiar to me as the place so many End to End attempts* on the Land's End to John o'Groats cycling record seem to come unmoored, and say a hurried goodbye to my chauffeur, eager to get going on the basis that the sooner I start, the sooner I'll finish.

The map suggests the climb won't start until after the village of Blair Atholl, which, as I heft my way up a mercifully brief 8 per center just outside Killiecrankie, is proven almost immediately to be a lie. More worried than ever, I stop for a fortifying coffee at the House of Bruar, the 'Harrods of the Highlands', a surreal luxury department store in the middle of the Perthshire

---

* Paul Jones's book *End to End: The Land's End to John o'Groats Cycling Record* (2021) is well worth a read.

countryside, which apparently boasts Scotland's largest collection of knitwear, as well as sections devoted to fishing tackle, art, dog accessories and, more usefully, fruit cake. I pick up an emergency loaf in case things get hairy later, clipping self-consciously past a well-heeled crowd in quilted gilets on my way to the till.

I'm grateful for this foresight when, not long afterwards, I find myself confronted by a friendly WARNING! sign: 'Cycle track climbs to 457m. Weather conditions deteriorate without warning and can be severe even in summer. No food or shelter for 30km. No snow clearance or gritting on cycle track.' Balancing Eddy against it for a photo, I almost topple into a gully. Great start, I think, getting back on before I can knock myself out on a rowan tree or trip over a wild haggis.

In spite of these dire claims, the climb is almost imperceptible, the track alternately hugging and straying from the main road, hills rising gradually on either side, the only flash of colour this grey day the vivid yellow of gorse flowers. The summit comes as a genuine surprise: if it weren't for a discreet sign, smaller than the notice about deer-stalking regulations, informing me I'm at the highest point on the Scottish cycle network I'd never have guessed – though I certainly wouldn't have missed the much larger one welcoming me to the Highlands a few hundred metres further down the road.

Almost immediately, the clouds above decide I've had it easy for long enough, and what has been a light drizzle all morning turns torrential – I barely remember much of the descent, so preoccupied am I with the pressing question of how waterproof human skin might be.

Passing the snub chimneys of the Dalwhinnie distillery, I call in hoping for a café, or at least a visitors' centre, but of course, thanks to the pandemic, everything is closed apart from the shop. They don't even do miniatures, so I have absolutely no excuse to linger after they've kindly filled my water bottles for me, agreeing mildly it's 'a bit dreich right enough'. Yet, having conquered the pass, I comfort myself that I'm over the worst, which is funny because, though it's basically all downhill from here, by the time I get to Aviemore almost four hours later, I'm furious with the world, Eddy, and most of all myself for ever having come up with this ridiculous idea. The last segment drags so slowly I spend the final 20km riding through thick, lichen-crusted forest wondering angrily if 'Aviemore' is actually a figment of the cartographer's imagination.

Aviemore, as I should well know having visited before, very much exists. Despite its beautiful setting, it's a practical place – a strip of shops and services that puts me in mind of a ski resort (when I make this original observation to my sister, she tells me it was in fact redeveloped in the 1960s with Alpine glamour in mind).

Nevertheless, it's also so popular with walkers and tourers that the Italian restaurant attached to the High Range motel (would recommend for the fact that you can turn the heating on to dry your socks while you lie on the bed watching Gaelic-language programmes about cattle auctions) is full all evening, and I have to trudge to the Indian next to the Hungry Haggis takeaway for sustenance. 'How many poppadoms?' the waitress asks, puzzled, looking at the empty spot opposite me. 'Four, please,' I say. 'And a large beer. Thanks.'

———•◦•———

Much as I love ski stations, I've chosen Aviemore for its proximity to the village of Carrbridge, 12km north, home of the World Porridge Championships, commemorated on a large roadside sign, just like Alsace's Capital of Choucroute. Though the golden spurtle competition, named after the implement traditionally used to stir the pan, has been held online for the past couple of years, organiser Charlie Miller has generously agreed to get a couple of the team together at his house to talk to me in person.

When I arrive, logistical kingpin Fiona – the only person who knows whose porridge is whose on the big day, Charlie says with some reverence – is already sitting on the sofa drinking coffee (no porridge appears to be on the menu, I note with a pang of disappointment, having skipped breakfast). Just as Charlie's cheerful wife brings in a plate of biscuits ('You'll no want to be tasting my baking!'), Heather, 'the quartermaster', arrives; she's responsible, I learn, for ensuring there are enough pots and pans for the competition to take place, not to mention oats and salt, and much else besides.

• •

Tea Break:
PORRIDGE

If there ever was a universal dish, Heather Arndt Anderson claims in her *Breakfast* book, 'it is, unequivocally, porridge'. Once cereal cultivation began in the Fertile Crescent about 10,000 years ago, porridges of various sorts, cheap, easy to prepare and filling, became ubiquitous, from the emmer wheat puls with fatty bacon mentioned by Ovid to uji, a fermented millet porridge popular in modern Kenya, and kasha, the buckwheat porridges of Russia and Eastern Europe.

Oat porridge has been found in the stomachs of 5,000-year-old neolithic bog bodies, and continued to be a staple food in the north of these islands well into the twentieth century (further south, dried pease pottage, as in the nursery rhyme, or frumenty, a wheat porridge, were more widely consumed). Rabbie Burns's lament of the married man harassed by the cries of his bairns for 'crowdie'* three times a day reflects the fact that for many this dish, a thin, cold gruel of oats soaked in water, buttermilk or broth, was not just breakfast.

Rolled oats, the steamed, flattened grains most of us now think of as porridge oats, were developed by Quaker Oats in the States in the 1920s as a convenience food – the same company was also responsible for the advent of instant oatmeal in 1966. Neither, I hasten to add, are dishes the folk at the World Porridge Championships would recognise as porridge.

●●●

Always a staple, albeit one that lost out to quicker, sweeter cold cereals in the twentieth century, porridge has seen its popularity surge in the last couple of decades as Britons rediscover the benefits of wholegrains. A Mintel study in 2013 found one in two of us were porridge eaters, and many manufacturers, including Scott's, Hamlyns and Quaker, reported a further boost in sales during the recent pandemic. Every cloud.

The championships began in 1994 as a way to get visitors to Carrbridge outside the traditional tourist season, and now attract entrants from as far afield as Oregon and Australia, though the Swedes have been the mainstay of the competition recently, apparently. 'Mind you, remember the Finnish ladies in the leotards?' Charlie muses. 'I couldn't take my eyes off them!'

The competition is always oversubscribed these days, Fiona says hastily; 'we have to draw the names out of a hat'.

---

* Also the name of the fresh cheese I saw on the menu at Gleneagles. Presumably those who ate them could tell them apart.

Those who get lucky must make two bowls of porridge for the judges, one traditional, using just oatmeal, water and salt, and one 'speciality', to which other ingredients can be added.

Oatmeal, rather than rolled oats, though Charlie admits he always uses the latter at home. Steamed and rolled flat, they soften more quickly in the pan than oatmeal – chopped raw groats – but connoisseurs insist the latter makes a superior porridge. Contestants can use any grade (fine, medium or coarse-cut) of oatmeal they like; they can even bring it from home.

Using the oatmeal you've practised with makes sense but some also arrive with their own salt ('you would not get an inch past our judges' noses if you didn't put salt in'), spurtle, and a few even their own water. 'I mean, you don't get better water than here in the Highlands,' Charlie sighs, 'but they think it makes a difference.' One man claims to collect his from the same spring used by his local whisky distillery.

Pre-soaking of the oats is allowed, but no other advance preparation is permitted – and they've had to crack down on gadgets too. 'I've really noticed a change,' Heather says. 'They used to come with a carrier bag of stuff, now it's a house move with bain maries, electric mixers, all sorts. We've had to put a stop to that though – we've only got limited space in the hall.'

Nevertheless, Fiona, who sees every single porridge that goes into the judge's room, 'and that's a lot', says it's surprising how much they differ given they're all made from the same thing. 'I've seen some that were quite smooth and others that . . . well, I won't say lumpy, but there's a lot of consistency there,' she concludes diplomatically. I wonder if I might actually have a chance here.

The judges, an eclectic mixture of past winners, chefs and celebrities – Britain's strongest schoolgirl, best-selling crime writer Lin Anderson and a reincarnation of Rabbie Burns have all done the honours in the past – assess entries 'on the consistency, taste and colour of the porridge and on the competitor's hygiene in the cooking process' (somewhere I fear I might fall down, given my tendency to be followed around by a small, hairy dog). The speciality competition also takes into account how well the contestant's choice of flavourings 'blend and harmonise' with the porridge itself, which must demand a certain open-mindedness on the part of the judges, faced with a bowl spiked with smoked fish or squeezy cheese when all they really want is some cream and brown sugar.

Indeed, the days of just sticking some fruit on top are long gone, Heather tells me – 'now people just go wild'. Last year's winner was *crunch sa bheul* (Gaelic for crunch in the mouth), an oat-based version of the classic French *croquembouche* choux puffs, filled with cream and dipped in caramel – 'and he made it in just half an hour!' Other submissions included confit duck oatmeal tacos and a pina colada porridge, the idea of which makes me feel very odd, though that could be the three Viscount biscuits I've put away while we've been talking.

In between the heats there's whisky tasting – 'for the crowd', Charlie adds quickly, 'not the judges, they don't drink' – and unsurprisingly, it's usually standing room only in the village hall. 'It always looks amazing,' Fiona says wistfully. 'We decorate it with flags, we raid people's gardens, there are tartan tablecloths, the lot. Then, once it's all done and dusted, there's a celebratory village ceilidh – though to be honest, we're all exhausted.'

Are you porridge fans yourself? I ask, secretly hoping to detect a shudder. 'Well, if I remembered to steep it I'd have it every day, but I probably only have it two or three times a month,' Charlie confesses. 'There's one member of the committee, Denise, she eats it every day though. If she doesn't have it for breakfast, she'll have it for lunch.'

Though a true-born Scot, Fiona admits she likes demerara sugar on her porridge, while Heather, English born, but who's lived north of the border all of her adult life, waxes lyrical about brose, raw oats covered in water or milk and eaten with cream.

'Och, my mouth is watering just thinking about it!' Charlie says appreciatively. Mine too, I agree, stopping myself from reaching for yet another biscuit.

I ask them, before I go, if they have any tips for amateur porridge fanciers like me. They're unanimous: 'Never be in a hurry,' Charlie says firmly. 'Have patience,' Fiona adds. 'Yes, take your time,' Heather chimes in. 'Those microwaveable packets, they might be OK, but they destroy the ethos of it for us.' 'Oh, my father used to stand for ages over the porridge pot,' Fiona agrees.

'But,' Charlie says kindly, 'you must make it the way you want it, don't worry about history or whatever.'

'Unless you come and make it for us,' Heather says firmly. 'Then you'll make it our way!'

PORRIDGE

The World Porridge Making Championships' Spurtle Specialities cookbook is tight-lipped on the subject of 'traditional porridge', including a whole page on the subject without much in the way of detail, apart from 'the habit of making it with milk in the microwave is all wrong'. Follow the instructions below, however, and I reckon you'd be in with a chance of that golden spurtle.

Amounts per person

50g coarse oatmeal

⅛ tsp salt

If you fancy a clootie dumpling-flavoured porridge (don't tell Carrbridge)

⅛ tsp mixed spice

25g mixed dried fruit (currants, chopped prunes, sultanas, etc.)

½–1 tsp treacle, plus more to taste

If you fancy whisky cream

25ml double cream

1 tbsp whisky

1 Heat a dry frying pan on a medium-high heat, and add the oatmeal. Cook, stirring, until it smells deliciously toasty.

2 Bring 300ml of water to the boil in a small (relative to the amount of porridge you're making) and preferably thick-based saucepan to which you have a lid, or can improvise one with a heatproof plate or foil.

3 Just as it's about to boil, sprinkle in the oats, stirring continuously as you do so. Once it comes back to the boil, turn the heat right down (if you have a heat diffuser, use it), partially cover the pan* and cook for 10 minutes, stirring occasionally.

4 Stir in the salt, re-cover and cook for another 10–15 minutes, again stirring periodically, until thickened to your liking – if

---

* If you have a range cooker, or another way of keeping the heat very low, then cover the pan completely – you probably won't need to stir it either.

you're making the clootie dumpling flavour, then after 5 minutes stir in the spices, fruit and treacle, then re-cover.
5 Spoon into bowls and serve with milk or cream; to make the whisky cream, simply warm the cream and stir in the whisky.

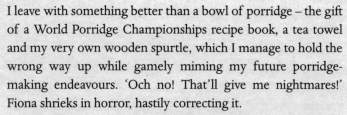

I leave with something better than a bowl of porridge – the gift of a World Porridge Championships recipe book, a tea towel and my very own wooden spurtle, which I manage to hold the wrong way up while gamely miming my future porridge-making endeavours. 'Och no! That'll give me nightmares!' Fiona shrieks in horror, hastily correcting it.

On my way out I spy the golden spurtle trophy on the telephone table, awaiting collection by the winner of last year's virtual competition. 'I can't wait for it to get back to normal,' Charlie sighs as he sees me to the door. 'Whatever normal is.'

Originally I'd planned to cycle across the Cairngorms to Aberdeen from here, but given the nature of the terrain, I'm slightly relieved that I don't have time – my marmalade contact in Arbroath is leaving town the day after tomorrow, and I need to catch him before he goes, which means taking a train down to Perth, where I can jump on one heading up to Aberdeen.

The stressful element of proceedings is that, though I've managed to book a bike space on the second leg, there seems no way to do so on the first. The ScotRail man I speak to outside an antiques shop in County Down informs me that if no bike spaces show online, it either means that no reservations are required . . . or there are none available. I'm keeping my fingers crossed that this is a case of the former, rather than the latter, but just to make sure, I've decided to get on in sleepy Carrbridge, rather than one stop further down the line in Aviemore.

In lieu of porridge, and with 90 minutes to kill before this train south, I decide to ride over to the Speyside Centre where I'm told I might get a slab of clootie dumpling, sometimes described as a sweet haggis, though in truth this mixture of flour and breadcrumbs flavoured with treacle, fruit and spices and boiled in a cloth, or cloot, reminds me strongly of Christmas pudding. I bolt down a comfortingly solid portion doused in thick yellow custard, in the 'sitooterie', a wonderful Scottishism for the terrace, before bolting back across country to Carrbridge's little station.

It's unmanned, so there's no one to ask about bikes – but, hearteningly, no bikes waiting to board either. In fact, there's no one at all. Feeling increasingly anxious, I change into my trainers and haul Eddy and my panniers across the bridge onto the correct platform, where I tell myself I'm being silly, and try to enjoy the scenery instead – after all, it's not every day I find myself in the Highlands – but it's no good. This is the only train I can get that delivers me in time for tomorrow morning's meeting at the marmalade factory, and I'll be extremely relieved once we're both safely on board.

The clootie dumpling lurches inside me as the locomotive chugs into view, and I realise with some trepidation that despite the number of stops it promises to make, it's a big fast thing rather than a local plod-along, the kind of train that usually comes with Rules. I'm limping hurriedly down the platform in search of the bike carriage when a woman in a guard's cap steps off and shouts, 'We're full!'

Hoping I've misunderstood – though really, there's no room for any other interpretation – I jog awkwardly towards her, Eddy bumping against my hip – 'Sorry?'

'We're already full. There are no free bike spaces.'

I look at her, and, to my eternal shame, start to cry.

Ridden: 457.32km
Climbed: 3,842m
Breakfasts eaten: 7 (porridge with whisky cream;
vegetarian fry; morning roll with lorne sausage, black
pudding and egg; haggis Benedict; morning roll with lorne
sausage and egg; full Scottish; clootie dumpling)

RED SAUCE OR BROWN?

Andrew: 'I prefer no sauce at all, unless it's a roll with square sliced sausage and then it's tomato ketchup for me.'

Harry: 'I'm a ketchup girl and Jay is brown sauce all the way. It's amazing we ever got married in the first place, such is my incomprehension at what he does to a sausage sandwich (his Saturday-morning favourite treat).'

Charlie: 'I use brown sauce with bacon. Ketchup is for fish and chips.'

Heather: 'Brown all the way.'

Fiona: 'I do occasionally have a fry-up but I don't put any sauce on it. However, I fry my mushrooms in butter and add Worcestershire sauce and that makes my fry-up tasty.'
[Hmmm . . . not sure if that counts as no sauce at all?]

11

CARRBRIDGE TO EDINBURGH
Marmalade

A wise bear always keeps a marmalade sandwich in his hat in case of emergency.
– Michael Bond, *A Bear Called Paddington* (1958)

The guard looks somewhat alarmed, as well she might at a grown woman having a meltdown in front of a trainload of people. 'Now now, there's no need to scream,' she says hastily, and even in the pink heat of my embarrassment, I think, hang on, I am at least snivelling silently here. As she tries to direct me to the telephone on the other platform, I carry on spluttering; I did try to get a bike reservation, and I do have one onward from Perth, and if I don't get this train I won't get that one ... and her expression changes.

'You're getting off at Perth? And you'd do anything to get on this train?'

I nod snottily, wondering where this is going.

'Would you stand all the way?' she asks. 'It's nearly two hours.'

'I'd travel on the roof if it got me there,' I say, confident no one is going to make me get on the roof.

'OK, I'll tell you what we'll do,' she says, in the slow, calm voice with which one would address a heaving toddler. 'You get on up there, in the disabled section, and I'll come and see you once we're off and we'll chat.'

Still blubbering, I thank her with a slightly uncomfortable level of sincerity, and scurry up the platform with Eddy, getting on at the first door I find before the train has a chance to go without me. Wedged sideways in the vestibule, I see eyes watching me from the carriage and, worried I'll be accused of crocodile tears (they came on so suddenly!), I carry on hiccoughing softly, awaiting the arrival of my saviour, who cuts off my squeaky apology with a firm hand.

When we get to Aviemore, she says, you get off and run the bike down to the carriage with the picture of the bike on the door – as fast as you can, mind! – and I'll bring your bags along when we're on the move again. As the buffet car isn't in operation, she explains, I can stay there all the way to Perth. I'm so grateful I start crying again, but only once she's out of earshot, because I am not proud of this unexpected flood of tears – brought on, I can only assume, by panic at missing out on marmalade – though I am, it turns out, grateful for it.

I slip out of the door at Aviemore like a well-buttered whippet. Once Eddy is safely installed in the correct carriage, albeit blocking an emergency exit (save your indignation, no one's here but me), my new friend appears with my bags, indicates two bikes already hanging neatly on the designated hooks, then, with a finger to her lips, opens the hatch to show me a third, illicit bike, stowed behind the bar. The problem is, she sighs when she returns later to help its owner off, there are

ScotRail bigwigs on the train today who would certainly frown upon such bending of the rules, and the confusing booking system means she's already had to turn someone with a reservation away back in Inverness. 'It's a complete shambles, with all the talk of sustainable travel, and all the cycle routes round here,' she tuts. 'In the old days you'd just chuck all the bikes in the guard's van and that was that.'

'Aye, well, it's all in the name of progress, isn't it,' my fellow cyclist says gruffly. We all laugh, somewhat hollowly.

The Pass of Drumochter, the highest point on the British railway as well as cycle network, seems to go on for miles – I'm gratified to hear the engine straining as I peer out of the window to enjoy the view hidden from me yesterday by the mist and rain. I cycled this, I think. And it wasn't even hard. Well, this bit wasn't anyway.

Abruptly, my regrets at leaving the Highlands, bonnier than ever in the sunshine, turn to guilt as I realise that it's not just Eddy who doesn't have a ticket for this leg of the journey. I accost the guard as she passes. Honestly, she says, clearly relieved I've finally stopped crying, don't worry about it. Just make sure you get off in Perth.

I have no intention of doing otherwise, because I have a connecting service to catch, which deposits me at tea time in the port town of Arbroath, a little way north of Dundee, a fully paid-up bike reservation for the second leg still stuck sanctimoniously between Eddy's brake cables. As I approach the harbour, where I'm staying tonight, I catch the mingled smell of smoke and fish in the air, and, after passing two shops advertising 'smokies', the town's famous smoked haddock, remember I haven't eaten since the clootie dumpling, and yield to temptation. A smokie quiche topped with vivid orange Scottish Cheddar, and a punnet of absurdly perfect strawberries,* prove a satisfactory, if substantial, pre-dinner snack.

The many signs warning of the risks of walking the harbour walls in stormy weather suggest this place can get quite dramatic in winter, but this evening it's perfectly still, the sun breaking through the clouds above the piles of lobster creels and fish boxes and lighting up the flock of cheerfully painted little boats at anchor.

I'm surprised to see so much evidence of activity given everything I've read about the parlous state of the British fishing industry. Later, I discover that while Arbroath once had a thriving white fish trade, the last big boat to operate from here ceased operations in 2013 – now the fleet is made up exclusively of small inshore boats focusing on shellfish, most of which is sold to mainland Europe. (How Brexit will ultimately affect this remains to be seen, though the town, like fishing communities around the UK, is reported by local media to have been pro-Brexit – at the time of the vote anyway.)

I eat downstairs at the pub where I'm staying; a bowl of cullen skink, the famous Scottish fish soup, which here is thick enough to stand a spoon in, a plate of stovies (another regional riff on mince and potatoes) and yet another clootie dumpling, because it's there, and I feel a bit defensive of it after hearing two English yachties at the next-door table compare it unfavourably to spotted dick. I only realise halfway through that it's not the kind of thing you should eat twice in one day.†

---

* Scottish berries in midsummer are the best in the world, and I will take on anyone who wants to fight me on this point, unless they come from Scandinavia.

† Walking it off afterwards I come across a chippie offering battered smokie, which reminds me of the battered smoked cod I had in Portrush – I've never seen smoked fish on offer in a chippie down south.

Breakfast the next morning is served in the room, 'because of Covid'. As I'm only staying one night, I happily order a smokie, grilled with butter and served with a generous portion of scrambled eggs. It's salty and savoury, tangy with woodsmoke, if less deliciously rich than my beloved kippers, and the perfect companion to the blandly creamy eggs. I leave the bedroom window wide open in silent apology to the next occupant, and set off in search of Arbroath's other attraction: the marmalade factory.

Though they're based in a light industrial estate on the outskirts of Arbroath, Mackays are, in fact, the last remaining producer of Dundee marmalade – quite something when the city was once synonymous with the stuff. It's often claimed, in fact, that marmalade was invented there by Janet Keiller, which is pure nonsense – the name may come from the Portuguese word for quince paste, but there's a wealth of evidence it was made from bitter oranges in this country long before the Keiller family established their confectionery shop in Dundee in the late eighteenth century.

Most significantly, the first English-language recipe recognisable as marmalade, as opposed to earlier orange pastes, was published in 1714 in Mary Kettilby's *Collection of Above Three Hundred Receipts in Cookery, Physic and Surgery,* though she does not seem to have been a fan of the bitterness which is the hallmark of a good marmalade, so it must be admitted that hers was probably a bit rubbish. (Sorry, Mary.)

What the Keiller family was (probably) the first to do, some time around 1800, is produce marmalade commercially, allegedly after James Keiller purchased a load of Seville oranges at a knock-down price from a Portuguese ship sheltering from the weather in Dundee harbour. Realising they were too bitter to eat, he gave them to his mother Janet, who turned them into a sweet preserve instead.

Given that Seville oranges, and marmalade recipes, were hardly unknown in Scotland at this time, the idea that this was entirely her own invention smells fishier than a smokie sandwich to me. Janet may, however, have been unusual in making her marmalade spreadable; earlier versions were thick enough to slice, and tended to be served as a sweetmeat or as part of a dessert course.

Indeed, it was almost certainly in Scotland that marmalade first migrated to the breakfast table, Samuel Johnson noting in his travels in the Western Isles in 1775 that Highland men always started their day with whisky, and:

> Not long after the dram, may be expected the breakfast, a meal in which the Scots, whether of the lowlands or mountains, must be confessed to excel us. The tea and coffee are accompanied not only with butter, but with honey, conserves, and marmalades. If an epicure could remove by a wish, in quest of sensual gratifications, wherever he had supped he would breakfast in Scotland.

In any case, though James Keiller and Sons was to become the world's leading marmalade manufacturer in the latter half of the nineteenth century, with factories in Guernsey (to avoid a punitive sugar tax) and later east London and even Germany, the company went out of business in 1992, thanks, I later learn, to maladministration, rather than a lack of demand for their marmalade.

In fact a Keiller's marmalade is still produced, albeit for export only, down in Cambridgeshire, by the same American company that makes Hartley's jam. There's a jar of the stuff, purchased in the States, waiting for me on the boardroom table at Mackays when I arrive for my meeting with Martin Grant, the company's managing director, before he heads off to Cornwall on holiday.

'I've just come from there!' I say, stretching the truth slightly. He asks how long the journey took, and I have to confess about three weeks. (Fortunately, unlike him, I didn't have any small children in tow.)

Martin took over Mackays, originally based just down the coast in Carnoustie, from his father, Paul, who bought the business from his old employer United Biscuits in 1995. They in turn had acquired it as part of a larger package in the 1970s and turned 'the Jammie', as the Carnoustie jam factory was known locally, over to making the filling for their jammy dodgers. According to Martin, the Jammie's manager Les wasn't too happy about this turn of events. Having worked for Keiller's, he found it difficult to muster much enthusiasm for this sugary pink gloop, so, on Fridays, when the factory was idle, he used the copper pans to make marmalade to sell out back.

It was Les's expertise, as much as the factory itself, that Paul Grant purchased back in 1995, and though his son concedes that they're not, strictly speaking, in Dundee, the business still regards itself as 'the custodians of Dundee marmalade: the last ones left standing'. He's not allowed to claim, legally, that they use the Keillers' recipe to make their marmalade, but, he says, it is the one that Les brought with him. 'Make of that what you will.'

(Plus, he adds, they do have a Dundee postcode.)

I ask what happened to Keiller's. He sighs as he tries to explain just what a big deal they once were in Dundee – 'to give you an idea, the family are buried in the Western Cemetery opposite D. C. Thomson'. (Thomson was the man who gave the city one of its famous three Js, jute, jam and journal-ism, when he started the media empire that still publishes the *Beano* and the *Dandy* to this day. He also apparently refused to employ Catholics or recognise trade unions, but that's another story.)

'Keiller's built an empire on sugar, but what they lacked was succession planning. Just because you've got an enormously successful business, that doesn't mean you always make great decisions.'

Fortunately, however, Dundee marmalade is bigger than just one company. The difference is in the shred of the peel, I discover – 'We use what, in the industry, is called the Dundee cut. It's not thick and it's not thin ... it's somewhere in between.' The raw ingredients are the same as with every other marmalade though: oranges, sugar and pectin. The real artistry, according to Martin, occurs in the pan.

The bitter oranges arrive by boat from Spain in barrels ready cut, much like the ones amateur marmalade aficionados can buy in tins all year round if they can't wait for the fresh ones to appear in January. The similarities with home marmalade making don't end there: at the heart of this modern factory are rows of copper-lined cauldrons which are 'basically just a big version of a copper pan you might have in your kitchen'. (Copper is, after gold, the best conductor of heat there is, and rather more practical for everyday use.) Covid restrictions mean I can only see them from a distance, but even allowing for perspective, they look surprisingly small, the diameter, perhaps, of a wine barrel – Martin explains that if they were any bigger the copper would snap as it cooled down, 'so we've just had to add more and more pans'.

The other important tool, it seems, are the 'boiler boys and girls' – marmalade-making is still a very manual process;

'no robots here!' – who quickly learn how to read the molten mixture within. The pans are steam-heated to keep the contents – oranges, sugar and pectin – at a constant temperature. When it hits 106°C, 'it's like a volcanic eruption – we don't have to stir it, we don't have to agitate it at all, we can slow cook it, because rushing marmalade doesn't allow those deeper, richer flavours to develop'. I nod, wondering if I'm guilty of rushing my marmalade. Maybe I need to invest in a copper cauldron to really take things to the next level.

MARMALADE

Seville oranges are never waxed, but most lemons, apart from organic ones, do tend to be. If you can only find shiny fruit, give it a good scrub under hot water before use. I've added whisky to this recipe in honour of Mackays' Scottish heritage, but you may wish to substitute another spirit of your choice, or indeed leave it out altogether. Information about how to sterilise jars can easily be found online.

Makes 6 small jars
1kg Seville oranges
1 unwaxed lemon (see above)
1kg soft light brown sugar
1kg white sugar
3 tbsp whisky (optional, see above)

1 Balance a sieve or colander over a very large saucepan – you'll need to have enough room for the marmalade not to bubble over later. Avoid aluminium or scratched enamelware. (If you're lucky enough to have a copper preserving pan, transfer the mixture to that in step 5.)

2 Cut the fruit in half and squeeze it through the sieve into the pan, collecting the pips in the sieve (do not throw these away!). Cut the squeezed shells into strips of your desired thickness, discarding any green bits of stalk; don't worry about the pith, that will dissolve during cooking. (If you'd prefer a peel-free marmalade, cut it into rough chunks instead and stick it with the pips in the sieve.)

3 Add the shredded peel to the pan. Tie the contents of the sieve up in a piece of muslin, knotting the neck securely, then add this to the pan along with 2.5 litres of water. Bring to the boil, then turn down the heat and simmer gently for 2 hours, or until the peel is soft.

4 Remove the muslin bag from the pan and, once it's cool enough to handle, squeeze vigorously over the pan, so the gloopy pectin oozes through the muslin and into your marmalade. This will help it set. Put a couple of saucers into the freezer.

5 Bring the marmalade to a simmer, then add both sugars and stir to dissolve. Bring to a rolling boil, skimming off any scum from the surface, then leave to bubble away for about 15 minutes.

6 If you have a thermometer, test it: the setting point for marmalade is 104.5°C. Either way, turn the heat right down and put a little of the marmalade onto one of the frozen saucers. Leave for a minute or so, then push your finger through it; if it's ready the top should wrinkle in protest. If not, bring it back to the boil, and repeat every few minutes until it does.

7 Take off the heat, stir a couple of times and leave to settle, skimming off any foam from the top. Stir in the whisky if using, then pour into sterilised jars, filling each right up to the top, and put the lids on. Tighten them again once the marmalade has cooled.

As well as their Dundee marmalade, Mackays produce a Seville orange version with finely cut peel, and a vintage one which broods more darkly in the jar. The British consumer, Martin reports, tends to prefer a tawnier, chunkier preserve, whereas overseas customers are happier to embrace less traditional flavourings because they didn't grow up with the stuff – 'The champagne version is very popular abroad,' he assures me.

Curious about such perversions, I ask about their biggest overseas markets; the USA, Scandinavia, Germany, apparently, but also Japan, India '. . . you can even find us in Nepal!' he says proudly. In Northern Europe, he's heard they pair marmalade with fish. I tell him I put it in a bacon sandwich, which isn't that much of a leap when you think about it.

Emboldened by Mackays' apparent success abroad, I gingerly raise the topic of marmalade's rather fuddy-duddy image. To my amazement, Martin shrugs it off. Trade magazines often ask him if he's worried that his market is dying out, he says – 'and I say no, I don't want to attract a younger audience. Once your palate develops, and you begin to enjoy wine, coffee and cheese, then you're ready for marmalade. And then you're a fan for life, and you get very particular in terms of peel, flavour and so on.' Like Campari, I say thoughtfully, or olives.

'Exactly!'

So, for home cooks, I ask, what's the secret of great marmalade? Well, it's not complicated, he says, before going on to add that, of course, at home it is a bit more difficult because you don't have such control over your raw materials, you can't test pectin levels and so on. 'But really, with marmalade it's all about the peel – do you want it soft, or do you like it really chunky. And the sugar levels – start low, work up – and how long you leave it on for: the more you cook it, the closer it gets to burnt. It's all down to personal preference, but it's a skill knowing when to stop.'

Feeling anxious about next January already, I change the subject; what's his favourite way to eat marmalade? 'Ooh, on sourdough toast, or soft white bread with salted butter. That's delicious.'

❖❖

Tea Break:
WORLD MARMALADE AWARDS

The World's Original Marmalade Awards have, as the rather defensive name suggests, been much copied, but surely never bettered – Jane Hassell-McCosh came up with the idea to celebrate her own love of marmalade back in 2005, and they retain the slightly batty air of all the best passion projects.

Held at Dalemain, the Cumbrian country house which has been in her family for the past three centuries, they now regularly attract several thousand entries from as far afield as Australia, Brazil and Japan, where it's even spawned an official spin-off competition. Classes are divided into homemade and commercial entries, and into a plethora of esoteric subcategories such as Seville Orange Medium Cut (peel approx. 4.5mm diameter), Octogenarian's Marmalade and Marmalades Made by Campanologists (bellringers).

Marmalades are judged on appearance, consistency and flavour, with points available, according to former judge Olivia Potts, for 'lack of smudges on the jar, colour, brightness, peel distribution, jar filled to the top, balance of jelly to peel, set, size of peel, texture of peel, balance of flavours, balance of acidity, length of finish, and "overall harmony"'.

The best 11 entries from Britain compete against the best from Australia in an additional contest known as the Marmalashes, and all the entry fees go to the local hospice at home charity.

In 2021, the top overall prize in the homemade competition was scooped by the winner of the children's category, nine-year-old Flora Rider from the Isle of Wight, who beat entries from over 30 countries to take best in show with her Seville orange and orange blossom marmalade on her first attempt.

❖❖

I'm not done in Arbroath yet – it would have been extremely remiss, knowing I was coming here for marmalade, not to try and get in some smokie action too, given that, like kippers, they're popular at breakfast time, though in yet another sad ripple of the pandemic, the first producer I contact, fifth-generation fish dealer Iain R. Spink, isn't in town. Covid has affected business so badly, he writes, that he's not working full time – but he does helpfully put me in touch with his friend Alex Spink (Spinks are, apparently, Big in Smokies).

Alex's business operates from a narrow terrace by the seafront, in the area known as the Fit o' the Toon, the epicentre of the smokie industry since, it's claimed, the idea arrived in Arbroath in the early nineteenth century from nearby Auchmithie along with fishing families attracted by the town's new harbour. At Auchmithie the fishermen's wives were forced to carry them out to their boats so they could at least start work dry – no wonder, with an average sea temperature of 10°C, the women were keen to move somewhere where their chauffeuring services would no longer be required.

Alex Spink & Sons is so tucked in among the ordinary houses that I ride past once before spotting it – there's just a low office and a gap between buildings leading to the yard, where I meet Gary, wreathed in smoke as he arranges salmon on a rack. The little smokehouse is hardly bigger than a garage, with a big square brick kiln at one end and a tall one at the other, inside which haddock fillets, some dyed a lurid yellow, some a natural creamy white, hang limp like socks.

Everything but the fish is black as tar, and the whole place feels genuinely timeless – though Gary himself has only been here four years. Before that, he worked in the fish shop, 'but the guy who was doing this, well, it's heavy work, it's not easy, so I took over', he says, effortlessly shifting a sooty rack to give me a better view.

So, I say, coughing a little – tell me about the smokie. 'Well, you're only allowed to call them an Arbroath smokie if you make them in Arbroath,' he shepherds me outside, where the air is marginally less thick. 'I suppose you could call them smokies, but you just can't replicate them anywhere else really, though people have tried. And failed.'

First off, they have to be haddock – here they use pretty much all North Sea fish, some from the Faroe Islands, but mostly Peterhead or Shetland – 'wait, I'll fetch some to show you'. They're surprisingly small, not much bigger than mackerel, with glistening snakey skin and huge eyes like sightless marbles. 'You're not wanting them too big, or they'll fall off the sticks and onto the fire,' he explains. They head and clean the split and gutted fish, tie them in pairs at the tail and pack them in salt for 'between four hours and overnight' (his vagueness on this point makes me wonder if he thinks I might try this at home, which I most certainly will not), before hanging them over wooden planks in the smoker for about an hour and a half.*

---

* Kippers, by contrast, are made from herring, and cold smoked – so, unlike the smokie, they're not cooked during the process, just cured.

'It's all hardwood logs,' he says. 'You want to use good wood because the smell of the wood is the taste of the fish. You get to know when they're done just from the look: the skin dries up and turns golden, and the tails get a bit crispy looking. We use a temperature probe to check, just to make sure – it sounds stupid, but different fish behave differently.'

Remembering the difficulty of choosing between oyster stalls in Brittany, I ask if all the producers I've passed in these narrow streets are essentially selling the same thing. Not exactly, he says, everyone has their own style – 'Some of them,' he says confidentially, 'well, I think they over-smoke them personally, they're all dry and crunchy.'

I can't help wondering how much of a market there still is for the smokie – you rarely see them outside Scotland, and not too often here either, in my experience at least. 'There was a bit of a downturn in sales a few years ago,' he admits, 'but they seem to be really popular again now.' I want to believe him on that, despite the gloomy tone of Iain's email.

He eats them all the time, he assures me. 'Sometimes, if they drop off the stick, then I stick them in a bowl and eat them right here. I probably eat about three or four a week.' But what's your favourite way to have them? I prod. 'Ah, hot out of the skins, just like that. Nothing better!' (I can confirm that, should you lack access to your own smokie kiln, they're also pretty good grilled and clapped between the two halves of a soft, well-buttered roll.)

———◆———

I leave Arbroath feeling faintly anxious about the future of both marmalade and the Arbroath smokie. It's all very well hoping people will just discover you at a certain point in life, but I wonder if my Nutella-loving nephews and nieces will ever graduate to Dundee marmalade, let alone fancy a piece of fish for breakfast. Perhaps, I think, I need to start forcing it down them.

Testing Martin's claim that Arbroath is almost Dundee if you squint hard enough, I head back down towards the Tay. I have to be in Edinburgh tomorrow evening – well, I've promised my sister and two friends coming up from London for the weekend that I will be – and the only thing I have to do between now and then is get there, a distance of some 130km, if you go direct. I plan to follow the coast instead, largely motivated by a desire to eat fish and chips in Anstruther and the pleasant feeling of having no particular plan besides pushing pedals around for the next couple of days. The weather seems to be on holiday too, the sky a deep, vivid blue, the yellow dunes fringed with poppies, the sea breeze playful on my face.

Turning west at Carnoustie, former home of Mackays, I stop in Dundee for a warm steak bridie, a kind of deliciously greasy hand-held pie that makes the Cornish pasty look positively Puritanical, before tackling the Tay Bridge for a second time. This time the length comes as less of a shock, though without Jay's company the roads on the other side seem endless. Even the prominent signs for Scotland's Top Secret Nuclear Bunker fail to raise their usual smile, though the sight of hairy Highland cows gladdens the heart, as does a marmalade ice cream in St Andrews.

Happy again, I continue on to Crail, where the coast joins the Firth of Forth (a bona fide fjord!). Pretty as this little fishing village is, however, I'm only here because there wasn't a single affordable room available in neighbouring Anstruther. To be honest, there wasn't much in Crail either, and when I reach my hotel, which wasn't cheap, I realise why it had space. The owner is friendly enough, but the place reminds me strongly of a tartan Fawlty Towers.

My room, naturally, is right at the top of the house, up approximately 45 flights of plaid-carpeted stairs with a view on to a large caravan site. Following a visit to the avocado ensuite, where someone hasn't flushed the loo, I begin to wish I was staying there instead. (After coming back later to find the same thing, I decide that potentially the plumbing is just a bit mixed up, which, if you think about it, is potentially a lot worse, though not as bad as there being a random shitting ghost, which is of course the other obvious possibility.)

I gallop back downstairs, barely noticing my lopsided gait after almost three weeks of injury, grab Eddy and fairly sprint the 7km to Anstruther, where the queue outside the famous fish bar, a favourite of our old friends Wills and Kate, already stretches around the corner. Scotland are playing Croatia at 8 p.m., and the town has a restless, anticipatory air – though my only concern is getting my haddock, chips and mushy peas. (I can't help laughing, however, at the disappointed face of the German in front of me in the queue who wants to know if his fish supper comes with salad.)

To my annoyance I spy a pleasant-looking campsite on my way back to Crail – a proper campsite, with actual tents – in a field by the road, which no doubt would have cost me a tenth of what I'm paying for my poky room, though then of course I would have missed out on the dubious pleasure of watching the football alone on the world's smallest television, as the hotel, and indeed the entire village, appears to be in hibernation. As Scotland lose 3–1 and plummet out of the tournament, perhaps it's for the best.

After a mediocre night's sleep thanks to the diaphanous curtains – which I suspect are intended for ornamental use only – I wake early, in a bad mood. Glowering my way through a surprisingly decent bowl of porridge topped with milk and sugar filched from the tea tray, I try not to think about how much I've paid for the experience, wheel Eddy out from behind the bins, and wearily set off for Edinburgh.

A buttery, the salty, almost croissant-like bread roll peculiar to this coast (see page 245–246), helps, as does an hour or so in the surprisingly fascinating, and quite unfairly deserted Scottish Fisheries Museum in Anstruther. It's hard to feel sorry for myself when confronted by the very real hardship of making a living from the sea.

I'm particularly struck by the vital but little recognised role women played in the industry in addition to their domestic duties, as can be seen in this account I read from 1799:

> The fishwives lead a most laborious life. They assist in dragging the boats on the beach, and in launching them. They sometimes, in frosty weather, and at unseasonable hours, carry their husbands on board to keep them dry. They receive the fish from the boats, carry them fresh or after salting, to their customers, and to market at the distance, sometimes, of many miles, through roads and in a stormy season . . . it is the province of the women to bait the lines, collect furze, heath . . . for fuel, to make the scanty stocks of peats and turfs prepared in summer, last till the returning season.

From the nineteenth century, they also travelled with the Scottish fishing fleet as it chased the herring down the coast as far as Great Yarmouth in Norfolk, and even across the country to the Isle of Man. The fish's high oil content means it must be eaten* or cured as quickly as possible after landing – herring lasses had to process and pack the catch within 24 hours before it spoiled.

---

* The late Keith Floyd shared fond childhood memories of 'crisply fried herring for breakfast with doorsteps of warm, crusty bread and butter'.

Working outside in all weathers, they gutted and graded the fish, wearing cloths wrapped around their fingers to protect them from the blades, and then packed them in salt. A good gutter was expected to process 60 fish a minute, and the women were often at it until the small hours to clear the decks before the boats came in again the next morning. In a good season, they might earn £17–£20; about £1,500 in today's money.

That said, life had its lighter moments: as Shetland herring lass Christina Jackman remembered, they didn't work Saturday nights, because they went out dancing – 'we did geng out an we wid be picking da scales aff wir arms as we gied alang, an wi da heat a da ballroom da chaps smelt da herring in wir hair. It didna matter how much time we washed wir hair, it always smelt.'

The displays culminate in a curiously unsettling model fishmonger's in which the mannequin behind the counter appears to be Nicola Sturgeon in a bloodstained yellow apron. Shivering pleasurably, I depart Anstruther much happier than I arrived.

The route onwards along the north coast of the Forth is mostly stunningly pretty, wide fields already tinged with gold, the bulk of the Pentlands rearing above the smudge of Edinburgh on the other shore and a couple of decommissioned oil rigs sitting incongruously in the middle of the channel. (Occasionally, as in many former mining areas, it is, I have to admit, a bit grim.)

I stop for a superb hot dog in a pile of pickles and caramelised red onions in a Polish café on the front in Kirkcaldy, accompanied by the first actual salad I've seen for weeks, but being able to glimpse my destination across the water has made me impatient, and I hurry west, the mighty Forth Bridges tantalisingly close, yet always frustratingly just around the next corner.

This being Britain, I pass a ruined medieval kirk casually scattered along the cycle path, but my mind is already on an almond Magnum in South Queensferry, so I don't stop to look, pushing on past the scary warnings of radioactive materials in tranquil Dalgety Bay, and finally on to the Forth Road Bridge itself. It's a route I've driven often, and run and walked too, but I've never cycled it and I've certainly never really noticed how you can see the water, almost 50 metres deep, through the gaps in the footway.

I'm so relieved to be on the other side that I forgo the ice cream in favour of heading straight for Edinburgh and the noisy bosom of my family. By sheer coincidence, my parents are here too, and already occupying my sister's spare room, which means I'll be spending the next four nights sleeping on a mattress in the playroom. It has no curtains, diaphanous or otherwise, but it does have the distinct advantage of being free.

—•◆•—

Woken at dawn by the light, I'm on time for my breakfast date on Calton Hill with friend and fellow writer Dan Richards, fresh out of ICU after contracting, and surviving, 'the worst Covid case in a young – well, a relatively young – person they'd ever seen', as he tells me proudly while I'm trying to work out where to start on the tray that's just been set in front of me. (Not that I'm not sympathetic, but I find it hard to concentrate when there's food around.)

In the end, I decide to kick off with the little croissant,* followed by the French set yoghurt in the dinky glass jar, and then move on to the savoury courses: smoked salmon with tomatoes and crowdie cheese; charcuterie, more cheese and a soft-boiled egg with rye bread, before finishing up with the

---

* Not bad at all, though a touch too *bien cuit* for my taste.

bowl of strawberries and clotted cream. (I abstemiously leave the watermelon wedges: it wouldn't do to be greedy.)

Afterwards, Dan escorts me to his local butcher where I pick up the wherewithal to make a proper Scottish breakfast for my family. An ostensibly generous move on my part, it's actually motivated by greed: my sister Rosie is the kind of person who happily exists on a single slice of toast grabbed on her way to work, while her husband Craig, currently struggling to stay sane with a house full of in-laws, enjoys a fry-up, but has probably been sent to the shops at least five times already this week. I exit Crombies with a rare sense of triumph and a bag full of lorne sausage, mealie pudding (as white pudding is also known; an unappetising name, which always puts me in mind of a mealworm), Stornoway black pudding and Ayrshire bacon, as well as a packet of tattie scones and some eggs, just in case.

(As Dan walks me back to my bike, a girl pops out of a café to ask how he's doing and give him a box of cakes. 'It's like being a celebrity,' he says. 'Everyone's heard about how ill I was, and they're all being so nice.')

That evening, my university friend Ali arrives from London – four months pregnant when she joined me on an electric bike in Burgundy, she's opted for a stationary leg this time, despite having no such excuse – or at least I assume she doesn't from the speed with which she suggests a negroni.

Waiting for the arrival of Alice, the third member of our greedy college gang (an alliance initially formed by a shared devotion to Nigel Slater and Ben's Cookies), we reconsecrate our friendship the next morning by putting away two breakfasts in quick succession, though to be fair, the first, a cardamom bun, is just a ruse to shelter from the rain while waiting for the second. Once we finally get our table at the Pantry in Stockbridge, I'm nearly cheated of my full Scottish by the waiter, who looks at his watch, and regrets to tells me that they stop serving breakfast at 11 a.m. My bottom lip begins to quiver dangerously. As you may have guessed, I am not very articulate in moments of stress.

Ali, a professionally trained mediator, points out, very calmly, that it's only 11.03. 'Can you not just put one more order through?' she says, as I hold my breath and look away, trying to pretend that not only am I very much not about to cry, I'm not even that bothered. I am though, and rightly so, because good as it all is – the plump, perfectly Marmite-coloured sausage, the golden streaky bacon, the Stornoway black pudding, the tomato, the confit mushroom, even, I suppose, the superfluous hash brown and the baked beans – the haggis is truly excellent, so crunchy I can't help but wonder if they found it at the bottom of the fryer when they turned it off. I cannot, however, approve the micro leaves on top, which have no place on a breakfast, particularly not in Scotland with its proud tradition of unapologetic salad dodging.

Satisfied, we waddle off to pick up Alice, who has planned a whole afternoon of entertainment, including a trip to see the Galloway Viking hoard* at the National Museum of Scotland (where I get told off for JOKINGLY getting out a haggis Scotch egg during the video bit) and a massage. Not a relaxing massage either – she's of the opinion that after all my woes, I need something a bit stronger.

'Have you had a deep-tissue massage before?' the masseuse asks, in a manner that suggests she hopes I know what I'm letting myself in for. She's young and vigorous, with a wrestler's physique. 'I . . . think so,' I say doubtfully. Five minutes in, I'm

---

* She's a medieval historian. This is what they do for fun.

almost certain I have not, but by then it's too late to admit it. (Of course, she also tells me to let her know if it's too much but I decide, in a very British way, that the harder she presses, the better it must be for my poor muscles, so, apart from the occasional involuntary squeak when she ventures near my hamstring, I spend the next half an hour screaming silently into my mask.) 'How was that?' she enquires solicitously as I peel myself off the bed like a well-chewed piece of gum. 'Lovely,' I say brightly. 'Thank you so much!'

If my leg feels no better it certainly feels no worse for the experience. Alice hoots as I limp brokenly across the road to meet her, though we're both surprised to see Ali floating towards us on cloud nine a few minutes later. 'Oh, when they asked me if I'd had one before I said no, and that if it hurt could I swap to a nice relaxing one instead,' she explains. 'It was bliss,' she adds, somewhat unnecessarily.

'Thank you, Alice,' I say humbly. 'I'm sure it will have done me good in the long run.'

We go so big at dinner that I'm glad of my forward thinking the next morning – there's no better task to refocus a brain shattered by too much wine than the quietly enjoyable, methodical process of breakfast prep, cooking everything in order, so it's all ready at the same time – the lorne sausage (which gives off a really startling amount of fat), the bacon, and then the black and white puddings in the same pan, and finally the eggs and tattie scones in the grease rendered from it all.

Even my niece Sofia, who claims to be 'kind of a vegetarian but I eat bacon but not ham?' is persuaded to try a bit of white pudding too, which I consider a minor educational triumph. Teddy the cockapoo, who, unlike his non-biological cousin

Wilf, is a delicate eater, leaves my gift of lorne sausage untouched in his bowl all day, however, suggesting I am indeed less discerning than an actual dog. 'At Granny's, he gets chicken,' Sofia explains, seeing me looking sadly at it later.

As it's my birthday tomorrow, there's a little party in my honour that evening – my oldest nephew Finlay brings out a Cyril the Caterpillar cake (other brands of caterpillar are available) festooned with candles and a big pink 40 (which I most certainly am not) and behind him Sofia falls about with the evil glee of someone who can't even imagine being quite so old yet not actually dead. You just wait, I say, letting her brother Harry blow out the candles, and then relighting them for him to have another go. You're not having a single one of poor Cyril's feet for that.

My brother-in-law makes me stay up drinking whisky until it is my actual birthday (I admit there may not have been that much coercion involved), and when I roll off my mattress and into my newly sweet-smelling Lycra the next morning I am not feeling terribly jolly about the whole event.

'I knew you'd regret all that booze,' my sister says happily, offering me a cup of tea. I'm getting old, I say sadly. The dog licks my knee sympathetically. My parents just laugh.

Ridden: 197.56km
Climbed: 1,352m
Breakfasts eaten: 6 (Arbroath smokie and scrambled eggs;
porridge; croissant/yoghurt/smoked salmon and
crowdie/cured meats and cheese/strawberries and
clotted cream; cardamom bun; full Scottish × 2)

RED SAUCE OR BROWN?

Martin: 'Neither: pork sausages with marmalade, in a roll!'

Gary: 'Red sauce.'

Dan: 'Brown.'

Ali: 'Yeaaaaaaaauuuuuuuuuuuuuuuuuuuuuuuu ccccccccccccccccccccccchhhhhhh: neither. UGH! Disgusting. Sugary pap on my bacon sandwich. I wouldn't even eat it. Have always been mystified by being so out of step with the majority about this.'

Alice: 'Ketchup and butter on a bacon sandwich. No sauce really with cooked breakfast. Perhaps a smidgen of ketchup?'

Craig, Rosie and Sofia: 'Ketchup.'

Finlay: 'Barbecue!' [outlier]

Harry: 'He likes barbecue. Or sweet chilli.'
[Teenage boys, eh?]

[I have never seen either of my parents eat a cooked breakfast in the nearly but not actually 40 years I've been on this earth. When questioned afterwards they claimed they do eat them in hotels (again, never witnessed this) but lack the time to do them at home. They are both retired.]

12

EDINBURGH TO NEWCASTLE
Stottie Cakes

'What the hell is a stottie cake?'
– Muhammad Ali

The sky is a dull, hungover grey as I reluctantly manoeuvre Eddy in the direction of Waverley station, strenuously avoiding Edinburgh's treacherous tramtracks. Even in the rain, I find Auld Reekie, with its towering old town and handsome Georgian squares, hard to leave.

My friend Suse once pointedly sent me an article claiming that the habitually late are simply chronically over-optimistic. Today, I'm running true to form. Having arrived at Waverley unexpectedly early for my train south I decide to ride over to my favourite local bakery, Twelve Triangles, for a birthday croissant. As I wait at temporary traffic lights on the perilously slippery cobbles by Holyrood Palace, I realise this is a stupid plan. And yet, instead of turning round and getting one from the station instead, I stubbornly carry on, eventually throwing myself, and my croissant, onto the train with barely a minute to spare.

I eat my hard-won and rather squashed celebratory pastry with a watery coffee from the buffet trolley rather than the punchy little noisette I washed it down with in France, but the Scottish croissant (9/10, savoury, buttery, in the bready tradition but still with good flakeage) is much better than the one in Trilport, Seine-et-Marne (7.5/10), a fact which unfortunately does nothing to put me off such over-optimistic timekeeping in future.

I get off in Berwick-upon-Tweed, which strictly speaking is in England, though as the River Tweed itself has been the border since 1237,* and the station sits on the north bank, I feel justified in a pang of regret as I cross the bridge. (The huge Scottish saltire flying outside the Berwick fish factory shortly afterwards, however, suggests loyalty round here is still a bit fluid.)

Having travelled the east coast mainline from London to Edinburgh more times than I've had gins in a tin, I always try to bag a seat on the sea side of the train to drink in the glorious Northumbrian views en route; humpy dunes, white sand beaches and, most intriguing of all, the Holy Island of Lindisfarne, splendid in its watery isolation. Now I'm finally on the ground, it's no less beautiful, but the cycle track, for a pernickety person who finds most tarmac roads unacceptably rough, occupies most of my attention; initially promising, it quickly gives up any pretensions of paving and disintegrates into cinders, craters and, finally, close-cropped grass.

Riding into a herd of sheep that flee bleating from my wheels, I stop and spend several minutes zooming in on Google Earth trying to work out if the surface is more likely to

---

* Geeky fact: it wasn't until 1746 that Berwick was officially declared part of England, rather than just under its rule; before that, it was described as 'of the Kingdom of England, but not in it'. The town has swapped nationalities a befuddling 13 times during its history.

improve . . . or turn into an actual bog. It's unclear from the grainy images, and the old boy I meet leaning against a bridge doesn't improve my mood when he advises me to watch out for the surface ahead; 'I always get punctures down that gravel track,' he says, 'and all my friends do too. Always.'

Cheery. The noble Eddy is made of sterner stuff though, and I'm soon leaning him against a thrilling sign warning of the risks of crossing the sands to Holy Island below a photo of a 4×4 engulfed in waves with the legend 'This could be you'. Not likely, I think. Having read *The Woman in Black*, I've checked the tide times before setting out, and pedal on across the causeway with confidence, my destination shimmering enticingly on the horizon.

I've always wanted to see Lindisfarne; a place cut off by water twice a day is necessarily possessed of a certain mystique, even now a paved road has replaced the old pilgrim's poles marking the safe route across the sands. Today visitors are welcomed by a slightly anticlimactic yellow sign blocking the only road in: COVID-19 HOLY ISLAND VILLAGE PARKING PERMITS ONLY. I decide bikes are surely fine – they're modern-day donkeys after all, and probably what Jesus would arrive on, if He decided to action the Second Coming – and carry on past trestle tables selling honey, cakes and strawberries; one somewhat testily declaring itself 'The only Holy Island-owned stall, support local business'. There's a whiff of angry-letter-to-the-parish-council about this, a suggestion that mainlanders are fairly swarming across to sell their cauliflowers and cookies, though today relations seems friendly enough, despite my gentle probing.

I'd imagined Lindisfarne to be principally inhabited by monks and ghosts, the air thick with incense and spirituality, so it's a bit of a shock, as I push on, to find it's actually a bustling tourist village, with pubs and shops, and as many people, this warm late June day, as Mont-Saint-Michel. Perhaps the penny should have dropped when I was passed on the sands by an Argos delivery van.

Slightly disappointed, I clip around the church, have a brief stare at the jagged abbey ruins, which seem more suited to tempests than the current sunshine and, sensing any lunch will involve a lengthy queue, plonk myself on the war memorial and finally unwrap the haggis Scotch egg I've been carrying around since the incident in the National Museum of Scotland two days ago. Perhaps I should have just left this as a place glimpsed from a train window, I think sadly as I get up to go.

Though the sands look distinctly damper than on the way over, my fear of drowning has nothing on the terror of crossing the A1, the Great North Road, with its endless lorries strung out along the carriageway like beads on an infinite, noisy necklace. I can't die on my birthday, I think, taking a deep breath and making a dash for it.

Thankfully after that it's all rolling lanes and quiet coaching towns – I even take a little diversion to see the magnificent Bamburgh Castle before I realise with a shock I'm running late again. Very late in fact. Somehow, the generous window of time I've given myself to make it down the coast as far as Alnmouth, where I can catch a train into Newcastle, has eroded such that, if Google's timekeeping is to be believed, I'm going to miss it by two minutes. This would be less of a problem if I didn't have birthday plans to keep, but I do, so naturally, I immediately set off in the wrong direction. Mistake rectified 15 very angry, sweary minutes later, I pedal as hard as I can for the next 90, and somehow make the train with four minutes to spare. After the stress of almost missing two trains in a single day, I reward myself by spending the entire journey looking out of the window, rather than at my phone. It's my birthday, and I can switch off if I want to.

—◆◆—

I may have had a Michelin-starred dinner – alone, but with sparklers and champagne and a kiss from the maitre d' – in Paris three years ago, but tonight's plan eclipses even that. Having put out a slightly plaintive tweet asking the best place for a birthday meal in Newcastle on a Monday in jeans, I get a reply from Mumbai-born food writer Maunika Gowardhan inviting me to dinner at hers.

Given that we've only met a couple of times, and briefly at that, this is exceptionally generous, and I immediately accept before she can suggest any alternatives. (It seems she already has the measure of me though – as I'm contemplating the shortbread next to the kettle in my handsome, and surprisingly cheap, Victorian railway hotel she sends me a text: 'Don't eat, save yourself for dinner, I've made lots.')

Maunika, her husband Bharat and their son live in leafy Jesmond, just east of the city centre. Also in residence, to my utter delight, is their beagle Brudo, whose furry company is perhaps the best birthday gift of all, though he has some stiff competition, because she's not lying when she says she's been cooking (she claims it's all recipe testing for her next book* so not really any extra work at all). We sit down to khade masale ka murgh (chicken with whole spices and caramelised onions), fish curry and bhindi (okra) with potatoes and dried mango . . . and salad and dal and rice and chapatis and profiteroles for dessert (not homemade, she's quick to tell me – that kind of

* *Thali: A Joyful Celebration of Indian Home Cooking* (2021).

baking isn't really her thing), and gin, and whisky, and conversation that ranges from cultural appropriation to dog hotels (Brudo goes to a place with actual bunkbeds, which strikes me as inordinately hilarious), and of course, breakfast.

I tell them about my desi experience in Birmingham, and ask Maunika for her thoughts on the subject. The thing is, she explains, Indian food is extremely regional; 'every 20 or 30km, the ingredients, the vegetables, the water . . . even the techniques change'. She tells me about a place, Prakash, in Mumbai where she sometimes used to go with her mother: It's been around forever. It opens really early, before people leave for work, and there's always a queue. There are these really ugly blue communal tables, but seriously, the food is no frills, but to die for, the service is quick and it's all very reasonably priced.'

They have a fixed menu, she says, and not much has changed since her childhood. (Later she sends me her breakfast favourites there – 'traditional dishes from the Maharashtrian community; what people from Mumbai grow up eating. I ate these when I was six years old, and I still go back for the very same things:

Sabudana khichdi: Stir-fried sago seeds with chunks of
     potato, cumin, green chilli and crushed peanuts.
Batata vada: Spicy potatoes coated in a gram flour batter
     and crispy fried, served with coconut chutney.
Puri bhaji: Fried fluffy puris that are golden brown and
     served with spiced fried potatoes.
Shrikhand: Strained sweetened yoghurt with saffron,
     cardamom and pistachio, delicious served with puris.
Misal pav: Sprouted bean curry with ground spices, curry
     leaves and grated coconut. Serve with coriander, chopped
     onions and lime. It is eaten with soft bread rolls and is so
     good. Next time you see me I'll make it for you!')

Food, the pair agree, was a big part of life growing up in India. Maunika reminisces about breakfasts of steaming idli and spicy omelettes, fluffy uttapam with coconut chutney – Bharat, she says, particularly loves sabudana khichdi, a dish usually associated with religious fast days.

He smiles, explaining that, as a child, when his father would fast, he'd take advantage of it to eat a pile of sago 'mounded up like this' (he describes the shape of a vast hillock of starch) and claim to be fasting too. 'Everyone else dreaded the fast because there wouldn't be much to eat, but I – I was so happy!' Maunika sometimes makes it for weekend breakfast, and she says that her son 'always laughs when he sees me, because he knows Dad is going to be so, so pleased'.

Her tone turns more serious, as if she's handed me a baby and is worried I'm going to drop it. 'Felicity, if *you* make it, don't be putting loads of spices in there. Cumin, salt, roasted peanuts – perfect for a bit of texture – green chilli, that's it.' I nod obediently.

Parsis, she goes on, her tone softening now she's done her duty by the sago, are known for putting eggs 'on everything' – like kanda papeta per eda (fried onions with potatoes and eggs, a firm family favourite) and keema per eda, spicy lamb mince with eggs. Recipes for both, she assures me as I scribble notes, are available on her website.

They even insist on paying for my cab back to the hotel, which is so kind I can't bring myself to sneak Brudo out in my bag as planned. As in France, the generosity of (near) strangers has made my birthday ... though this time I'm not quite so drunk that I start crying about it.

—◆—

Sadly Central Newcastle doesn't offer much in the way of Maharashtrian breakfasts, but I have high hopes of starting the day with a stottie cake, the flat bread rolls, sometimes as large as a dinner plate, which are so peculiar to the North East that Greggs, the national bakery chain with local roots, only sells them up here.

The name comes from the dialect word stot, to bounce, provenance unknown, though given stotte is the Old English for bullock, anyone who's seen cows jumping for joy on spring grass might not find it hard to see the etymological link.

Unprepossessing as they look, stotties have the wonderfully bouncy open texture of a ciabatta or a decent 'English' muffin of the type so rarely seen in England (and no, McDonald's doesn't count), and the chewiness of a proper bagel. I'm determined to have one before I leave, even if it's too early for the traditional ham and pease pudding filling. Bacon and egg though, that would work.

❖❖❖

Tea Break: BREAD ROLLS OF BRITAIN. OR HOW TO START A TWITTER WAR

Every six months or so, a war erupts on social media about the proper name for a bread roll – wild claims are thrown around concerning what they were or weren't called in north-west Somerset in the late 1970s, and everyone gets Extremely Angry before something else comes along to make them Even Angrier.

Though I should know better, I blundered into this debate when, in the course of writing this book, I found myself standing outside a chippie in Lancashire, taking a picture of the hot beef teacake advertised in the window (for a very reasonable £2.55). A teacake to me suggests something studded with currants, and served toasted with butter, so I was puzzled – and, as the shop was closed, unable to go in to solve the mystery. Thanks to the wonders of modern technology, it wasn't long before I stood corrected.

Originally cake simply referred to a small bread, as opposed to a larger loaf, hence the terms tea, bread or barm cake (barm being the foam scooped off fermenting beer to leaven bread in the days before commercial yeast). A cob, meanwhile, meant a stout, roundish lump – from which we get cobblestone. Bap, which I would use to describe a flattish, floury soft roll, is of unknown etymology, but has been used since at least the seventeenth century.

Barm cake: North West, taking in Manchester, Wigan,
   Preston, Liverpool and Blackpool
Batch: Midlands, Liverpool
Bap: nationwide, but particularly common in Northern
   Ireland, the Isle of Man and Birmingham
Bread cake: Yorkshire (less common)
Bun: found nationally, but most popular in the North East
Cob: Midlands, particularly Nottinghamshire
Huffkin: an enriched Kentish bread roll, made with lard or
   butter, with a soft crust marked with a pronounced dimple,
   which is popularly said to invite the addition of jam. I'll be
   honest, I spend a lot of time in Kent and I'm yet to see a
   huffkin in the wild, but I like the sound of it and sometimes
   call Wilf my little huffkin when no one's around to hear

Morning or Scotch, Softie or sometimes Glasgow rolls: the
fluffy rolls of Scotland, available in soft or well-fired (crusty)
variants

Muffin: North, particularly just north of Manchester in areas
like Rochdale and Oldham

Oven bottoms (muffins or cakes): Lancashire

Roll: found nationally, but most popular in London

Rowie: somewhere between a pastry and a bread roll, these
salty, lardy, buttery pleasures are a staple in the north-east
of Scotland. Also known as a buttery, for obvious reasons

Scufflers: An oven-bottom bread much like the stottie below,
triangular, floured, and found under that name in parts of
West Yorkshire

Stottie: a muffin-like bread roll, a flat, chewy oven-bottom
bread almost exclusively found in Tyneside and Sunderland

Tea cake: North West, particularly areas north of Manchester,
like Leeds and Blackburn (elsewhere this refers to a fruited
bread roll)

. . . and, inevitably, at least one I haven't heard of, but which
someone will inform me of after this book has gone to
print.

(With thanks to the My Dialects project website headed by
Dr Laurel MacKenzie, Dr George Bailey and Dr Danielle
Turton for additional material.)

❖❖

The first bakery I target seems, like so many city centre businesses around the country, to have closed during the pandemic
so, determined not to be late for another train, I speed limp in
the direction of the Geordie Stottie. I find it in a promisingly
unprepossessing location across a dual carriageway, down a

little back street next to a wholesale drapers and textile importers and opposite a Nigerian Pentecostal church. The shutters are still at half-mast; I ask a woman smoking outside if they're open.

'Oh aye,' she says, 'mind, she's just got in and put the fryers on so it will be a while yet, I think. You want to try that place,' she gestures with her fag to a nearby office block, 'it's really cheap, all the students go there. Their curry and chips are beautiful. But then,' she adds, perhaps worrying she's been disloyal, 'you have to have the Yorkshires here, they're amazing, that's what they're famous for.' Yes yes, but where will I get a stottie, my good woman, I ask impatiently (I paraphrase).

'There's a Greggs opposite the station, pet.'

Happily on the way back I stumble, quite by chance, upon the tiny Pink Lane Bakery, where they're just putting some very handsome-looking stotties in the window between loaves of bread and pretzel buns.

'You don't do them with fillings, do you?' I ask plaintively – a dry bread roll isn't my idea of a good breakfast, however much of a regional speciality it may be. 'We do a cheese savoury,'* she says, 'but they're not made up yet, sorry.' I have to content myself with a plain one instead, so as I'm passing Greggs anyway, I pick up a cheese savoury stottie there too, just for good measure – they don't seem to do them with bacon for some reason, though they're doing a roaring trade in ordinary bacon rolls.

Once safely on the train south, I buy a bacon sandwich from the buffet. Not wanting to offend the chap who delivers

---

* AKA cheese and onion mayo, sometimes bulked out with grated carrot. Not one for a first date, perhaps, but an excellent hangover remedy the day afterwards.

it, I wait until he's safely out of sight, strip out the filling and arrange it in the Pink Lane stottie along with a thin smear of Tracklements mustard. The quality of the bacon may leave something to be desired, but the stottie itself is pleasingly springy and elastic – why Greggs keeps them from the rest of us I have no idea.

STOTTIES

Or how to get your fix if you live outside the stottie catchment area. The tip about leaving them in the oven to cool comes from fellow food writer and Tyneside native Olivia Potts, who recalls her mum serving them for lunch on Saturdays, 'with bacon and mushrooms and lots of ketchup', while her grandma's 'were proper South Shields fare: stuffed with pease pudding and breaded ham'.

Makes 6 small, 4 medium or 2 large stotties
15g dried yeast
A pinch of sugar
500g strong white bread flour, plus extra to dust
2 tsp fine salt
60g lard, or butter, put into the freezer for 30 minutes before use

1 Measure out 330ml of warm water, and stir the yeast and sugar into a little of it. Leave it until the top becomes foamy.
2 Put the flour and salt into a large bowl or food mixer and grate the fat across the surface. Rub in with your fingertips until no lumps remain.
3 Add the yeast mixture and the rest of the water and stir until it comes together into a sticky ball. Knead on a lightly floured work surface (try not to add too much flour) for

10 minutes or until elastic and smooth. You can also use a mixer fitted with a dough hook for this if you prefer.

4 Cover and leave in a warmish place until doubled in size. This should take about an hour, but may be longer depending on your room temperature.

5 Tip out onto a clean work surface and divide into equally sized pieces. Flatten into rounds the size you want them. Line two baking trays with lightly floured baking parchment.

6 Divide the stotties between the trays and poke a dent in the middle of each with your thumb. Prick each all over with a fork. Cover with a tea towel while you heat the oven to 220°C/200°C fan/gas 7.

7 Put the stotties into the oven and bake for 15 minutes. Turn the oven off and leave to cool in there for an hour before tucking in.

◆━━━━◆

The guard returns just as I'm trying to shove his uneaten roll into the bin. I'm unrepentant; I've done what I came to do, and I've got one in the bag for later.

Ridden: 84.81km
Climbed: 637m
Breakfasts eaten: 2 (birthday croissant; bacon stottie)

RED SAUCE OR BROWN?

Maunika: 'Ketchup forever!'

13
NEWCASTLE TO HARROGATE
Tea and Pikelets

With tea welcomes the morning.
– Samuel Johnson

Y ork station, my first stop after Newcastle, has an unusually festive air for a Tuesday morning thanks to the crowds of men in ankle-baring jeans and England shirts, as exuberant as boys as they head to Wembley to watch the game against Germany. Remembering the headlines that accompanied the same pairing back in 1996 (the *Mirror*'s 'Achtung! Surrender! For you, Fritz, ze Euro '96 Championship is over' being a particular lowlight), I'm relieved to see, as I wait for my connection, that the worst it gets this time is the *Sun*'s 'Come on, Harry, Even Hancock scored!' in reference to the former Health Secretary's recent indiscretions. Not that anyone wants to be reminded of that either, frankly.

I've come to Yorkshire to talk tea – the central pillar of the British breakfast, without which nothing else tastes quite right. Coffee is all very well, but it's a bit intense and shouty first thing, whereas a cup of tea leads you into the day gently, like someone tenderly half opening the curtains to let your eyes get used to the light.

The tea meeting's tomorrow though, which leaves me a day to kill in the UK's* largest county first. I'd thought about cycling from Newcastle, but on learning that it's 140 hilly kilometres from there to York, where I have a bed booked this evening, I immediately decided I'd rather see a bit more of Yorkshire instead. Which bit, however, has been giving me low-level anxiety for days. I consider heading west in the direction of the Dales, reversing a route I did with Gemma last autumn when we rode from Morecambe to Bridlington, or alternatively going up to the North York Moors.

In the end, I decide to indulge myself with a trip to Castle Howard, 'one of the great palaces of Europe' according to its website, in honour of what most of us regard as the ultimate British breakfast: a silver row of chafing dishes and buttered toast at some grand Edwardian country house party, in those sunny years before things all kicked off abroad.

Diplomat and author Harold Nicolson described such a breakfast, around 1910, thus, in his 1937 book *Small Talk*:

> Rows of little spirit lamps warmed rows of large silver dishes. On a table to the right between the windows were grouped Hams, Tongues, Galantines, Cold Grouse, ditto Pheasant, ditto Partridge, ditto Ptarmigan. No Edwardian meal was complete without Ptarmigan. Hot or cold. Just Ptarmigan. There would also be a little delicate rectangle of pressed beef from the shop of M. Benoit. On a further table, to the left between the doors, stood fruits of different calibre, and jugs of cold water, and jugs

---

* Well, largest historic county; it's been subdivided for practical purposes.

of lemonade. A fourth table contained porridge utensils. A fifth coffee, and pots of Indian and China tea . . . The centre table, which was prepared for twenty-three people, would be bright with Malmaisons and toast-racks . . . Edwardian breakfasts were in no sense a hurried proceeding. The porridge was disposed of negligently, people walking about and watching the rain descend upon the Italian garden. Then would come whiting and omelette and devilled kidneys and little fishy messes in shells. And then tongue and ham and a slice of Ptarmigan. And then scones and honey and marmalade. And then a little melon, and a nectarine or two, and just one or two of those delicious raspberries.

Thanks to its starring role as Brideshead Castle in the 1981 television adaptation of one of my favourite books,* Castle Howard was every Brit's fantasy country house long before *Downton Abbey* came on the scene. It sits in a part of Yorkshire that's entirely new to me, just on the edge of the rolling Wolds. I disembark in the market town of Malton (so polite it even has a sign on the way out urging 'Do Come Again'), whose neat streets quickly give way to the gentle Howardian Hills – in fact, there's no mistaking the fact that I'm in Howard country† round here.

It's soon fairly obvious that I'm on estate land too: the villages are chocolate-box affairs of uniform stone houses, all

---

* *Brideshead Revisited*, obviously. Yes, I know, I know, so basic: it's not even Waugh's best work.
† A name familiar to anyone who's battled through Tudor history, whether at school or in the pages of Hilary Mantel's Cromwell trilogy, the Howard family includes the dukes of Norfolk and more earls than you could shake a sceptre at; they're so rich in property that their eponymous Yorkshire castle is occupied by a relatively minor branch of the clan.

with the same paintwork, and there's not a Bargain Booze in sight, though there is, annoyingly, another idyllic-looking campsite to reinforce my mild sense of regret about leaving the tent in Cornwall.

I glimpse a flash of cupola through the trees as the road spools out straight in front of me, a tree-lined avenue with an obelisk visible at the far end and a sequence of rollercoaster bumpers that makes it quite the thrill ride on a bike. I'm the only one out enjoying it though; the car park is rammed, the bike racks empty. I change my shoes, shove the pannier with the cheese savoury stottie as far into the shade as I can manage, and queue, self-conscious in my shorts, for a ticket behind three collies showing even more flesh than me. (Though I suppose they are at least somewhat hairier.)

Eschewing the dreaded audio guide, which always feels like being trapped at a party with someone who won't stop talking, I ask the lady on the door if any of the kitchens are open, or if there are any food-related displays – I've been imagining batteries of gleaming copper pans . . . perhaps even a fully laid breakfast table. She shakes her head; not even a single plastic pork pie. It seems I'll just have to imagine the Howards sitting down to their kidneys and kedgeree.

Once visitors have processed dutifully through the sculpture gallery, single file like mourners paying their respects to a succession of plaster aristocrats, we're free to wander through the magnificent rooms, or at least, the few, comparatively speaking, open to us out of the 140-odd available. I comb the information boards for food-related scraps like a vulture picking over a carcass, discovering that an eighteenth-century visitor reports the 5th Earl sitting 'like a nightmare' at the head of the dinner table, while the same earl's friend, essayist Sydney

Smith, described Castle Howard as 'so far out of the way, that it was 12 miles from a lemon'.

Said grumpy earl's daughter, meanwhile, travelling on the Continent with her husband, found their carriage accosted by two riders near Rome. 'Fearing bandits,' the display informs me, 'Lady Cawdor reached for the pistols she carried with her, but in the dark she caught hold of a cold chicken leg instead, which had been crammed into the coach compartment as a snack.' (Annoyingly, it does not elaborate on what happened next with this drum-stick-'em-up. I'd like to think the bandits produced some mayo, they all laughed, forgot their differences and sat down to a picnic.)

It's all very beautiful, of course, but there's barely a mention of Brideshead, and certainly nothing about the breakfasts of scrambled eggs and bitter marmalade, salmon kedgeree and Bradenham ham favoured by the novel's narrator, Charles Ryder. (Later I discover I've missed Castle Howard's chief attraction: a black cairn terrier called Blodwyn who 'works' with their operations director. According to a blog on the house's website, Blodwyn, unlike Wilf, enjoys a swim 'during the summer months and has been known to jump into the Atlas Fountain, although we probably shouldn't admit to this'. Perhaps not a match made in heaven, much as I'd like Wilf to marry into such a fine estate.)

I exit via the gift shop, have a brief wander around the lovely gardens, positively thrumming with bees, find myself disappointed by the farm shop, with its vacuum-packed beetroot and plastic bags of Spanish celery when the chard grows lush and thick on the other side of the wall, and return to the car park to eat my cheese savoury* stottie, which, gloopy and aggressively oniony in the afternoon sun, is not an item I can imagine Evelyn Waugh's characters embracing with open arms, even after a night on the Brandy Alexanders. I, however, enjoy it immensely.

The ride out towards York proves the best part of the whole visit: another wide and undulating avenue punctuated by a series of gatehouses, one pointy and Gothic, another round and Romanesque, framing a final obelisk, a memorial to the 7th Earl of Carlisle, topped with a brazier of gilded fire, like a beacon declaring the Howards' might to the local populace. Not that they needed reminding, I imagine.

The landscape gradually spreads and flattens into the Vale of York, punctuated by the occasional sight, such as a sturdy twelfth-century church in tiny Bossall – now the smallest parish in Yorkshire thanks to the ravages of the Black Death – built when the Howards were still mere Norfolk lawyers, and the vanished village of Henderskelfe went about its business on the land now given over to Castle Howard.

I have my very own brush with death when two elderly sorts, chatting by the roadside on the outskirts of a village, wave frantically as I approach a thickly hedged corner. I've already spotted the top half of a lorry approaching, and adjusted my speed accordingly, but such is their urgency that I screech to a halt, and, steadying myself on a deceptively solid-looking verge, topple over into the vegetation. The lorry passes, on the other side of the road as I'd anticipated. 'Are you all right?' the lady calls over kindly. 'They do come round this corner very fast.' Fortunately I don't seem to have done myself any further mischief. I thank them for their kindness, and move on, wobbling slightly in shock.

Somehow, I fall over again in the middle of York – the slippery brick surface gets the better of me as I stand consulting a map, and Eddy skitters to the ground and I with him. A woman rushes to help, trying to pick him off me, but my leg is somehow threaded through his frame, and it takes a good minute or so for me to stand up, hot with shame. 'Are you sure you're OK?' she asks. 'That looked like it really hurt!' No, no, I assure her, it wasn't that bad, though in fact it's not just my pride that's dented this time. The bruise is going to be a belter – but at least my hamstring is still apparently attached, which is some comfort.

I seek solace in a Yorkshire pudding wrap, a concept that has long intrigued me from afar, and turns out to be best appreciated from a distance too. It's not that the idea of a roast dinner in a sandwich is a bad one, problems of gravy aside, but that a good Yorkshire pudding has qualities diametrically opposed to those of a good wrapping material, being light and airy, rather than flat and sturdy. This one is, perhaps necessarily, a bit like soggy styrofoam, and I guiltily deposit it in a nearby bin, muttering an apology to the animals that died to satisfy my morbid curiosity.

With time to kill before I can impose myself on Sam, my host for the night, I wander aimlessly around the market, have a trifle ice cream near the Minster, and, feeling restless after the disappointments of the day, decide to ride the straightest road I can find to Rufforth, a village with an airfield, a shuttered pub and so little to detain me that I turn round and come straight back. (Having hoped to beat my mileage from the French trip, I'm becoming increasingly concerned that a week out of the saddle in the Midlands might have scuppered my chances.)

York's pubs are already filling up with football fans, some singing uproariously in beer gardens, all of which seem to have televisions balanced precariously on outside tables to circumvent social distancing regulations. I sit in a park next to a seventeenth-century Plague Stone, so called because victims of a previous pandemic would leave money for food in a well of vinegar in the middle, and look at the map, trying to decide where to head next on my southerly journey. There's a sudden ROAR in stereo, much singing and cheering . . . and then, as if on cue, the wail of sirens. Seems we've won, I think, picking up Eddy and wondering belatedly if I should have brought Sam and his boyfriend Gareth something better than a Castle Howard tea towel.

The two of them, I'm surprised to discover, live in a proper house, in a proper street – I always think of Sam as about 23, but clearly he isn't, because it even has a proper spare room, with a dressing gown and slippers laid out, as well as balloons (birthday balloons!!) and a bottle of expensive English fizz. I'm honoured, I say, looking at the label. 'Oh, I got it from a taste test,' Sam, the food editor for a group of women's magazines, says, deftly popping the cork, 'don't worry, I didn't buy it for you.'

When he'd asked me a couple of days ago what I fancied eating, I'd requested vegetables (good, he said, we're both skint), which, as he writes recipes for a living, means we sit down to a squash pie topped with bronzed waves of filo pastry followed by an actual birthday cake. My third, admittedly, when you consider Cyril the knock-off Caterpillar and Maunika's profiteroles, but the first homemade one, a Norwegian 'success tart', which turns out to be a crunchy sugar almond cake with a rich, buttery filling and on this occasion, a thick coating of chocolate. 'I thought it would be a good omen for your trip,' Sam says, cutting me a hefty slice.

I'm well aware of the need to be on time the next morning – I'm having breakfast at the original Harrogate branch of Bettys, Yorkshire's favourite tearooms. It opens at 9 a.m.; I arrive at 8.40 a.m., laden down with Sam's homemade parkin* and an apple he thrusts upon me as I leave (apparently I'm looking a bit peaky), to find a polite queue has already formed outside.

At the front is Abi Taylor, who handles press for Bettys' sister tea and coffee company Taylors of Harrogate, and has, she says, been waiting under the colonnaded verandah since 8.30 a.m. – no special treatment is accorded to staff, it seems, even those accompanying Very Famous People like me. She and Kate Halloran, Taylors' Tea Innovations Manager, recall having to once wait with a group of Rwandan tea growers who became so cold in the northern weather that 'they were in about four Yorkshire Tea coats each. I kept saying, we're nearly there, I promise!'

As we study the menus, Kate asks me what kind of tea I like. I tell her I favour an Assam-heavy breakfast blend, with just enough milk to turn it the colour of damp sand. It's one of the few things I miss when I'm away, I say, slightly mournfully. She nods sympathetically, recommending the Bettys breakfast tea, a strong Golden Tippy Assam from India's Brahmaputra Valley,† which arrives in a gleaming silver pot with a neat strainer and a jug of milk. It's robust, but bright and fragrant: the tips of the bush, she tells me, yield a more delicate flavour.

---

* If you're not familiar with this sticky ginger and oat loaf, traditionally made for Bonfire Night, I commend it to you; it's one of those cakes that rather than going stale, just keeps getting better in the tin.

† NB: Though Taylors blend their famous Yorkshire Tea in Harrogate, the plant itself tends to like a bit more sunshine than is common in God's own county – the leaves come from over 20 countries across the Indian Subcontinent and Africa, to the regular amazement of people on Twitter who seem to think they're drinking something grown on the Dales and tended by tiny terriers.

Tea tasted, we turn to the matter of breakfast. Founded by Swiss patissier and confectioner Fritz Bützer* back in 1919, Bettys is famous for its baking, so I opt for a pastry and pikelet selection – though in truth I'm only in it for the pikelets. These floppy free-form crumpets, buttercup yellow with a crunchy frill of darker toast around one edge, are the perfect sponge for butter and leave a very satisfactory ring behind them on the plate once I've polished them off. I could eat at least a dozen, but I restrain myself from asking for seconds, and turn the talk back to tea, because Kate, who describes herself as 'a tea obsessive', doesn't have long before she has to get back to the office.

It's Assam season, she explains apologetically, and she and the other Taylors buyers are currently inundated with samples of garden-fresh leaves to drink their way through before deciding what to buy for the year ahead. (Most of the tea we consume in this country is, I learn, between six months and a year old.) We discuss breakfast blends: she recommends I stick to Scottish or Irish ones, which tend to contain more Assam than English versions, and taste thicker, richer and maltier in consequence.

One of the first things she asks people looking for tea recommendations at any time of day is whether they plan to drink it on its own, or with food, she says. Assam is the perfect choice to cut through the richness of a traditional fry-up (I knew there was a reason why I liked it), but if someone starts the day with yoga and a few slices of papaya, a more delicate Darjeeling might be in order. And, she adds, warming to her theme, if you like porridge, well, you have to try our toast and jam tea – a splash actually works really well in the porridge itself. (I'm

---

* His wife's name was Claire; no one really knows who Betty was, a detail which makes me feel better about the missing apostrophe.

momentarily distracted by a vision of the World Porridge Championships committee spinning like angry spurtles at this revelation.)

Taylors is most familiar, however, as the manufacturers of Yorkshire Tea, a brand that's recently gone from niche to national treasure. I remember laughing to myself when I saw it in the foreign and speciality food aisle of Morrisons in Hackney about a decade ago; now it's everywhere, from Highgrove (it holds a royal warrant for the Prince of Wales) to the corridors of power.

Not that all publicity is good publicity: last year Chancellor Rishi Sunak tweeted a picture of himself making the budget team a brew with a vast catering-sized bag of Yorkshire Tea and social media responded in its typically unhinged fashion, calling for boycotts and claiming the association was the 'kiss of f*cking death' for the brand. So heated did things get (people generally feeling more emotionally invested in tea than politics) that Yorkshire Tea's Twitter account was forced to issue a response calling for a bit more kindness online: 'On Friday, the chancellor shared a photo of our tea . . . We weren't asked or involved – and we said so the same day. Lots of people got angry with us all the same. For some, our tea just being drunk by someone they don't like means it's forever tainted, and they've made sure we know it.'

('That was quite the week to be honest,' Abi says. 'Everyone thinks we set it up, but I promise you, we really didn't.' She sounds weary at the memory. Lest anyone doubt Yorkshire Tea's impeccable impartiality, Jeremy Corbyn posed with a similarly large bag during a visit to York in 2017, suggesting he'd like to discuss climate change over a cuppa with Donald Trump. This did not happen; Trump, of course, only drinks Diet Coke.)

I ask how they've achieved this success; why does everyone suddenly want a splash of Yorkshire in their mug? 'People want a quality cup of tea,' Kate says, 'and we never compromise on that. You can't fool a tea drinker.' Clearly she's never had a cup from Starbucks.

•••

Tea Break:
QUICK-FIRE ROUND WITH KATE HALLORAN OF TAYLORS OF HARROGATE

Loose leaf or tea bags?
'I mean, I'm in the tea industry and even I only drink loose leaf in the afternoons and at weekends. It's a convenience thing – the "dust" people claim is swept off the floor to go into teabags [it isn't, by the way] is actually designed to brew faster, so you get a powerful tea in a fraction of the time.'

Pot or mug?
'I'm unusual in that I always use a pot, because I'm greedy, I always want a second cup!' I'm sure I remember my grandma telling me never to wash a teapot. Is this correct, or am I just lazy? 'I give my teapot a good rinse, but it should never see detergent. Ever.'

Is tea better taken black? I mean, I don't care, but is it, strictly speaking?
'No, plenty of teas taste better with milk.'

Milk first or tea first?

'When I make it in a pot, I add the milk to the cup first, when I make it in a cup I add it afterwards, because otherwise the water won't be hot enough to brew the tea' (gavel down, case closed).

Kate's recipe for the perfect cup of tea:

'It sounds obvious, but for breakfast, go for a classic English Breakfast blend or even a pure Assam. They are robust teas, which are best with milk. The strength of those types of tea cuts through rich food so is perfect for a fry-up. If you prefer a non-dairy alternative, I really like Assam with coconut milk. They work really well together.

'If you are having a proper breakfast – rather than grabbing it and running – make your tea in a pot. Not only does it give the tea more space to brew, but you get an instant refill without having to put the kettle back on! Tea likes hot water, but a chilly teapot cools things down so always warm the pot. I pour the hot water from the pot into the mugs to warm them too.

'For loose tea, I recommend a heaped teaspoon per person and one for the pot. If you prefer to use teabags, I would recommend 1 teabag per person. Nothing for the pot though. Experiment with what works best for your teapot. For my favourite four-mug pot, I will use three teabags and brew for 4–5 minutes. If you are brewing tea in a pot, it is milk in first as the brewing has already taken place in the pot. If you are making it in a mug, the water goes in first to give the tea time to brew.'

We ponder why people are prepared to invest so much time and money in coffee, but anything other than a mass-market tea bag is seen as an affectation ('Don't get me started,' says Kate darkly). Is it a generational thing? I suggest. The younger demographic is certainly drinking less tea, Abi admits, but they're still drinking it. Maybe, I think, it's something, like marmalade, that you grow into. Certainly if I was forced to choose between tea and coffee, I say, I'd go for tea every time. And I'm not just saying that because you're here, Kate.

'For me, coffee has a certain formality about it; it's an occasion, something you might go out for, whereas tea . . . it's honest, it's . . . cosy,' Abi muses. I couldn't agree more. At a time of day when I don't always want to be challenged, a comforting cup of breakfast tea hits the spot. Sexy espressos and their ilk are for when I've actually woken up.

❖❖

Tea Break:
PAUSE–CAFÉ: THE TAYLORS' COFFEE TEAM TIPS FOR A PERFECT CAFETIÈRE OF COFFEE

We recommend 60g coffee to 1 litre of water as the perfect
    ratio for a cafetière.
Coffee doesn't like boiling water, so after the kettle has boiled
    leave it to stand for 5 minutes.
Pour the water over the coffee and then give a little stir to
    make sure the coffee is free to brew properly.

Leave to brew for 4 minutes before plunging.
As we chat, I mention my trip to Castle Howard, and how disappointed I'd been not to find out more about its domestic life. Kate lights up, explaining that it was once common for big estates to have their own house blend of tea, and that Taylors' founder, Charles Taylor, is sure to have been responsible for a few locally. 'I have absolutely no evidence for that yet though,' she admits, 'and I'm desperately trying to find some.' Once all that new-season Assam has been tasted anyway.

BUTTERMILK PIKELETS

Bettys use yeast to raise their pikelets, which is indeed a lovely thing, but sometimes you want breakfast now, rather than in an hour's time. (In fact, I almost always want breakfast now.) This recipe is based on a 1914 version from May Byron's Pot-luck; or, The British Home Cookery Book *and will give you pikelets in mere minutes.*

Some tips courtesy of Bettys Cookery School: 'If your yeast or raising agents are old, stodgy pancakes not pikelets will be the result! Pikelets are at their best the more patient you are; the longer you wait the bigger the bubbles! A warm pan is key; too hot, they could burn or become bitter and the top undercooked.'

Makes about 8
Fat, to grease
175g strong white flour, or plain will do
¼ tsp bicarbonate of soda
½ tsp fine salt
About 300ml buttermilk

1 Lightly grease a heavy frying pan, griddle or crêpe pan –
   Byron suggests with a little bacon fat, but oil will do – and
   place over a medium heat. Whisk together the flour, bicarb
   and salt, then stir in the buttermilk to make a batter about
   the same thickness as double cream.
2 Put a small ladleful of batter onto the pan, flatten and leave
   until set on top – there should be a wealth of small bubbles
   – then turn and repeat. It should be golden on the bottom; if
   it's dark brown or burnt underneath, your pan is too hot.
3 Keep warm if eating immediately, or simply stick in the
   toaster to reheat. They also freeze well.

As previously noted, Yorkshire is a very large place – it's almost
100km just to the border with Nottinghamshire. One hundred
very scenic kilometres, no doubt, but my next appointment is
in Cambridgeshire in a couple of days, and I don't want to miss
out on the East Midlands completely. Thus, after a lot of
prevaricating (now my hamstring is stronger, it pains me to
take a train), I've decided to go by rail from York to
Peterborough. My last train of the trip, I promise myself. From
here on in, it's all about the legs.

To salve my conscience I ride back to York, through
Knaresborough, passing, on a route closed to cars, and which
thus feels like a real cyclist's perk, the shrine of Our Lady of
the Crag (closed due to coronavirus restrictions; woe betide
anyone counting on her help in avoiding this particular plague),
the site of the Battle of Marston Moor, and signs for Mother
Shipton's Cave. The last bills itself as England's oldest tourist
attraction, and promises great riches including petrified teddy
bears and Queen Mary's shoe, plus a life-sized figurine of the

fifteenth-century prophetess herself. I very much regret I do not have time to stop and admire these treasures, but as ever, I have a train to catch.

By the time I'm on board I've got half the carbs in Yorkshire in my panniers: a Bettys fat rascal and a Yorkshire curd tart too, plus a comfortingly warm pork pie for lunch. I feel I've barely scratched the surface of the North, but it's time to head south and home.

I'm not sure I'm ready for it.

Ridden: 98.96km
Climbed: 533m
Breakfasts eaten: 1 (buttered pikelets)

RED SAUCE OR BROWN?

Sam: 'I'm brown sauce all the way. Gareth likes to put red sauce on one slice of bread and brown on the other.'

Abi: 'Bacon sarnie is always ketchup. However, as soon as sausages come into the mix it is HP (and it has to be HP) – I crave tamarind as a flavour. I increasingly also love a couple of splashes of Tabasco on either. As my husband will tell you, I am really heavy-handed with both sauces – they are more than a garnish. I will happily have both with a bit of butter on toast.'

Kate: 'Brown on bacon, red on sausages.'

14
PETERBOROUGH TO CORBY
Weetabix

'Weetabix are unbeatabix . . . Though for preference for breakfast,
Mr Speaker, you'll know what I like – it's Nanny's homemade
marmalade on toast.'
– Jacob Rees-Mogg in the House of Commons, 11 February
2021

Though I feel like I'm leaving the North behind as I pull out of York station, it strikes me when I get off in Peterborough, not much closer to London than it is to Hull, that this probably doesn't count as the South either. Despite the unhealthy English fixation with binaries, Peterborough feels, to me, born in Cambridge, more like the East than anything else.

An ancient city, with an important twelfth-century cathedral and a pretty market square, it suffered, architecturally speaking, from its promotion as a New Town in the 1960s. Butchered by dual carriageways, overshadowed by office blocks, the road out of town from the station is unlovely, to put it kindly. I cycle past a scuffle between daytime drinkers, and an evangelical church promising the desperate 'supernatural manifestations' to empower them in their faith, family, finance and future. This at least is a more enticing offer than the undertakers in nearby Eye whose window display jauntily encourages passers-by to PLAN YOUR OWN FUNERAL.

I have other business to attend to first, however. Of just over 2,000 adults surveyed at the beginning of 2020, 29 per cent of them said cereal was their most frequent breakfast, followed by toast, at 21 per cent, and porridge, clearly its own category of cereal, at 14 per cent.* Today, I'm heading for Spalding in Lincolnshire, on the edge of the Fens, where much of that cereal grows – the East of England, (relatively) dry and (very) flat, is the country's arable heartland.

Indeed, though Weetabix, my childhood breakfast of choice, is made in neighbouring Northamptonshire, tomorrow's destination, I suspect most of the principal raw material hails from Lincolnshire, given it's the UK's largest producer of wheat. (The county also supplies most of our potatoes and poultry, is home to one of Europe's major fish markets at Grimsby and has its very own cheese (Poacher) and colony of grey seals. It doesn't get enough love in my opinion.)

Down here, the skies are vast, bigger even than in the flat-lands near York, confirming my impression that things are about to get distinctly East Anglian. As I pedal past Crowland, noting the faded UKIP poster on a lamppost, something large looms beyond the little terraced houses that back onto the main road, an intriguing bulk of medieval stone. It looks significant enough for me to turn off to see what's what – and what I find is, to me at least, genuinely jaw-dropping; an ordinary parish church with the ruins of a Norman abbey hanging off

---

* A fry-up came fifth.

one side, its vast window open to the sky, its façade covered in sculpted saints, those within arm's reach now sadly headless.

I feel like I've walked into an M. R. James ghost story – how is this place, which, I learn from the information board, pre-dates the Norman Conquest (it was founded by the Anglo-Saxon St Guthlac in the early eighth century), just sitting here, so far off my beaten track I've never even heard of it, let alone visited? I immediately message Lucinda. Even she doesn't know Crowland Abbey and she knows everything, or at least claims to.

The church itself is locked, so I sit on the welcoming stone benches in the porch, worn smooth by generations of bottoms, and eat a Bettys Yorkshire curd tart, thinking how, in a car, I would probably have missed all this completely.

After that, the rest of the ride into Spalding is a bit of an anti-climax; a lot of blank skies and big lorries hefting agricultural produce around and a few people gawping open-mouthed at a lone woman on a bike. I am, therefore, particularly thrilled to see an owl flying low over wheat fields near Cowbit with something small and dangly of tail in its beak. When I describe it later, my friend Doug, a gamekeeper, immediately identifies a barn owl on a twilight hunt. It's ages since I've seen one and, just like the red squirrels in the Highlands, a timely reminder of the privilege afforded to the cyclist to become part of the landscape, rather than just travelling through it.

Following the river, and a handsome line of Georgian houses, into town, I'm surprised to discover my hotel, the Red Lion Inn, boasts a blue plaque commemorating the time, back in 1967, when it hosted Jimi Hendrix after 'Spalding's remarkable Barbecue 67 gig, which also included Pink Floyd and Cream'. (The White Hart, a couple of doors down, claims to have put up the philosopher Jean-Jacques Rousseau exactly two centuries earlier. Both feel so unlikely I begin to wonder if that curd tart was spiked with something.)

Eddy spends the night down in the beer cellar with the barrels, and I, seized with a sudden yearning for something not wrapped in pastry, amble over to the Crystal Inn Chinese Restaurant, where I spend a pleasant hour with some aubergines in black bean sauce and a beer. As she clears the table, I ask the waitress what she eats for breakfast. She looks startled. 'Toast?'

◆◆

Tea Break:
RICE PORRIDGE.
GREEN EGGS AND HAM

Chinese 'breakfasts' aren't hard to come by anywhere with a takeaway – congee, or juk to give this rice porridge its Mandarin name, is on most menus, and if it isn't, it never hurts to ask. A staple across East and South-East Asia as well as southern India and Sri Lanka, the kitchen will almost certainly know how to make it.

David Yip of the Wing Yip chain of Chinese supermarkets fills me in on the attractions of congee: 'It's filling but it's very light because the vast majority of it is water; you'd be surprised how much you can make from one cup of rice.' His mum used to make it on Sundays, he says, but when I ask if that was for breakfast, he explains that in Chinese culture they don't really separate things like that: you can eat anything for breakfast you might have for lunch, but just less of it.

For him it's a comfort food, though he's been with friends who have struggled with the texture; 'Rice has a different consistency to oats, doesn't it?' It's usually cooked with stock, though it can be made with water, and the most popular toppings, in David's reckoning, are century egg and shredded pork. Similar to the British taste for eggs and bacon then, though in truth, a century egg, cured for a few weeks in an alkaline solution until the white is a beautiful translucent amber, and the yolks a chalky sea green, bears little resemblance to anything you'd get on a fry-up.

But, like soup, he says, congee is infinitely adaptable: you can throw anything in you want. He used to work with someone in Manchester who liked the sweetness of carrot in there, and he's heard of people adding sliced abalone, a shellfish that sells for £150 a kilo, for special occasions.

'You do get a lot of differences between families; obviously the first ones who immigrated here tend to be quite traditional, and then their kids are more westernised.' He himself likes to add crisps, for example, while his mum would sometimes serve congee with spring rolls, and youtiao (deep-fried dough sticks, like savoury churros) are a very common accompaniment. It's a textural thing: the congee is soft, he explains, so you need something crunchy to go with it.

Wait, I say urgently, tell me more about the crisps. What flavour do you go for?

Cheese and onion, he says, obviously. 'My kids now do it too.' He pauses. 'They've moved on to Wotsits though – a bit too much that is really.'

Spalding, on my post-prandial perambulation, feels like a pleasant place, combining gunmakers and country clothing specialists with takeaways and Polish and Lithuanian help centres. Indeed, many of the people I pass are speaking Slavic-sounding languages, with the exception of a teenage boy on a bike, who demands indignantly of his mate, 'Yeah, but has she even knobbed you off yet?'

I hurry into the hotel before I can hear the answer. There's a sign on the door up from the bar requesting guests remove muddy work boots before ascending and, at 9.45 p.m., already a sonorous snore coming from the room opposite. From Hendrix to this, I think. How the mighty have fallen.

◆◆

Tea Break: ŚNIADANIE

Poles, who according to figures from June 2020, account for by far the largest number of foreign-born British residents, eat what used to be known as a 'continental breakfast', as Ren Behan, author of *Wild Honey and Rye*, explains. 'Cold cuts are very popular (smoked hams and meats) as well as cheese, especially cottage cheese with radish and spring onion, served with a sourdough or rye bread, with tomatoes and cucumbers on the side and perhaps a hard-boiled egg,' she tells me.

'Also, all types of eggs, such as softly scrambled eggs with Polish ham or kiełbasa. We love oats with berries and honey and Polish pastries or pancakes (with sweetened curd cheese and berries or with stewed apples). We usually drink lemon tea with it.'

Unable to find anywhere in Spalding offering such a feast, I settle for a trip to the Olawa Bakery, whose windows hold a dizzying array of pastry-based possibilities. A small chain with branches from the North West to Tooting Bec, it was started by Miroslaw Zubicki, an energetic baker from the south-western Polish town of the same name, who arrived in Worksop in 2004 to work in a sandwich factory.

'After the deduction of room costs, he was usually left with £70 per week,' the company's website informs me. 'He would leave £15 for himself and send the rest to his wife. He used to live with 10 roommates and bread with butter, eggs and chips were his only meals.' In 10 years, he'd saved enough to open his first bakery.

I can see why he's done so well; the choice is bewildering. The man behind the counter suggests a poppy seed croissant, of the original, bready mittel-European variety (puff pastry croissants being a twentieth-century French innovation) and I add a cabbage roll for good measure, which he confirms is very good, 'if you like cabbage'.

I eat the roll in the market square, observed by a predatory pigeon and an endless stream of shouting schoolchildren. The pastry is bready and nicely seasoned, the cabbage, slightly sour, studded with mushrooms and faintly spiced.

It's so filling I can't even make a start on the croissant, and feels like just the thing to set me up for a day on the road, or in the fields – which is what a significant proportion of the local Eastern European population came here for in the first place. It's estimated that 150,000 Polish citizens alone have left since the Brexit referendum.

Picking up a pork pie from George Adams butchers as a gift to my hosts this evening, I put the Corby Weetabix factory into my navigation app, and get on the road.

East Anglia, with its scrawled adverts for CAULIS, huge fields of wheat and sprawling houses with unfeasible numbers of cars outside, some in an advanced state of disrepair, gradually gives way to the wealthier East Midlands. The villages are increasingly clustered together, stone replaces brick and thatch starts to appear on roofs again. Helpston ('formerly in the Soke of Peterborough, geographically in Northamptonshire, subsequently in Huntingdon and Peterborough, then in Cambridgeshire, and administered by the City of Peterborough unitary authority') boasts one such thatched cottage with a plaque to the 'Northamptonshire Peasant Poet' John Clare, who was born here in 1793. He died in Northampton General Lunatic Asylum 71 years later, his medical diagnosis: 'years of poetical prosing'.

Small climbs and descents break the monotony of the flat as I ride through Rockingham Forest, once William the Conqueror's favourite hunting ground, now so reduced by agriculture and development that the only clues to its existence on my route are a few arrestingly large and ancient-looking oaks by the roadside.

I stop in the picturesque village of King's Cliffe, eye caught by an elderly man arranging fruit outside the village shop. When I enter, clutching a peach, I discover the shop is of the traditional, dimly lit kind; a ramshackle assortment of fly papers, shoelaces and discounted flour 'past sell-by date' as well as the usual requisites of everyday life, like Vimto and Prawn Cocktail Spirals. The fruit arranger, now back behind the till, compliments me on my choice, telling me he had one of the same himself for breakfast: 'lovely it was'. I eat it along with the Polish croissant, savoury and fluffy, with a delicate sprinkling of poppy seeds.

Sticky fingered, I press on along roads increasingly hedged in by hedges (not a fenland speciality, the hedge) until, eventually, down a narrow but liberally pot-holed lane that speaks of an infinite amount of heavy traffic, I find myself on the outskirts of Corby. It's a name chiefly famous to hotel guests worldwide in relation to trouser presses, though disappointingly it seems these were actually invented in Windsor by a John Corby, as if Windsor didn't have enough to show off about already.

Corby does have a proud, if unlikely, heritage in the cereal aisle though, as this transcript from the NASA website of communication between ground control in Houston, and Neil Armstrong on his way to the Moon in 1969, proves:

053:56:39 McCandless: In sports, the Houston Oilers are showing plenty of enthusiasm in their early pre-season work-outs at Kerrville, and Coach Wally Lemm says he is impressed with the fine group of rookies. National League baseball for yesterday, Thursday: St Louis 11, Philadelphia 3; Montreal 5, over Pittsburg 4; Atlanta 12, Cincinnati 2; San Francisco 14, and Los Angeles 13. American League: we have Baltimore 3, over Cleveland 2; Detroit 4 to Washington's 3; Minnesota 8 to Chicago 5. Boston at New York was rained out. And in Corby, England, an Irishman, John Coyle, has won the world's porridge eating championship by consuming 23 bowls of instant oatmeal in a 10-minute time limit from a field of 35 other competitors. Over. [Pause.]

053:57:48 Armstrong: Roger. I assume Houston didn't play yesterday.

053:57:51 McCandless: That's correct.

053:57:55 Collins: I'd like to enter Aldrin in the oatmeal eating contest next time.

053:58:00 McCandless: Is he pretty good at that?

053:58:04 Collins: He's doing his share up here.

053:58:13 McCandless: Let's see. You all just finished a meal not long ago, too, didn't you? [Pause.]

053:58:20 Aldrin: I'm still eating.

053:58:24 McCandless: Okay. Does that – that . . .

053:58:27 Collins: He's on his – he's on his nineteenth bowl.

There is now a crater on Mars named Corby, which, whether or not it's in tribute to the town, is still surely cooler than any trouser press. Corby's other claim to fame is more solid: its Weetabix factory. Until recently, it had two, but one shut in 2019 after the Chinese state-run Bright Foods, who'd taken control in 2012, hoping to crack the home market, gave up trying to interest 1.4bn Chinese citizens in breakfast cereals, and sold it on to the Americans.

When I google it to find the address, I discover Weetabix workers are taking industrial action over pay, conditions and health and safety concerns, which has led to several strikes. This may explain why my polite request for a factory tour has gone unheeded, though then again, it could also have something to do with Covid. Most things seem to.

Instead, my schoolfriend Alex, who lives nearby, comes from a family of farmers and boasts a cousin whose photo sometimes pops up on the side of Shredded Wheat boxes, has kindly agreed to come and meet me outside for a bowl of 'bix. She's bringing the ingredients; I've got the spork and an appetite for making a fool of myself in public.

◆━━━━◆

Tea Break:
MORAL FIBRE. OR THE
SURPRISING HISTORY OF
BREAKFAST CEREALS

Breakfast cereals are a nineteenth-century American invention, a product of the Popular Health and Clean Living movements which also favoured vegetarianism, brown bread and regular exercise. According to historian Heather Arndt Anderson, 'bacon and eggs, pancakes with syrup, and hot coffee were now considered as "injurious" to one's health as masturbation'.

Cereals were thus developed as a health, rather than a convenience, food; the first on the market, Granula, required overnight soaking before consumption and was so jawbreakingly tough it was nicknamed 'wheat rocks'.

The more palatable flakes we're used to today were, it's said, discovered accidentally by the thrifty Kellogg brothers, who were determined to find a use for a dried-up pan of cooked wheat at their fashionable Michigan sanatorium. Passed through rollers, the crispy pieces proved a big hit with their dyspeptic clientele, and a phenomenon was born.

Weetabix, however, is an Australian creation. Originally known as Weet-Bix, when that business was sold in 1928, to the company that still make it in Australia and New Zealand to this day, its inventor Bennison Osborne started afresh in South Africa, bringing it to Britain under its new name in 1932.

Following a brief spell of Chinese ownership, Weetabix is now under the wing of Post Holdings, a business set up by

C.W. Post, a former patient at the Kelloggs' Battle Creek sanatorium, in 1895, and which debuted its first breakfast cereal, Grape Nuts, two years later. (His own take on cornflakes, Elijah's Manna, was so controversially named that Britain refused to register the trademark.) Today the company also manufactures Chips Ahoy!, a box of miniature chocolate chip cookies masquerading as breakfast, which, to be fair, makes no claim to be a health food.

Interesting fact: Australian friends inform me that Weet-Bix are commonly eaten as biscuits as well as with milk due to their alleged superior 'structural integrity': butter and honey, or Vegemite, appear to be the favourite toppings. This may have been the initial inspiration for the increasingly worrying serving suggestions on British Weetabix boxes: having tried replacing the muffin in an eggs Benedict with a dry Weetabix, I wouldn't recommend it.

•••

'I thought it would smell of toasted wheat,' Alex says, disappointed, stepping out of the car. Me too, I say, I've been cycling with my mouth open for miles. Built, like Marmite HQ, of flimsy-looking corrugated metal, Weetabix nevertheless offers a distinctly superior picnic spot in the form of a freshly mown grass verge rather than a roadside smoking area.

She doles out two biscuits each – the recommended serving suggestion, though in truth I generally find I'd prefer three – and douses them in whole milk, which always feels like a treat to someone brought up in the fat-phobic Eighties. Just enough so the bottom goes soggy; you want to retain a bit of crunch on top. I add a sprinkling of brown sugar from a packet I've been carrying around for emergencies and we tuck in. No one comes out from the sentry box to ask us what on earth we're doing sitting down for a bowl of cereal on an industrial estate, largely because no one seems to be in there. Perhaps they're all on strike.

••

Tea Break:
WEETABIX FACTS

- All the wheat for Weetabix comes from a 50-mile radius of the company's mills in Burton Latimer, Northamptonshire.
- It takes about 365 grains of wheat to make each biscuit: sorted, cleaned of stone, dust and broken grains, soaked, steamed with vitamins, malt, salt, water and sugar, then dried, crushed, shaped into biscuits and baked.*
- During the Second World War, Weetabix was only available in the Midlands and north-east England to reduce waste and maximise efficiency.
- Sir Ranulph Fiennes took Weetabix, and sister brand Alpen, on his Transglobe expedition in 1979.
- Weetabix is the bestselling cereal in the UK according to Nielsen, while Weetabix East Africa, based in Nairobi, is Africa's.
- Weetabix is constantly suggesting new ways to enjoy its products, from topping them with smashed avocado to blitzing them up as a coating for fried chicken. Personally I'm not sure you can beat cold milk and sugar, but that's

---

* There's a fascinating video of Weetabix East Africa's Nairobi factory on YouTube, shot for the Made in Kenya series. (Fascinating if you have a special interest in cereal anyway.)

unlikely to send Twitter into a tailspin, or indeed prompt
discussion in the House of Commons, as occurred when
the company recommended adding baked beans back in
February 2021. Jacob Rees-Mogg, it turns out, likes his
Weetabix with hot milk and brown sugar, and probably
made by Nanny.

◆◆◆

We load Eddy into the back of the car, and I spend the evening
with Alex, her family, her border terrier Bob, and my small
godson Hamish, who, the next morning, proves the perkiest
person in the house, giggling as he puts away a quite astonishing number of Weetabix. 'He's never gone beyond three
before,' Alex says adding another half to his bowl. 'It must be
the effect you have on people.' I'm proud, I say. If that's my
legacy to him it will be a fine one.

I help myself to a third too, just to keep him company. I'm
usually more of a muesli girl these days, but there's no denying
the convenience of any kind of cereal when you're pushed for
time or energy, whether that's before work or when you roll
back in at midnight having been so thirsty you forgot to eat.
The Kelloggs may have been odd, but they had at least one
good idea.

MUESLI

Note that this is my perfect combination; feel free to swap the grains around, simplify them, add different fruit, leave out the nuts, etc. – the beauty of making your own muesli is that not only is it cheaper than fancy brands because you're making a lot, but it saves you picking out all that dried papaya or wondering who's stolen all the best nuts.

Makes about 1kg
400g rolled oats
200g rye flakes
50g almonds, roughly chopped
50g pecans, roughly chopped
50g pistachios, roughly chopped
100g mixed seeds
A pinch of salt (optional)
100g dried apricots, roughly chopped
50g stoned dates, roughly chopped
100g dried sour cherries or figs, roughly chopped

1 Heat the oven to 200°C/180°C fan/gas 6. Put the cereals, nuts and seeds on a clean baking tray, spread out well, and bake for about 10 minutes, shaking halfway through.
2 Leave to cool, then mix with the remaining ingredients. Store in an airtight jar.

Alex kindly drives me as far as Stamford so I can retrace my steps. Having made a detour to admire the façade of a shed turning out dehydrated wheat biscuits, I'm heading back to East Anglia for something altogether more substantial: black pudding.

Ridden: 96.38km
Climbed: 352m
Breakfasts eaten: 2 (Polish cabbage roll and croissant; Weetabix) (or maybe 3 if you include both helpings of Weetabix)

RED SAUCE OR BROWN?

David: 'I'm ketchup really . . . you go up north though and it's brown, isn't it? Once you get past Birmingham, up to Lancashire or Yorkshire, brown sauce is more and more popular. Even in Birmingham you don't really see it. There's a line, a line of sauce. Red one side, brown the other.'

Man in the Polish bakery: 'Ketchup and mustard. Both.'

Alex: 'Ketchup and loads of butter for a bacon sandwich (ignore those marmalade freaks). Likewise ketchup for the sausage element of a cooked brekker only, though may also add mustard on the side.'

Hamish: 'Definitely a ketchup man.'

15
STAMFORD TO CAMBRIDGE
Black Pudding

From black pudding to pickled jellyfish, beauty lies in the eye of the beholder.

– Laurence Mound, entomologist, in his introduction to the
1988 reprint of *Why Not Eat Insects?* by Vincent M. Holt (1885)

Having been thwarted in my hopes of a black pudding bap in the North West, I'm hoping to have more luck at the Fruit Pig Company in East Anglia. I'll be honest, they were the back-up plan once it was clear Bury was out of bounds – I knew their puddings to be excellent, because my local butcher stocks them, but I didn't know, until I googled them, that they're the only commercial producers to use fresh rather than dried blood, and as such are also something rather special.

These gloomy-looking sausages are made, in various forms, around the world: blood, though extremely nutritious,* does not keep well, so packing it into intestines to be cooked or smoked makes sense from a preservation point of view. Irish

---

* High in both protein and iron.

black pudding giant Clonakilty uses beef, while a fifteenth-century English recipe calls for the fat and blood of a porpoise, which I think, as I head east from Stamford, even I'd struggle with on my breakfast plate.

My ride into the Cambridgeshire plains feels like yesterday in reverse, the horizon sinking, the hedges disappearing, the architecture turning from warm stone to red brick, and then to the same sandy yellow brick of my primary school. In Gorefield I see the first flint church – which somehow feels significant to someone christened in one. I celebrate the milestone with the last of my Glasgow tablet and push on deeper into the fens in search of the black pudding factory.

◆◆

Tea Break:
THINGS FOR SALE BY THE ROADSIDE IN THE 122KM FROM STAMFORD TO CAMBRIDGE VIA WISBECH IN EARLY JULY 2021

Rhubarb
New potatoes
Goose eggs, duck eggs, hen eggs, quail eggs
Horse carrots
Manure
Jam
Guinea pigs

◆◆

I find Fruit Pig in a light industrial park just south of the little town of Wisbech, near a caravan repair shop and a bait and tackle merchants. Leaning Eddy against the side of the building, and having no luck with the doorbell, I accost a man who's just pulled up in a van.

'Hi! Grant?'

No, he says, that's who he's here to see. Suddenly the door opens, revealing Grant Harper himself. At almost 2 metres tall, he fills the frame – come in, come in, he says, just a small electrical thing I've got to deal with and then I'll be with you. Sure, I say, secretly relieved; I'm always grateful for a moment with a mirror before sitting down to chat – after 50km on the bike, one doesn't unfailingly look one's best.

Hair brushed, sparky sorted, I ask Grant how one ends up in the blood sausage game. Well, he says, by accident really: Matt, his partner in Fruit Pig, came out of the RAF after a career as a fighter control officer, and decided to buy a smallholding – 'and then a friend got him into the butchery business, which was never his intention when he started out'.

Grant, a Hertfordshire boy with a diploma in horticulture, moved up to Norfolk with his parents as a young man, and came on board when he saw Matt advertising for a meat cutter – 'I was the same really: I just thought I'd give it a try.'

They worked with traditional breeds from the start – Matt had Gloucester Old Spots, Grant's family Oxford Sandy and Blacks, 'the plum pudding pigs', but with so many good butchers locally they needed something else to set them apart. That something turned out to be black pudding. He estimates '99.9 per cent, probably' of pig's blood in this country goes to waste, so they decided to buck the trend – 'though at the time,' he admits, 'we didn't really realise no one else was doing it.'

They soon understood why; though using fresh blood 'is possible, you have to jump through a lot of hoops first'. The closure of many smaller abattoirs, coupled with regulations restricting its sale in the wake of the BSE crisis, led producers to favour the convenience of dried blood over fresh, and now the demand, and thus the infrastructure, is no longer there – 'I could pick up the phone and get a pallet of dried blood here tomorrow,' Grant says, 'like I do with the oats and the fat. Instead we drive an hour and 20 minutes each way to collect it ourselves, fresh.'

And when he says collect, he means it literally; both he and Matt have qualified as slaughtermen, 'and I tell you that makes a difference when you walk into a place like an abattoir, a dangerous place that most people would turn around and walk right back out of'. Their nearest, H. G. Blakes in Norwich, kills 300–400 pigs a day, and allows them onto the line to take the blood from 30 or 40 of them for their puddings.

'Without wanting to be too heartless about it, you're literally holding the pig until the life drains out of it, and that takes about 30 seconds. It's very labour intensive work.' The blood must then come down to 3°C before they're allowed to take it away, which means leaving it there to chill and then coming back the next day to get it – 'though we usually do it on a Friday to give it the weekend to cool'.

It sounds an extraordinary amount of work, I point out – like getting a sourdough starter going to make your own pizza, rather than buying one of those cardboardy bases from the supermarket – but he insists it's similarly worth it. Even when you rehydrate dried blood, he says, there's always a lingering grittiness. 'We're making a real product; it has to be fresh. We don't do it by hand or anything, we use modern methods, but it's a traditional pudding. We don't use raising agents or preservatives, and when you're making it in small batches, you can concentrate on not over-mixing it.'

Indeed, the pudding, when he fries some on a sandwich toaster in the kitchenette for lunch, is rich and creamy; more like a really good French boudin noir than anything I've had on the trip so far. I don't mind a bit of grittiness in a black pudding, if I'm honest; as with shortbread, it adds to the texture. But it can't be denied that this – luxurious, full and round in the mouth, almost moussey – feels a cut above.

In fact, Fruit Pig makes two versions. The original Grant describes as 'quite Scottish' with barley as well as oats, 'which opens up the texture of the pudding and adds a nuttiness that we both really like. My mother's from Edinburgh, and for her, black pudding has to have barley.' The Fruit Pig 53 (named because it's particularly popular north of the 53rd parallel, which runs through Boston, Nottingham and Stoke on Trent) is Bury-style, with pearly lumps of cured back fat. (That's hard to get hold of too, he sighs, because of the taste for leaner meat. Local abattoirs know who to call if they have a very porky porker in.)

They've tried to find a more local East Anglian black pudding recipe too, but without success – 'My guess is round here it would probably be quite Scandinavian,' he muses. 'The Danes do one with fresh horseradish.'

To my delight, there are also a couple of slices of white pudding on my plate, rich and soft and warmly spiced. 'From my research, the spices were shipped into Plymouth and Portsmouth, hence the link with their hog's pudding,' Grant explains. 'We've had West Country people say to us that ours isn't a hog's pudding, and Irish people tell me it isn't a proper white pudding either, but whatever it is, it's still going ridiculously well.'

Most daringly of all, they make a haggis. 'People do say, Wisbech is a strange place for a haggis,' he concedes, but the proof here is very much in the pudding; Fruit Pig haggis is served as part of the full Scottish breakfast at several cafés in Edinburgh and Glasgow . . . though presumably not with its provenance listed too prominently lest things get a bit *Braveheart*.

It seems outrageous, I say, wiping the delicious fat from my plate with the last of the bacon bap, that we waste so much in this country – fat, blood, offal, none of it very Instagrammable of course, but all full of goodness and ripe with culinary possibility. Grant shakes his head sadly. 'I think it's because food comes in packages these days – people don't want to know what goes into it.'

When I think of the love and care that goes into these puddings, and into Sally Lugg's and Andrew Ramsay's too, I feel depressed by how squeamish some people – and I'm talking about people who have the luxury of choice – are about such things when they'll happily tuck into low-welfare bangers. I respect those who don't eat meat, but if you do, I believe you should show the living animal some respect in return.

We part on a cheerier note, as he hands me a stick of black pudding for my host this evening, fellow food writer and *FT* restaurant critic Tim Hayward. It doesn't look far to Cambridge, it's dead flat, and it should be a nice ride, I think, as I set off south.

Famous last words. I would comfortably rank the 70km between Wisbech and Cambridge as the worst of the entire trip. Not because of the scenery, which is beautiful in a way that only somewhere with landmarks like the Forty Foot Drain can be – Midwestern and empty, the fields vast, the roads dead straight – but because there's so little else here. So few farm buildings, so few villages, so few corners; nothing to look at but the sky, and, in a landscape this flat, no other position but sitting down, which means by the time I'm navigating the soul-sapping dullness of the Cambridge Guided Bus Way, I'm almost rage-crying with pain for the first time in weeks.

How I long for a Cornish cliff, or a Highland ski station to aim for, rather than these endless vistas of crops and coppices. Struggling to keep my spirits up, I do something I rarely allow myself to do – as it's not really a road as such, more a cycleway, I put some music on. There's nothing like a bit of Beyoncé to perk up the flagging spirits.

More perking still is the Campari and soda Tim makes me when I arrive at his house, angry and sweaty and bearing a black pudding like a weapon. 'Go and have a shower, dinner's in 20,' he says kindly. If this isn't heaven, I think, standing underneath a hot jet of soul-soothing bliss, it must be very close.

Ridden: 122.26km
Climbed: 138m
Breakfasts eaten: Well, I had black pudding, white pudding and bacon for lunch . . . does that count?

RED SAUCE OR BROWN?

Grant: 'Bacon sandwich is ketchup, sausage is brown sauce, fry-up is brown sauce . . . and a curveball, if there's an egg in the sandwich (with anything else) it's Stokes Chipotle Ketchup.'

16
CAMBRIDGE TO NEWMARKET
Sausages

A sausage is an image of rest, peace and tranquility in stark contrast to the destruction and chaos of everyday life.
– Tom Robbins, *Another Roadside Attraction* (1971)

Tim and his family, wife Alison (his co-owner in café and local institution Fitzbillies) and teenage daughter Liberty, are off to see Ralph Fiennes perform T. S. Eliot's famously difficult *Four Quartets* this evening – which will, at the very least, be a break from listening to me talk about my hamstring. They depart in a flurry of apologies for abandoning me to their sofa; I am being in no way polite when I assure them that an evening of Campari and Tour de France highlights is my idea of a rollicking good time right now.

They return, buzzing with Fiennes' energy – Lib enthuses about the lighting while Tim opens a bottle of Alsatian riesling and Al and I work our way through the sticky paper bag of Yorkshire brandy snaps I've been carrying around since Harrogate. We chew the (bacon) fat into the small hours, agreeing that the fry-up is the closest thing we have to a national dish, and disagreeing vehemently on the place of potatoes therein.

Tim tells me his tastes vary according to context – ideally, he says, a fry-up comes when 'I'm about to do something that'll work it off, [like] a day of physical work, or a long journey, or when I've done something that requires it, i.e. got massively drunk'. Confirming my own opinion that it's impossible to judge the quality of a fry from its surroundings, he professes not to be able to pick a favourite: 'I've had incredibly posh ones and incredibly bad ones and loved them equally in context.'

The one at Fitzbillies, he says, has been designed to be 'brilliant in any context', which is a wonderfully Tim thing to say, and which I have the opportunity to judge for myself the next morning, when we go there for breakfast. Lib and I cycle, me panting to keep up with her while also endeavouring not fall into a kerbside drainage channel like a tipsy fresher, while Tim drives. Having spent 10 days on life support with Covid back in November, he's lost movement in his right foot, and now walks with a stick, albeit still talking at 100mph as he does so. (His joie de vivre, happily, appears completely undiminished.)

We're first in the queue, and to Tim's credit, none of the staff look visibly terrified as they let us in – instead the talk is of which shifts Liberty is going to have to take on to cover for staff absence. Though things have been gradually opening up in the weeks I've been away, Covid is very much still with us, and with so many people either testing positive or in isolation because they've been in contact with someone who has, restaurants are shutting everywhere. Tim isn't sure Fitzbillies will last the week. 'It's weird, suddenly you're seeing the owners of restaurants waiting tables,' he says as we sit down. 'Not that I'd be much good right now.'

Naturally I go for the Full Fitzbillies breakfast: eggs (Tim is very keen I should have them scrambled), smoked streaky bacon, sausages, hash brown, grilled tomatoes and sourdough toast, with extra black pudding. I dimly recall Tim waxing fat on the subject of their hash browns last night. In general, as I may have already made clear, I do not approve of them, either homemade (they always taste raw) or frozen (they always taste like school dinners) on a fry-up. Potatoes are of course always welcome on my plate, but to my mind, a floury tattie scone, or an honest blob of bubble and squeak, provide a more satisfyingly bland, absorbent foil to all that fatty, salty meat.

I will concede, however, that if you must have a hash brown, the Fitzbillies version is a very high-class example; crunchy on the outside, soft and yielding within, though personally I think it would be better snugly tucked into a breakfast roll with a fried egg on top. (That said, I do agree with Tim about the scrambled eggs; creamy and thick, they are indeed even nicer here than the fried kind, which is not something I anticipated changing my mind about.)

He has eggs Bene't, a classic renamed in honour of a nearby street, and Lib a stack of pancakes with bacon and Chelsea bun syrup, on the basis that last time she was here she was made to share them, and they are not made to be shared. We also order a croissant and a bacon roll for the table because Tim is very keen that I try the roll itself, which, he says, is the secret of its greatness. In his opinion you can get away with merely ordinarily good bacon – people don't really want anything too distinctive or challenging in a bacon sarnie. The soft white packaging, pillowy enough to comfort, strong enough to stand up to sauce, is what makes the difference.

The recipe for theirs came from a local baker, Alan Ackroyd, who did his early training at Fitzbillies and remembered how they made a particular, rather superior bread roll Tim found listed on a menu from 1958. The kitchen simply splits them, butters them and pops them on the griddle to lightly toast before applying streaky bacon and, in Tim's case, brown sauce. I have my half au naturel because in my opinion, it's so good it needs no such adornment. I'm coming round to brown sauce, but it's still a work in progress.

Thus set up for the day, I'm ready to meet my new peloton, the first people to offer to ride with me since Jay back in the Cairngorms. Tim, Lib and I part ways in the Fenland morning drizzle, me triumphantly clutching three of Fitzbillies' famous Chelsea buns, buns so beloved of Stephen Fry he tweeted a lament for them when he heard Fitzbillies was up for sale in 2011. Tim and Al both saw his tweet, and the rest is finger-lickingly sticky history.

—•◆•—

Matt and the second Caroline of the trip arrive just as I'm carefully stowing this precious cargo at the top of my panniers. Matt, a university friend, accompanied me on the Grand Départ in 2018, a willing receptacle for almost all the shellfish Brittany had to offer, though he wisely swerved the freakishly large oysters that still haunt my nightmares. Having inspected my proposed route this time, he's opted for the East Anglian leg on the basis that it's sure to be nice and flat.

Caroline, meanwhile, is the woman who got me into this cycle touring business in the first place when she invited me to ride to Brussels with her back in 2014. Having produced two (delightful) small girls since, she was the first person to reply to my recruitment drive back in early spring, which suggests she's desperate to get back in the saddle. I'm less sure about Matt. I receive a cryptic message from him a few days before we meet – 'Did I mention I've invested in a new bike with a number of modern improvements? Some friends seem to think you'll hate it but I'm confident it will make the mountains of East Anglia more bearable.'

Is it electric? I shoot back, immediately suspicious.

'One of many modern improvements . . .' comes the evasive reply.

(Actually I'm relieved; Matt is a man who works extremely hard doing something important for a ministry, and the last year of excitement hasn't left him much time for exercise. Hopefully this will mean he enjoys the whole escapade as much as Caroline and me.)

GLAMORGAN SAUSAGES

I'm not giving a recipe for meat sausages here because, although it's perfectly possible to make them at home, unless you go down the McDonald's route of reclassifying a pork burger as a 'sausage patty', you need to invest in casings, and various pieces of equipment for a truly satisfactory result. The vegetarian Glamorgan version is both easier to execute and a rare, though not unique, example of a meat-free sausage that's as delicious as the real thing, and that, I think, is largely because it's not attempting to ape it. A speciality of the lush Vale of Glamorgan, which has been a hotspot for dairy production since the Iron Age, it instead makes good use of the local abundance of cheese, mixed with stale bread, leeks and herbs to make a sausage shape, which can then be fried until golden.

I'm not convinced that they're ideal on a full cooked breakfast, but they are rather nice with fried eggs and bubble and squeak, and perhaps bacon if you're of an omnivorous persuasion. Sadly

Glamorgan cheese is no longer in production, but tangy, lactic Caerphilly works very well, as does Crumbly Lancashire – or Cheddar at a pinch. (Really, there's no such thing as the wrong cheese, is there?)

Makes 8
50g butter
1 large leek, washed and finely sliced (use as much of the green part as isn't tough and dry)
Salt, to taste
Nutmeg, to taste
200g fresh breadcrumbs
1 tsp fresh thyme leaves, finely chopped
175g Caerphillly (see above)
1½ tsp mustard (I like wholegrain)
2 eggs, separated
2 tbsp milk
50g flour

1 Melt half the butter in a frying pan over a medium-low heat and sweat the leek with a pinch of salt until soft but not brown. Add a good grating of nutmeg and set aside.
2 Mix 100g of the breadcrumbs with the thyme, and grate or crumble the cheese into the same bowl. Stir the mustard and egg yolks together and add this too, along with the leeks and milk. (No need to wash the frying pan yet.)
3 Use damp hands to shape the mixture into 8 sausages, adding a little more milk if they won't hold together. Put into the fridge to chill for half an hour.
4 Heat the oven to 200°C/180°C fan/gas 6. Whisk the egg whites in a shallow bowl until frothy. Put the remaining breadcrumbs on a plate and the flour on another. Roll each

sausage in the flour, followed by the egg whites, followed by the breadcrumbs to coat.

5 Melt the remaining 25g of butter in the frying pan over a medium-high heat and fry the sausages until lightly golden all over, then transfer to a baking tray and bake for about 20 minutes or until golden brown. Eat immediately, while they're still warm and gooey inside.

◆——————◆

I lay out our plans, such as they are, over coffee: due east towards the coast, with a stop for sausages in Newmarket. Beds booked at a pub near Bury St Edmunds this evening – 'and I can promise it's totally flat until we get to Newmarket!'

Then what happens? asks Matt suspiciously. Oh, it's a bit more up and down, I say, but look – I show him the gradient profile – literally nothing over about 80 metres. Anyway, you're all right, aren't you? You're cheating. He gives me a look, and mutters something about not having charged the battery, which feels somewhat remiss in the circumstances.

Off we go, down the lovely lanes of Cambridge, past a sign for Six Mile Bottom, which Caroline and I use as a Hilarious Photo Opportunity, and off the main road through a succession of comically pretty villages with names like Swaffham Bulbeck, all half-timbered façades and mysteriously grand churches.

'It's nice how this Komoot app you're using takes us down the smaller roads,' Matt says conversationally as we come into Newmarket. 'It's shown us some really out-of-the-way places.'

Caroline is looking ahead. 'Yes, like this Asda car park,' she says drily. 'Were we meant to take that last turn?'

As well as Asda, the horse racing capital of Newmarket offers two further attractions. The first is the prospect of seeing disgraced local MP Matt Hancock skulking around glad-handing his angry constituents. The second, and arguably more compelling, is sausage shaped: Newmarket sausages hold PGI, or Protected Geographical Indication, status, which means that only three butchers in the town itself are currently permitted to sell them as such. I'm keen to find out what makes them so special.

The first mention of the town in connection with sausages comes in 1618, when the Marquis of Hamilton brings 'four pigs incircled [sic] with sausages' to a royal banquet in the town to celebrate the birth of James I's son, the future Charles I. Two centuries later, a Victorian traveller records himself breakfasting on 'Newmarket sausages and water-cress' after going out to the gallops at sunrise – indeed, the Newmarket Sausage Association claims that pigs were once used by racing stables to keep their yards 'free of debris', though whether I'd want to eat a sausage from a pig that had fattened principally on manure is open to question. During big race meets, demand went through the roof: *Baily's* sporting magazine in 1860 reported, 'We heard on our arrival that every stall at Newmarket had its occupier, as every bedroom its tenant, and the sausage machines had never ceased working.'

•••

Tea Break: SAUSAGES OF BRITAIN

The sausage is a food that defies neat categorisation; bursting out at every attempt like a cheap banger from its synthetic skin, it's not necessarily even made of meat (*bore da,* Glamorgan) or, in fact, tubular (*halò,* lorne sausage).

Taxonomy is easier at an individual level. The UK has a proud regional tradition of fresh sausages. Pork is the principal ingredient, but beef gives it stiff competition in Scotland. Black pepper is a mandatory seasoning, and mace common.

Cereals, usually rusk, but sometimes breadcrumbs or grains, are often dismissed as a mere bulker, which indeed is their purpose, but they also soak up the fat and juice as the meat cooks – to me, many continental sausages seem dry in comparison to our own.

Cambridge: sage, cayenne, nutmeg
Cumberland: coarse-cut pork, high meat content, highly spiced with white pepper, marjoram, nutmeg and often sage, sold in a long coil rather than twisted into individual sausages
Glamorgan: cheese, leek or onion, mustard powder (meat-free)
Lincolnshire: sage and thyme
Lorne: fat beef, nutmeg, coriander, sold skinless in squares
Manchester: sage, cloves, nutmeg and ginger
Newmarket: coarse-cut, white pepper, thyme, parsley, nutmeg
Oxford: pork, veal, beef suet, sage
Tomato: coloured with tomato purée, popular in the Midlands
Wiltshire: ginger
Yorkshire: nutmeg, cloves and cayenne pepper

✦✦✦

The Newmarket Sausage Association to which the three chosen butchers belong is vague about what exactly sets one of their sausages apart from other regional British varieties, referring instead to 'a selection of herbs and spices'. The government's PGI specification is more helpful: to qualify as a Newmarket sausage, they must 'have a dry and coarse texture with visible pieces of lean meat and fat [at least 70 per cent prime cut pork; the rest can be rusk, breadcrumbs and water] which give the sausage a slight bite when eaten. The taste is predominantly of pork and moderately spicy from the herb and spice mix used in its production although the taste and colour may vary according to the butcher's particular blend of seasoning. Traditional seasoning for Newmarket Sausages include combinations of the following and must make up to a maximum 3 per cent of the finished product: black pepper; white pepper; salt; thyme; parsley; nutmeg.' It certainly sounds breakfast friendly to me.

I go into Powters, which claims to still be using its original recipe from 1881, and ask the man behind the counter what makes a Newmarket sausage different. He shrugs. OK, what goes into them then? I persist. Are there special herbs and spices? It's a secret, he says. I can't tell you. Did you want anything?

Leaving Matt and Caroline spewing flakes of sausage-roll pastry across the pavement outside, I say I'm just popping round the corner to check out a rival butcher's shop. This one sells Musk's, but they don't have any Newmarket sausages left. They do, however, have a packet of Marmite-flavoured bangers and, without thinking, I buy them. It's just too serendipitous to ignore.

'What on earth are you going to do with those?' Matt says when he sees what I'm putting in my panniers. It's my turn to shrug. I've been carrying a camping stove round for six weeks, I say, perhaps it's time to give it some use.

Tea Break:
THE FLOPOMETER. OR HOW TO JUDGE A GOOD SAUSAGE

A few years ago, I was honoured to be invited to help judge the British Sausage Week awards in the company of trade journalists, master butchers and members of the excellently named Ladies in Pigs group of female pork fanciers. It was a lot more serious than I imagined, despite the presence of the Fisher Sausage Flopometer, a handy chart to help assess their perkiness (eight points deducted for any unfortunate sausage that described a right angle when held up by one end).

Sausages were held up, prodded, cut open, probed for suspicious air pockets, rubbed between thumb and finger to check for gristle, and generally abused in a way that I wouldn't recommend if you want to enjoy them afterwards. Instead, here are a few pointers for picking a quality banger (which won't be a banger – the name comes from the wartime versions so sodden with water and full of air that they exploded in the pan):

1 Sausages can be made from anything, but should be a mix of lean and fatty cuts; naturally lean meat, like venison, is often too dry for the purpose, and should be mixed with something lardier. Low-fat sausages are almost always disappointing; better to just eat fewer.
2 Higher meat content isn't everything: according to fourth-generation master butcher Keith Fisher, beyond about

83 per cent, a sausage turns into 'a solid hunk of meat, and
... tend[s] to be drier too'.

3 Check for visible air bubbles underneath the skin – a badly
   packed sausage is likely to go pop. They should be evenly
   and plumply filled.

4 Never prick a sausage before cooking; you'll let the juices
   out and it'll end up dry and tough.

5 The best way to cook a sausage is to slow-fry it in a heavy-
   based pan with a little grease – baking dries them out and
   grilling is often too harsh.

••

We skip town, six sausages richer, if not much the wiser on the
matter, and still discussing what we look for in the perfect
breakfast sausage. Matt is of the opinion it should be fairly
neutral in flavour – 'pork, basically' – while Caroline favours
the idea of something spicier. I agree that warm, comforting
seasonings like mace and pepper are nicer than herbs first
thing, and share my theory that a slender chipolata is more
appropriate on a fry-up than a full-sized banger. Matt is
outraged by this suggestion. Fortunately, at this point, we
glimpse the gallops, deserted in the early afternoon, and find
ourselves busy with the first hill of the day. When I catch him
up at the summit, where he's paused to admire a manicured
stable yard, Matt seems to have forgotten all about the sausages.
'I thought East Anglia was supposed to be flat?'

To be fair it is pretty flat, but with a bit more variety than
the Fens – Tudor houses with overhanging second storeys,
endless dancing fields of wheat and, just outside Bury St
Edmunds, where we stop to eat our buns in the sharp scent of

the Greene King brewery, a hare by the side of the road, boxing the air before disappearing into the crop. We're into the golden hour, where the sun bathes the fields with a warmth that makes everything feel right with the world. 'I never see this time of day,' Caroline sighs. 'It's usually bath time. Isn't it nice?'

In Pakenham, we pass two straw hares squaring up on the apex of a roof as a fox sneaks up from behind the chimney. I love these animal sculptures on top of thatched cottages – I've seen pheasants, pigs, dolphins, even, on Alex-of-Weetabix-fame's brother and Australian sister-in-law's house, a kangaroo – and wonder if the thatchers themselves also enjoy the chance to let their artistic sides show, or if such decorations are just a whimsical annoyance at the end of a long job.

Our pub for the night sits on the edge of the village of Bardwell, and is not what you might call busy, though they push a television out into the pretty beer garden for the England–Ukraine match. To my relief, as I'm not sure I can be bothered to start faffing around with a gas canister, the girl behind the bar is completely unfazed by me sliding the packet of sausages in her direction – we get lots of guns in here, she says, they're always asking us to cook stuff for them. Sausages are nothing.

We eat two each as a starter, deliciously savoury and sticky and rich, not overpoweringly Marmitey, but not shy about it either. When the chef comes out to check if they're all right he admits he can't stand the stuff, which makes his efforts for us all the more noble. The whole place is silent and dark by the time we turn in, though I hear singing across the fields as I drift off; England has won 4–0, and the nation is en fête.

Ridden: 79.69km
Climbed: 488m
Breakfasts eaten: 1 (or 1.5: a full Fitzbillies;
half a bacon roll)

RED SAUCE OR BROWN?

Tim: 'Never ketchup, it's vile. We have a secret sauce in the restaurant kitchen: 95 per cent HP sauce with 5 per cent sriracha. That's the stuff. Amazing in a bacon bap. Supreme with Tuscan salsicce in a soft roll.'

Caroline # 2: 'I have thought deeply about your question: I would forgo all sauce, unless it was Heinz sauce. I really can't stand a cheap, vinegary ketchup or brown sauce, and remain deeply suspicious of anything that labels itself "artisanal" and comes in pretentious packaging with type-writer font.' [NB: Caroline does not work for Heinz.]

17
COGGESHALL TO IPSWICH
Bacon

There is nothing quite so blissful as the bacon sandwich you make
for yourself at midnight, when everyone else is tucked up in bed.
– Nigel Slater, *Real Fast Food* (1992)

Matt puts away a Full English the next morning in the time it's taken me to regret opting for scrambled eggs, which come in the form of a cloud of tight, pallid fluff that leaks water all over my toast. I don't mind solid curds, yolk yellow and dry, like a chopped-up omelette, and I certainly don't mind them oozy and creamy like at Fitzbillies, but this halfway house is a definite disappointment.

I'm not going to let them spoil my mood though; it's Sunday, my next appointment is on Monday morning in Peasenhall, a mere 50 pancake-like kilometres east of here, and Matt and Caroline are both on holiday, so we've decided to go to the beach. I haven't seen the sea since Northumbria, and I miss it.

While I'm inside paying the bill, I hear a man tell Matt and Caroline, 'I knew you was cyclists, your mate's in the bar clipping round like a bloody pony.' When I come out, he's

inspecting the bikes critically, more interested in Matt's electric
vehicle than Eddy's simple beauty, which annoys me – '70km
to fish and chips!' I say briskly. 'Chip chop!'

The route zig-zags along the border between Suffolk and
Norfolk, which, apart from signs for things like the Suffolk
Pet & Horse Crematorium or the Norfolk Feather Company,
are impossible to tell apart. Things With Feathers seem to be
big in both; we pass several clusters of poultry sheds hidden
in woodland, extractor fans whirring, and not a cluck to be
heard from any of them. Every village, however, has a sign
cautioning drivers to be careful of perambulating ducks. That
these things can co-exist, the things we eat pushed out of
sight and out of mind in battery sheds, even as we cherish
their cousins for their ornamental value, slightly boggles the
mind.

Coming into Brockdish, we run into a road block, stopping
traffic for a woman in a huge pink poncho on an old tractor,
who shoots round the corner at surprising speed, pink ribbons
streaming out behind her like a wedding car. She honks
merrily as she passes, quickly followed by a girl driving a
larger, shinier, more modern model covered in pink teddy
bears. The tractors keep on coming, at least 10 of them, until
there's a break and we're allowed through. We follow at a
respectful pace, whooping in general support whenever
another one passes us. 'Smart-looking tractor, that,' a wag at
the side of the road calls to me in a thick Suffolk accent.
Thanks, I say. Does the job.

Seeing spectators on folding chairs by the roadside, I stop to ask
what's going on. 'It's for breast cancer,' the chap tells me. 'They
do it every year, 20 odd miles. Ages it's been going, and they're on
track to raise a quarter of a million, I heard. Great event.'

A little way down the road, a child sitting on a wall falls silent as we approach. 'We can wave to *these* ladies too, darling,' her father says, smiling apologetically as she glowers darkly at us.

None taken, Matt mutters behind me.

———◆———

It's a warm day, and we stop at a garage in Halesworth to refuel, glugging down cold drinks and Calippos next to a vending machine selling fishing bait: red or white maggots for £3 a pop, a small sign reminding buyers to allow them to recover for an hour at normal room temperature before use.

Somehow, though, Southwold never seems to get any closer. Even I'm feeling dispirited. Indeed, I'm not sure anyone speaks until we're finally wedged into the queue for the Little Fish & Chip Shop, which, even at nearly 4 p.m. on a Sunday, is buzzing with London accents, red chinos hugger-mugger with expensive tracksuits, and everyone looking pink and frazzled by the crowds and the thick heat. We decide to beat a hasty retreat to the beach.

The sea, so blue the last time I saw it, has turned a distinctly unwelcoming muddy grey, and a little breeze is whipping the tops into white horses. Caroline and I swore we'd swim, but, perhaps aptly, now we're here I'm getting cold feet. After all, we still have 30km to go, and sand in one's cycling shorts is no laughing matter, so I'm relieved when she confesses she doesn't fancy it after all and we can get back on the road towards a cold pint and an early night.

Laxfield, our home for the evening, is yet another remarkable place I've never heard of, with a sixteenth-century guildhall of herringbone brick, a shop and two pubs, all of which are still open for business. Unfortunately, it's Sunday, and by the time Caroline and I have finished riding in giddy, exhausted circles to try to take us over 100km for the day (Matt is less interested in statistics and more interested in two rounds of lime and soda), the pub we're staying in has stopped serving. In fact, though we do get a beer in the other one, next to a table of young farmers who tell us they've been drinking since Friday, the only dinner available in there is a packet of crisps.

Back in the room, as Caroline takes a bath, I worry I might have broken Matt. Did you know he hasn't even brought any cycling shorts with him? I say through the door. No wonder he's suffering; it's like coming on a biking holiday without bringing a helmet!

'He hasn't got one of those on either,' a voice comes from within. 'Haven't you noticed?'

—●◆●—

Feeling bad about the lack of dinner, I'm at least quietly confident in our breakfast plans – surely we can't fail to score in a place that actually makes bacon? I think happily, as we gust along country lanes towards Peasenhall.

I've been to Emmetts before, years ago, when I worked for a food magazine and went to interview owner Mark Thomas about their cult Christmas hams. The shop is perhaps a bit lighter and shinier inside than I remember, and the hand-sanitising station is new of course, but otherwise, I get the sense that this is a place that sits a little outside time and space; a 200-year-old business in a pretty but unremarkable Suffolk village where you can buy whole crystallised oranges and Spanish goat's cheese by mail order. After last night's packet of cheese and onion, it feels like going through the back of the wardrobe and into Narnia.

Mark, who doesn't look any different from our last encounter over a decade ago, orders us out into the garden behind the shop where we've left the bikes, calling after us, bacon sandwiches all round? Matt's voice goes a bit high and squeaky in response. I fear yesterday may have taken its toll on his morale.

Drawn by a familiar and very appealing smell, I tentatively poke my nose into the shop's back door, where Mark is manning a frying pan. He beckons me in to inspect the contents – 'See, no white gunk at all, because we don't use nitrates.' It's the same story I heard from Andrew at Carluke's, though Emmett's goes one step further, leaving the meat a natural dull pink, rather than keeping it artificially bright with preservatives. (Grant at Fruit Pig told me they'd experimented with this too, but customers found the grey colour off-putting. It's odd, because naturally, bacon is almost exactly the shade of roast pork, but then when it comes to food we are rarely rational.)

The sandwich itself is a work of art, if also the antithesis of the perfect simplicity of the Fitzbillies roll. Served on local organic wholemeal bread with melted Montgomery Cheddar and a healthy dollop of tangy, sugary date and lime pickle, somehow the flavour of the pig still dominates; not overpoweringly salty, or smoky, but emphatically porky, which is, in my experience, a sadly rare thing with bacon.

THE GREATEST BACON ROLL
OF ALL TIME

If it seems extraordinary that the two best bacon sandwiches in the world both come from East Anglia, I can only advise you try the recipes below, based on the Fitzbillies and Emmett's versions, before calling for an official enquiry. I've left it up to you whether you prefer smoked or streaky bacon; though I usually go for smoked in a roll and unsmoked in the sandwich below, truth be told I can't decide which is more delicious.

Makes 4 rolls

8 thick rashers of streaky bacon
Butter
*Sauce of your choice (might I suggest English mustard and
    marmalade?)*

For the rolls
7g dried active yeast
10g butter
300g strong white bread flour, plus extra for dusting
8g fine salt

1 First, make the rolls. Stir the yeast into 50ml of warm water
   and leave until foamy on top. Melt the butter.
2 Put the flour and salt into a large mixing bowl or food mixer.
   Mix well to combine. Add the yeast mixture, melted butter
   and 130ml more warm water, then stir into a smooth dough,
   adding a little more water if it's dry or a very small amount
   of flour if it's too wet to handle.
3 Knead, either with a dough hook or on a lightly floured
   surface, for about 10 minutes until the dough is smooth and
   elastic; it shouldn't be sticky, but neither should it be floury
   – soft is the aim of the game here. Put under a clean tea
   towel and leave for 30 minutes.
4 Divide into 4 pieces. Lightly dust the surface with a little
   more flour, then shape into balls. (With the floury side at the
   bottom, stretch an edge out, bring it back to the centre and
   press it in. Rotate the dough slightly and repeat until you've
   gone all the way round – there are several useful videos on
   roll-shaping technique online if you're new to it.) Turn over,
   then roll gently under your cupped hand until pleasingly
   round, and rest again, covered, for 15 minutes. Line a baking
   tray with parchment.

5 Flatten the balls with a rolling pin to make ovals (no need to roll them out to pancakes, just lightly squash them) and then space out on the tray. Cover, and leave for about an hour or until roughly doubled in size (this depends on the temperature of your room, so pay more heed to the size than the time).

6 Heat the oven to 240°C/220°C fan/gas 9 and bake for about 10 minutes, or until lightly golden. Allow to cool slightly while you cook the bacon.

7 Put a heavy-based frying pan over a medium-high heat. Once hot, add the bacon and fry to your liking – good bacon should give out fat, rather than water, but if yours exudes a lot of liquid, tip this out or the rashers will steam rather than fry.

8 Cut the rolls in two, dip briefly in the fat rendered from the bacon, then butter well. Add the bacon and your sauce of choice, sandwich together and eat immediately.

AND THE GREATEST BACON SANDWICH

Makes 4 sandwiches
8 rashers of good back bacon
8 slices of good brown bread
Date and lime chutney or something similarly sweet and tangy
– decent brown sauce (see page 31) would not be a bad
call here
4 generous handfuls of good vintage grated Cheddar
Butter, to spread

1 Put a heavy-based frying pan over a medium-high heat and fry the bacon to your liking, as in step 7 above. Set aside somewhere warm.

2 Meanwhile, heat the grill to medium, then put the bread on a grill tray and lightly toast (if your grill isn't large enough to do all the slices at once, you can use a toaster for half).

3 Remove half the slices and set aside for now (stacked upright so they don't steam). Spread the chutney or sauce over the toast left on the grill tray and scatter the cheese on top. Put back under the grill until just melted.

4 Butter the remaining toast, or, if there's enough fat left in the bacon pan, dip it lightly in that instead. Remove the cheese on toast from under the grill, top with the bacon, and then put the buttered slices on top of that, butter side down. Cut in half and eat without pausing for breath.

———◦————————◦———

As we eat, Mark brings out a framed front page from the *East Anglian Daily Times*, dated 6 January 1971, and props it on the chair beside me. Alongside news about an urgent enquiry into the risks of cigarette smoking, and a warning of serious industrial trouble in the mining sector, there's a picture of the shop's previous owner, Frederick Jerrey, standing proudly with his royal warrant, declaring him official ham supplier to Queen Elizabeth the Queen Mother. His father Gilbert started the curing side of the operation just before the Great War, and Mark bought the business from the family in 2000 – Gilbert's great-great-grandaughter '. . . I think?' still lives next door.

Mark himself also comes from a food family; his father owned the Culpeper spice company. After school, where he was the only boy in the cookery class, he flitted around the world, selling clothes for children – 'and Ronnie Corbett, he used to come in and buy his socks. VAT free, you see, kids' clothes' – and charcuterie, working on a pig farm in Vancouver and a ginger plantation in Fiji, and setting up the Culpeper business in Japan before finally returning home to his native East Anglia.

When he bought this shop at the turn of the century, it was, he says, 'a real time warp: it sold dog food, cat food, tampons, knickers, individual cigarettes . . . people would come in at 8.15 a.m. for a single slice of ham, a pint of milk, a cigarette, and then they'd come back at 11 a.m. for another slice of ham – all on account, mind! – and I thought' – he shakes his fist at an imaginary old boy – 'for God's sake! This is just so time consuming.'

Playing the long game, he chose to wait for two years before doing anything drastic: 'We had everything for everyone at the start, cigarettes and all, but I knew change was coming. Supermarkets were coming.' Once they did, providing all things to all men at half the price, Mark was able to concentrate on what he wanted to do, which was, for the most part, curing meat.

Today, his closest customer lives opposite, and the furthest in Hong Kong, he's been name-checked by Delia Smith and chosen by Rick Stein as a local food hero, but I don't get the sense that he chases such publicity. Covid, he says with commendable honesty, was actually good for him – 'April and May 2020 were the easiest months I've had in retail. People from London came in and bought 20 of this, 20 of that, people who'd usually go abroad were in Suffolk instead, and it allowed me to refocus on driving the business, rather than the business driving me.'

He introduces us to Damian, his chief curer, who moved to the area from the bright lights of Ipswich, where he worked in music venues – 'Ed Sheeran was my last gig,' he says, herding us towards the sheds where the magic happens. 'Took me a couple of years to slow down.' Not that he gets much chance of that in December, he adds; Mark picks him up from home at 5 a.m., and they'll be here till gone 7 p.m.

'It's a different business at Christmas,' Mark agrees. 'The first ham order came in just after Easter this year. I thought they'd got mixed up, but no.'

The pork, Damian tells us, is free-range from Blythburgh. 'Oooh, I think we passed the pigs on our way to Southwold yesterday!' I say, pointlessly pleased by this coincidence. He nods: 'You will have done, yeah. They say there are more pigs round here than people.' (Later I discover that the pink colour of many Suffolk houses was originally achieved with a mixture of whitewash and pig's blood. This truly is pig country.)

The animals are slaughtered in Eye, then go to Bramfield to be dressed before arriving here in Peasenhall for their final and most miraculous transformation. Emmett's do several cures, but the Suffolk black hams and bacon are what they're really famous for – as Frederick Jerrey told the *East Anglian Daily Times* half a century ago, 'I do not know of anyone else who pickles hams like we do.'

'Suffolk people, they don't really like telling you much,' Damian says, summing up the difficulty of learning the trade. Happily, he doesn't share this general reticence, and talks us through the whole process, which takes place in these three small sheds behind the shop. Hams, or sides of bacon, are rubbed with rock salt, pepper and fennel seeds (a natural source of nitrates) and left for a week before they're rinsed and plunged into a pungent mixture of black porter, dark brown sugar and molasses. He opens a dustbin in which pale pieces of pig float in an inky black liquid, rather like a macabre apple bobbing game, and inhales appreciatively. 'If you come in here at the wrong time, you can get a bit drunk.'

There they sit for six weeks, quietly absorbing flavour, turned by hand every two days – 'it's a very labour-intensive process' – before they go across the yard to the smoker, a dim, sunken brick hole sprouting meat hooks from the ceiling, the walls sporting a thick coating of black residue much like I saw in Arbroath, and will see again in Peel in a few weeks' time. 'Careful sticking your head in,' he says. I'm used to it, I say, sniffing the air, thinking of the thousands of pieces of pig that have passed this way, some destined for royalty, others for people who bought one slice on pension day.

Even the slicer is antique, a hand-turned affair that has given Environmental Health sleepless nights trying, and failing, to fault it – 'There are no buttons to press,' Mark says, somewhat unnecessarily given the thing, though spotlessly clean and shiny, looks every day of its 80 years and more. 'It's all done with elbow grease. Just like out in the smokehouse.'

We pose for photos outside the front of what is perhaps the most extraordinary village shop I've come across. Like so many of the producers I've met, I think, waxing philosophical now I've eaten, Mark seems to have found his sweet spot: making just enough money doing the thing he loves. He's not particularly interested in taking over the world, or even working harder. There's a rhythm to the year, a time to work 14-hour days, and a time to kick back and enjoy life, and he's got bacon sandwiches on tap whenever he wants them. He's got it sorted, I decide.

I, meanwhile, have got my first puncture.

——◆——

It happens just outside Hacheston, a sinking sensation that I endeavour to ignore; I'm constantly thinking my tyres feel funny when in fact I'm just not pedalling hard enough. Eventually I reach down for a reassuring squeeze. 'STOP!!' I shout. We pull over by a barn, and I have a go at pumping up the offending tube. 'It'll have to come off,' I say finally.

What I don't tell the others is that it once took me three and a half hours to get one of these back on again; the advantage of puncture-proof tyres is that you don't need to worry about them very often; the downside is that when you do, it's like wrestling cooked spaghetti into a plug socket. Just as I'm releasing the brake in preparation, a woman walks past with a small dog. Matt hails her – is there anywhere nearby we might get a coffee, he asks? I wonder if we may be some time.

There isn't, but we're welcome to go and perform the mechanics in her garden; her house is just across the road and we can let ourselves in through the gate – she'll be back soon. 'Nicer than doing it by the road,' she says. At the sound of our voices, a chap comes out of the house we're standing outside, and asks whether we need any help.

Oh, it's just a flat tyre, I say, we're going to go over the road to your neighbour's to sort it out. He turns, looking a tiny bit disappointed – 'I do have all the tools,' he says over his shoulder. 'If you need any.'

I don't, but I recognise my knight in shining armour when I see him. Last time he took the form of a smartly dressed elderly Frenchman strolling with his wife and dog on the Côte d'Azur; this time it's Keith, who's lived in Hacheston for four years with his wife Ann, and turns out to have a garage full of helpful things, though he is, in truth, the most useful gadget of all. He has the tyre off in a jiffy, shaking his head sadly over its pock-marked surface; now I look at it – he dangles it in front of my face so I can bear witness to my shame – I'm forced to concede it has really been through the wars on this trip.

'Can't believe you haven't had one before,' he says, running his fingers along the inside to try to locate the source of the puncture. 'You won't get far with these I'm afraid.'

While he works, and I meekly hold things for him, Matt and Caroline talk to Ann about life in Hacheston. 'There's a real community spirit,' she says. 'A dog went missing the other week, a blind dog, and the whole village was out looking for it.' Somehow they get on to the subject of the charity the couple support, the Beehive Children's Trust, which works with young victims of rape and sexual abuse in Kenya to provide a safe space for them and their babies. Matt asks if we can make a donation, in return for their generosity – a kind idea I'm extremely grateful for.

I tell Keith, busy trying to centre my brakes, that I will be forever in his debt, and swear to buy new tyres at the first opportunity. He brushes off my thanks: 'Oh, I like fixing them as much as riding them.'

Ann nods. 'He just loves tinkering with things!' she says fondly. Were they sent from above? I wonder, as we ride off, waving furiously. Certainly it feels like someone was smiling on me given that this could have happened on any lonely country road or dual carriageway for the last five weeks but, in fact, happened here, right in front of Keith. Whoever it was, I appreciate it.

Back on the road, trying not to look at my terrible tyres, anticipating a second puncture at every turn, we wind south along pretty tree-lined lanes into Woodbridge, where I've agreed a group detour to see something unrelated to food, yet impossible to bypass – the Anglo-Saxon ship burial at Sutton Hoo. En route, I spot the words SMOKEHOUSE AND BUTCHERY as we pass the railway station, and execute a dangerous turn across traffic in my eagerness to check it out. When fate tosses a place like the Five Winds Farm Shop into your path, it would be extremely foolish to ignore it.

The fridges are packed with local meat, much of it smoked a mile away at Five Winds Farm itself, and smoked fish from Orford, the tables full of baps and cobs and baskets of Lincolnshire plum bread, but the real draw is the deli counter, with its billowing cheese straws, Scotch eggs, huntsman's pies and poacher's rolls – and, at the back, something called the Melton Bad Boy, which I'm powerless to resist. Slightly self-conscious, I ask the chap behind the counter what a Bad Boy might be. 'Well, it's a pasty, with sausage, bacon, cheese and ketchup.' And that's all one portion? I ask. It's like a house brick. Ah, what is a portion anyway? he says, putting it in a bag and handing it over.

I eat it, or some of it, at a picnic table at Sutton Hoo while watching a cairn terrier being dragged away from a particularly interesting tree, legs stubbornly splayed in familiar fashion. The National Trust's guide for canine visitors describes it as 'an important archaeological site which is popular with dogs and their families'. I imagine Wilf proudly appearing from a freshly dug hole with mud on his whiskers and an ancient bone clutched between his teeth and give an involuntary shudder.

There's a long queue to get into the exhibition hall, even on a Monday afternoon, thanks to *The Dig,* a film about the discovery starring Ralph Fiennes (him again) and Carey Mulligan that caused great excitement back in January, when the nation was locked down with literally nothing else to do but watch telly. Completely inaccurate, of course, says the man at the door, but he got the Suffolk accent right, no doubt about that. (I remember Mark mentioning, somewhat cryptically, that Voldemort was a fan of their bacon – perhaps it was Ralph who came down from London last year and bought 20 of everything?)

My favourite detail from our visit, however, apart from the cairn terrier, is the fact that the archaeological finds in Mound 17 included a 'miniature feasting kit' comprising a small cauldron, a bucket, a pot and a drinking bowl. The young warrior was also buried with a bag of lamb chops, 'perhaps a picnic for his journey to the afterlife'. Cold lamb chops wouldn't be my choice of death picnic, I think, but each to their own.

We stroll over to the burial mounds themselves, springy hummocks against the late-afternoon sky, fields of pigs rooting next door, unmoved, like the terrier, by the tides of history. It's a bit eerie as the clouds mass, blocking out the light, and I'm not sorry when we realise the site is closing on us. Come on, I say, there's a Travelodge with our name on it waiting in Ipswich – don't say I never treat you to anything.

———•◆•———

Ipswich is another city I can't recall having stopped in before, yet another ordinary place with a casual dollop of extraordinary history, with Lakeland operating from a fourteenth-century merchant's house, and a recruitment firm doing business from Thomas Wolsey's birthplace. It's raining hard by the time we get there, the boats in the marina next to the hotel are clinking mournfully, and I'm starting to feel the sadness that creeps up on me at the end of a journey, though I still have almost a week to go.

I hug Caroline tightly the next morning as she returns to the bosom of her family after a final fry-up by the waterfront – a plump, nut-brown Procter's sausage,* bacon, a fried egg, half a

---

* The benefit of having to order through an app – 'because of Covid',

grilled tomato, a potato cake and the inevitable baked beans. I plump for ketchup on the side as we're now in the South, and, as usual, slightly regret it.

The drizzle persists as, Caroline dispatched, I go in search of a fresh spare inner tube to replace the one now in residence on my back wheel, silently apologising to Keith for not immediately investing in two new tyres as promised. Matt is happily reading the paper when I return, and shows no particular sign of wanting to leave in this weather, but, though we only have 60km to cover, I'm feeling itchy-footed and impatient to be off – if distinctly less thrilled by the looming prospect of the Home Counties.

Ridden: 52.75km
Climbed: 372m
Breakfasts eaten: 3 (scrambled egg and tomatoes; an Emmett's bacon sandwich; a fry-up)

RED SAUCE OR BROWN?

Mark: 'It has to be our date and lime chutney with our bacon!'

Damian: 'Date and lime.'

---

naturally – is that it allows me to make requests I'd feel like a diva demanding of an actual waiter, like 'sausages well done, please'.

18
Ipswich to Chelmsford
Jam

> *You can lose a piece of plain bread and not think twice about it, but when you lose one spread thickly with strawberry jam it's an altogether more serious matter.*
> — Alexander McCall Smith, *Precious and the Monkeys* (2012)

Essex has been much maligned in recent decades, mostly by people who have never actually been there. Growing up in a neighbouring county, the acme of my ambition was to go swimming at 'the Harlow tubes', though we mostly just went cross-country running in muddy fields near Bishop's Stortford.

It's muddy today too, but despite the fact that half the roads have turned into fords overnight (I always make Matt go first to check how deep it is, on the basis that he's taller so less of him will get wet), the north of the county is a treat to cycle through, the narrow twisting lanes of the Dedham Vale AONB – 'Constable Country' – a particular highlight, ancient trees fluffy in midsummer splendour, the verges spilling over with greenery after the rain. The sun has come out for us at last, but every puddle mirrors the clouds massing ominously overhead.

The sky darkens still further as we pull into Colchester, a place I remember has Roman roots and also, I see now, a large hill. I vote we eat at the bottom of it, in a little café with a picturesque view of a vast 1970s 'landmark office building'. Matt, nervous about his fancy bike, wants to make it a picnic, but I, equally nervous about the weather, refuse, so we sit in the window, tucking into vast jacket potatoes stuffed with beans and cheese, and placidly watch people running for cover as the heavens abruptly open. The rain is so bad that the staff let us stay an extra 10 minutes after closing time, sweeping around us until it finally slows to a lazy drizzle.

Matt suggests that, as we're here, we may as well go and see the castle. It's up that hill, I say. He shrugs, indicating his battery. Up to you. So we go and see the castle, because I am a very proud person.

I'm pleased we do. As well as the aforementioned Norman castle, this modestly sized city-centre park contains the remains of a Roman temple, a memorial to the victims of the Essex Witch Hunts imprisoned there during the sixteenth and seventeenth centuries and an obelisk commemorating two Royalist officers shot by firing squad at the end of the Siege of Colchester in 1648, which is currently being weed on by a dog. 'I honestly had no idea so much had happened here,' Matt says. 'Remarkable.' I remain silent, as if to suggest I had, of course, been well aware but simply hadn't thought to mention it.

This time, the weather does not clear, and, in a sign that London is already breathing down our necks, Essex treats us to a road so astonishingly unfriendly, so packed with huge lorries overtaking at speed, forcing us through every huge pothole they've created, that by the time we find our pub for the night I'm a bit shaky.

I occupy myself with drying the sopping contents of my panniers on the towel rail, while Matt messages me juicy snippets from the book of Essex murders he's found in the corridor underneath a framed poster of 'Arsenal Legends' and some old photos of greyhounds.*

The food downstairs, somewhat surprisingly, is fantastic – proper pub stuff: hare pie and syrup sponge and custard – but the thrum of lorries on their way to Felixstowe keeps going all night long. It's clearly going to take me a while to readjust to being back in the South East, I think, reaching for my ear plugs.

———◆◆———

Though my home region isn't particularly known for its breakfasts, the Essex village of Tiptree has become synonymous with jam. Indeed the name of the village has somehow eclipsed the fame of the jam's manufacturer, Wilkin & Sons. Holders of a royal warrant since 1911, jam suppliers to first-class passengers on our national airline and first-class breakfast tables around the world, the brand conjures a certain idea of Englishness: Victoria sponges at summer fêtes, cream teas by the fire. Fortunately, however you feel about such things, it also stands for very good jam – still our favourite variety of spread, enjoyed by 19.2 million Britons according to figures from 2018: almost twice the number that opt for marmalade, and three times the number that favour Marmite.

---

* My favourite is the pre-war champion Mick the Miller, two times winner of the English Greyhound Derby, who Wikipedia informs me 'is still considered one of the greatest sporting heroes of the UK' (his Wikipedia page is, in fact, quite the ride).

While I love the bitter edge of marmalade, and could eat Marmite by the spoonful,* there's something very comforting about the straightforward sweetness of jam. It's good on toast, it's good on crumpets, it's great with yoghurt, or stirred into a bowl of porridge – truly it's the people-pleaser of spreads. (In fact, the only thing I can think of that it's not good for, unlike marmalade, is pairing with smoked fish or bacon, and that's probably only because I haven't thought enough about the flavours concerned. It's entirely possible a greengage preserve would be a delicious match with a kipper.)

As with Tracklements, I smell the factory before we see it, a sticky strawberry bootlace kind of smell that reminds me of a fruit-packing plant I passed near Arbroath. There's a visitor centre and café attached, but given that we've skipped breakfast at the pub, I'm disappointed to discover not much in the way of jam on offer at the latter unless you want to buy a jar from the shop and ask the waitress for a spoon. Matt can choose from Wilkin & Sons brown sauce, mustard or ketchup with his fry-up, but I have to breakfast on a toasted teacake if I want to try the company's most famous product, and even that only comes with a choice of two flavours (raspberry or strawberry. Very boring.).

It just seems a missed opportunity, I say crossly, double buttering each half in preparation for the deliciously seedy raspberry: they should be offering yoghurt with passion fruit curd, crumpets with damson jam, and toast with grapefruit marmalade – that kind of thing. Matt, reading the newspaper, makes a non-committal kind of noise in reply. I get the distinct feeling he's less bothered by this issue than I am.

---

* Well, one spoonful: as schoolfriends will recall, that game of truth or dare back in 1998 proved that was my limit.

I consider offering them my consultation services, but find myself distracted by a noticeboard displaying pictures of the annual Tiptree Strawberry Race, where professional and amateur pickers compete to pick the most Little Scarlet, Wilkin & Sons' signature variety,* in an hour. Despite some fantastic hats of the kind that used to be seen on Monster Raving Loony candidates, I note the last British winner was in 2005; Romania and Bulgaria now seem to have the fastest fingers, as well as potentially rather more sensible headgear. (I wonder how Brexit will impact this year's competition: having expressed concerns over the recruitment of pickers before new rules came into place, they must surely have been affected by the shortage of Europeans willing or able to come and work here this summer.)

Wilkin & Sons is unusual among jam manufacturers in growing much of their own fruit – although you won't find many Seville orange trees in Essex, the aim is to be self-sufficient in those fruits that do thrive here, which means that it's 'almost certain' that the strawberries in your jam have come from the Tiptree estate. In fact, they're the only commercial growers of Little Scarlet, a capricious variety, sensitive to changes in weather, which doesn't like to hang around after picking. They also cultivate more unusual crops like mulberries, quince and medlar (some of the mulberry trees are over a century old), as well as raspberries, cherries, loganberries, damsons, greengages, Victoria plums and rhubarb.

Once picked the fruit is washed and checked before being prepared for the Boiling Room; in the company museum sits a huge cherry stoner, bought from France in 1947, capable of processing almost a tonne of fruit an hour. There's also a

* James Bond's favourite flavour of jam, and apparently the Queen's preferred substitute when the homemade variety isn't available. Not, I think, that anyone's suggesting she makes it herself.

Wallace and Gromit-style 1930s orange peel slicer made from a bicycle chain, roller bearings and piano wire, and – joy of joys! – even a couple of antique apple corers to remind me of my trip to the apple tapping museum in the Loire Valley with Tess and Tor. One assumes these have all been replaced by more modern machines in the factory next door, though the oranges, I'm assured, are still prepared by hand.

Other problem crops for the large-scale jam producer apparently include three of my favourites, damsons, greengages and Victoria plums, the last of which also has to be cut by hand thanks to its sharp-edged pit.

Once it's ready for cooking, the fruit goes into covered kettles where it's boiled with sugar for about 15 minutes, depending on the variety, until it reaches setting point and is ready for packaging – Tiptree can turn out 50,000 jars a day. This is clearly a mammoth operation, even if the museum is barely the size of a double garage.

Remarkably, it still manages to entertain us for a full hour. It helps that the story of Wilkin & Sons is full of characters. There's polymath John Joseph Mechi who, having made his fortune in London in the 1830s with Mechi's Magic Razor Strop, a patented cut-throat razor sharpening device, managed to transform Tiptree from marshes to rich agricultural land in a generation, before dying in penury at Tiptree Hall in 1880.

He was followed by Arthur Charles Wilkin, Radical Liberal, Non-conformist teetotaller and fruit grower, who found himself inspired by the oratory of William Gladstone to start a preserving business at the age of 48, borrowing steam engines from neighbours to heat the pans. He sent some jam to the Prime Minister, and received a 'very encouraging' letter back, which, when it became public, prompted some media wags to suggest that Gladstone might also be better suited to running a jam factory than a country.

Arthur operated Wilkin & Sons along old-fashioned pater-nalistic lines, starting an Old Age Relief Fund in 1904, several years before the introduction of the state pension, though this came with strict conditions: beneficiaries were not to spend the money on 'wine or intoxicating drinks' for example. On special occasions, such as a big birthday in the Wilkin family, the firm's oldest worker was given the gift of being able to live rent free in the company cottages for the rest of their lives – though presumably not to sit around in them drinking liquor.

Best of all, however, was Arthur's son, Stanley Swinborne Wilkin, who fell out with his older brother, withdrew from the company and left preserves behind to become 'an enthusiastic breeder of White Wyandotte chickens – the most profitable birds you can buy' according to his promotional literature. He was also, the display assures me, 'world famous for his breed-ing of whippets'.

Even without his help, however, the firm achieved its first royal warrant, for jam, from George V, but it didn't get one for marmalade until 1955, perhaps because the Royal Family, always, it's said, at their happiest north of the border, were loyal to Scottish brands, or perhaps because – and I speculate wildly here – the Queen Mother liked to make her own. These days the warrant is simply for 'Tiptree Products', which sadly means we'll never know if the Queen is a brown or red sauce woman, or if she actually prefers a pina colada conserve with her sausage sandwich.

Among ephemera like a pair of the founder's spectacles and a locust found in a crate of Seville oranges in 1929, we hit the jackpot with the inevitable freakish farm animal beloved of all provincial museums. On this occasion it's a four-legged chicken bred, of course, by Stanley. Impressive indeed.

STRAWBERRY AND EARL GREY JAM

This loose, (relatively!) low-sugar jam is breakfast in a jar: just add buttered toast. The tea is optional, but gives the sweet fruit a subtly bitter, citrussy edge, while the slight crunch of the half-candied leaves makes it worth getting a few stuck in your teeth in my opinion.

Makes 4 medium jars
1kg ripe strawberries
4 tsp loose-leaf Earl Grey tea
675g caster sugar
Juice of 2 lemons

1 Hull the strawberries and cut in half, or quarters if very large.
2 Put the fruit into a large, wide, heavy-based saucepan with the tea, and leave over a low heat until the strawberries start to give off their juice. Put a couple of saucers into the freezer.
3 Add the sugar and lemon juice, stir and slowly bring to the boil, then leave to bubble away until it reaches 104.5°C on a sugar thermometer.
4 Turn the heat right down, then put a little of the jam onto one of the frozen saucers and leave for a minute or so. Push your finger through it; if it's ready the top should wrinkle as you disturb it. If not, bring it back to the boil, and repeat until it does.
5 Take off the heat and allow to cool for 5–10 minutes, stirring occasionally, then pour into clean jars and replace the lids, tightening them again once cooled.

Having exhausted the museum of its treasures, I eat a punnet of Tiptree's very fine strawberries in the car park while Matt quietly confesses that, fun as it's been, he has absolutely no desire to spend the rest of his holiday pedalling around the outskirts of London. I'm sad, but I don't blame him; the roads are becoming increasingly busy, and though we haven't said as much out loud, I think we both know that this flat bit stops as soon as you turn right into Kent.

——•◆•——

The least I can do for my final companion is offer a suitable farewell lunch. It seems apt, given our previous adventures in Brittany, that we're so close to Mersea Island, and I suggest heading there for some oysters before he makes his escape. They've been cultivated in this strange marshy landscape since Roman times, and three years after my unfortunate encounter with the giant Breton bivalve, I feel it's time to make my peace with the things.

West Mersea, the principal settlement on the island, is a remarkably ordinary little place; like Holy Island, it hadn't struck me that people would actually go about their everyday, non-oyster-related business here and yet there's a tip, a Tesco Express and a cemetery. There's also a pleasant view of the old Bradwell nuclear power station, which we tactfully decide to ignore as we tuck into our oysters at the West Mersea Oyster Bar, under a prominently displayed list of Famous People Who Eat Our Oysters on a Regular Basis, which includes Justin Timberlake, Posh and Becks and Kylie Minogue. The King of Belgium, it claims, gets a box a week, though one hopes someone has cancelled Queen Elizabeth I's standing order by now.

It's an odd place, a shed which manages to dispense both fish and chips with curry sauce and whole lobsters with an equal lack of ceremony – this, and a table of kids nimbly picking prawns reminds me how unusual it is to see seafood treated in such a democratic way in the UK. In my experience it's either pickled whelks from a van or fruits de mer on a starched white tablecloth, with not much in between.

We share half a dozen bracing, minerally rock oysters, my preferred creamy natives being out of season, followed by a seafood platter, chips and a big mug of milky tea, because we're in Essex, not Brittany. As we unlock the bikes, a man staggers past, pulling a boat along the road with the help of a large husky. No one else bats an eyelid. Mersea Island seems to be that kind of place.

———◆◆———

Our route to Chelmsford, where I'll be dropping Matt off at the station (he's already wearily wondering if he might be able to get his bike in a cab at the other end), takes us back past Tiptree – and, as if of one mind, we both say, 'Shall we stop for tea?' May as well, we agree – this time I have a little jar of gorgeously perfumed strawberry jam with my warm fruit scones, just for a change.

I'm very sorry to see Matt go, but I experience a familiar heady rush of freedom as I head south out of Chelmsford on the hunt for somewhere to stay for the night. It's Wednesday evening, and I'm expected back in London on Saturday morning, which gives me two days with no one to meet and nothing particular in mind, except eking out these last carefree hours as long as possible. Even after all these weeks, playing hooky from real life is still undeniably exciting.

Ridden: 83.71km
Climbed: 524m
Breakfasts eaten: 1 (toasted teacake and raspberry jam)

RED SAUCE OR BROWN?

Matt: 'Ketchup, please!'

19
STOCK TO RICHMOND
Eggs

An egg is always an adventure; the next one may be different.
– Oscar Wilde

Having found a bed for the evening in a pub in the village of Stock, 10km south of Chelmsford, I order a glass of wine and ponder my next move. The obvious way back into London is down through Kent and up through Surrey: I could ride straight in from the east of course, but not only would that not take very long – it's about 50km, a generous morning's work – it would miss out two counties that might well have something good to offer breakfast-wise.

That said, neither of them have any obvious specialities. I run through my camera roll, wondering if there are any glaring gaps in the menu, and suddenly it strikes me: we've covered porridge and cereal, oatcakes and jam, smokies and farls, bacon and sausages, black and white pudding – even bloody beans, but I've neglected the sun the whole fry revolves around: the mighty egg! So unassuming, yet so absolutely vital. Frankly, I'm ashamed of myself.

I decide to dedicate this penultimate stage to eggs. No egg with even a nodding acquaintance with breakfast will be passed uneaten in the next 48 hours, and that's a promise. It's good to have a mission again. Satisfied, I tuck into my dinner, which is, it must be admitted, an egg-free zone, in the almost deserted dining room. Excitement about the semi-final, England v. Denmark, has been simmering below the surface all day; IT'S COMING HOME writ large on dirty white vans, and chalked white on cracked suburban pavements. Suddenly everyone's buying beer.

As someone still, even at this stage of proceedings, more interested in watching people watching football, I'm not particularly invested in the game – aside from the fact that, should we win, the country is going to go bonkers – but there is an undeniable thrill on hearing a roar from the other side of the kitchen door as me and a lone businessman sit politely ignoring each other across our phones.

Did we just score? I ask the waitress. 'Yeah,' she laughs. 'I mean, I didn't see, but I can tell by Louis's reaction in the kitchen.' I head out into the twilight for a wander, enjoying the tense silence of a village utterly engrossed, catching the odd glimpse of a family clustered round a television as I pass. It's a friendly, communal sort of feeling, and I'm actively pleased when, half watching while wringing out today's jersey over the sink, I realise England is going into our first ever Euros final – which means everyone's going to be in a good mood for the rest of my trip.

The next morning, I make good on my promise and start the day with one of the fancier egg preparations, eggs Florentine, which I prefer to eggs Benedict and eggs royale because the earthy sweetness of spinach offers a more satisfying counterpoint to the rich sauce than either fatty, salty ham or smoked salmon. It also feels healthier – everything's relative.

My choice is proof of my confidence in the kitchen after last night's lovely solid brick of lasagne: this is not a dish I'd order just anywhere; there's too much to get wrong. The poached eggs could be hard, cold or tainted by too much vinegar, the hollandaise is likely to be either split or straight out of the packet, and the muffin is almost always soggy with either egg or spinach cooking water. This particular example turns up looking like two yellow eyeballs of sauce-drenched egg sitting plumply on a cushion of spinach. The eggs are perfectly cooked, the spinach well sautéed, rather than either raw or sopping wet, and the hollandaise delicious, topped with just the faintest sprinkle of nutmeg. As ever, the ratios are a bit off – you really need a great mound of spinach to mop up all that buttery sauce and yolk, but it's a satisfactory start on the egg front nonetheless.

..

Tea Break:
HOW DO YOU LIKE YOUR EGGS IN THE MORNING?

There's growing evidence that the demand for large and extra-large eggs is not good for the birds forced to lay the things – so I go for medium, or mixed-size boxes. Unless you're baking something very temperamental, a few grams of egg more or less is unlikely to make much difference to the recipe, and at breakfast time, use your common sense: if the egg looks very large, boil or poach it for a bit longer; if it's very small, whip it out a bit sooner. Note that the commercial UK flock is vaccinated against salmonella, and there's no need to keep your eggs in the fridge unless you live somewhere very hot, or you don't have room anywhere else.

Boiled: The simplest of all, and a great choice for eating with Marmite soldiers, mashed onto toast or sliced onto kedgeree. Lower the eggs carefully into a pan of boiling water, and turn the heat down to a simmer. Cook for 6 minutes (soft-boiled), 7 minutes (semi-set yolk still gooey in the middle), 8 minutes (fudgey) or 10 minutes (hard-boiled). Note, these times will vary slightly depending on the size and temperature of the egg, and (occasionally) your altitude. If peeling, dunk immediately into cold water.

Fried: The other simple option. I like them fried in butter, over a low heat, covered, for about 3½ minutes. If you like them crispy, fry them over a high heat in a lot of hot oil, basting regularly, instead. If you must have them cooked all the way through, keep them covered until the yolk is firm, or spoon hot oil over it as you go.

Scrambled: The most comforting choice, scrambled eggs are true nursery food, in that they're easy to eat; nutritious yet unchallenging on the palate, teeth and digestion alike. I also like the neutral, creamy element they bring to a cooked breakfast made thus: whisk together 2 eggs per person and season. Add to a small cold pan with a knob of butter. Place over a medium heat and cook, stirring every 10 seconds, until almost done to your liking, then take off the heat and stir in a dollop of crème fraîche, a dash of cream or another knob of butter.

Omelette: A dish in its own right. Beat together 2 eggs. Season. Heat a small frying pan on a medium-high heat

with a knob of butter until it stops foaming, then add the
eggs and swirl the pan to cover. Leave for 20 seconds, then
draw in the edge of the omelette to the centre and shake to
redistribute the liquid egg to the edge. Add any fillings,
cook until set but still slightly runny, then roll out of the
pan onto a plate.

Poached: The fussiest of all basic egg preparations, in that it's the
least forgiving, poached eggs are good on the Benedict family
of breakfasts, and also with things like kippers or on toast.
The fresher the egg the better here. Crack it into a jug or cup.
If you're tidy-minded, you might want to crack it into your
hand or a sieve and let any particularly runny bits of white go.
Add a dash of neutral vinegar. Bring a pan of water to the
boil, whisk vigorously and drop the egg into the middle. Turn
the heat down and cook for 3 minutes, then drain on kitchen
paper, tidy up and serve immediately. If you're nervous about
poaching, I'd go for a 7-minute boiled egg instead: still runny,
but firm enough to peel, and much less faff.

◆◆

Approaching the Thames I begin to see mini roundabouts
spray-painted with St George's crosses. A sudden rash of
England flags, as well as the increasingly impatient driving,
remind me it's not just football that's coming home. The traffic
is horrendous through Billericay and indeed in almost every
town I pass through, backed up along narrow roads not made
for cars and bikes to share, though there are at least nice views
across the fields to the towers of Tilbury when I'm not too
busy dodging discarded nitrous oxide cylinders to enjoy them.

I stop in a bakery and a man brazenly pushes in front of me.
I'm not in a hurry, so I don't say anything, but I sense I'm

entering the zone where people, though presumably no less kind at heart than people anywhere else, live less collectively, avoiding eye contact, keeping to their own space, quick to get one over on anyone who's too slow.

It's a surprisingly decent baker's though – unflashy, the counter stacked with Banbury and Eccles cakes, Bakewell tarts and bread pudding, as well as fancier things like chocolate operas and strawberry millefeuille. I choose a Belgian bun, whose white icing and jaunty glacé cherry feels faintly patriotic, and continue down to the docks, where colourful columns of containers sit waiting for their ship to come in.

Finally, I reach the river itself, wide and placid, the exact shade of a toad I almost ran over in the Fens. It's the first time I've set eyes on my old friend the Thames since the train crossed it at Maidenhead just over six weeks ago, and rarely do I ever see it at such an expanse, as if it's broken free from the confining walls of the city, and is finally able to stretch out and relax here, so near the open sea. Wheeling Eddy onto the wooden jetty that juts out over the lazy water, I can't find much information about the foot ferry that's operated here for centuries, so I sit back in the sun, eat my bun and hope it'll turn up at some point. I could cycle home from here if I wanted to, so I'm not too worried.

———◆◆———

When the little boat does hove into view, I'm almost the only person waiting to board, but the crew doesn't stint on the cheery banter – 'You go up front, the waitress will be along to take your cocktail order in a moment' – and for the princely sum of £4, I'm carried across to the Kentish shore and deposited in the historic heart of Gravesend.

Hunting for a cashpoint, I happen upon a pie and mash shop of the sort more often found in London's eastern hinterlands than in the capital itself these days. The menu – pie and mash, eels, faggots and pease pudding, boiled bacon, spotted dick, treacle pud – makes my mouth water and I consider stopping for an early lunch of egg and chips, but it's beginning to spit, I have no clear route or even destination in mind, and northern Kent is, in my recollection, a fairly hilly place, so regretfully I bookmark it for a return visit.

As soon as I'm out of town, the Komoot app takes me along some seriously lovely country lanes dotted with rose-hung red-brick cottages and weatherboarded pubs, one of which has a stern notice: 'No Horses Outside: You will not get served! (100 yard radius)'. I know I should stop at one for the egg and chips now weighing heavy on my mind, but I keep pushing on, through Eynsford with its medieval church, past the spectacular lavender fields of Lullingstone until I find myself in Shoreham, which is so pretty that every pub is full, apart from one that declares itself open but isn't. There's not even a takeaway Scotch egg – which, as it combines sausage and egg, surely counts as a breakfast food – in sight in the village shop.

I give up, and unwrap Sam's Yorkshire parkin instead, cursing my tendency towards delayed gratification, for always wanting to push on, rather than regret it later. Now, as so often, I'm repenting at leisure.

• •

Tea Break: THE EGG MCMUFFIN

'A call @11.30 this morning from an angry lady who stated that due to the queue at the McDonald's Drive Thru, by the time she got to the window the breakfast service had stopped and she couldn't order a breakfast. The lady was given words of advice about ringing the police.'

– Tweet from Inspector Darren Taylor (@InspectorDarren), 21 January 2021

'Of the UK breakfast "Informal Eating Out" market, our share is currently 10 per cent, and yes, we're the largest brand in the market,' a McDonald's press officer confirms when I contact them, curious to know how this American burger chain fits into our national breakfast habit. Strangely enough, however, the market leader doesn't serve toast, or cereal, or even a fry-up. The eggs in the McDonald's Breakfast McMuffin are apparently steamed, while the bacon is said to arrive ready-cooked.

The McMuffin represents a historic shift in American food habits: prior to its national roll-out in 1976, breakfast tended to be a sit-down affair. This was the first widely available option to eat on the go, the US equivalent of our breakfast baps, or Staffordshire oatcakes. Invented by a franchisee in Southern California, it was an immediate hit, allowing stores to open for several more hours a day, though it's also, anecdotally at least, the McDonald's meal that's been hit hardest by the pandemic. With fewer people going into work, there are fewer excuses to grab a sneaky treat en route.

I've not had a McMuffin since the age of 14, when I ate my first at the airport, feeling ever so sophisticated, and found the disk of egg so problematic I wasn't to repeat the experience for over two decades. Duty calls, however. Back in London, I call upon my friend Kaj, and Wilf, for moral support/egg disposal duty respectively, should either be necessary.

I regret to say it isn't. I take a tentative bite of my sausage McMuffin and then another, larger one – I want to hate it, but it's salty, carby, and fatty, and offers very little textural resist-ance. Even the bouncy egg is actually fine if you don't think too much about it. Within minutes, I've scoffed 423kcal, even allowing for the tiny piece of egg I give the dog.

I finally understand why they're so popular. One day maybe I'll even brave a Greggs vegan sausage sandwich. But not yet. Right now, I need a lie down.

◆◆

As no egg-shaped options have appeared on the horizon in the time it's taken for me to finish the parkin, I move on to an apple and look at the map. There's a clear choice to be made between the Kent Downs and Surrey Hills, beauty spots I am already somewhat familiar with, and the unknown, the places that I know principally from traffic reports and Boxing Day sofa sales; Bromley, Purley, Croydon, Leatherhead. The last name snags my eye. As I attempt to dislodge an oat flake from a back tooth, I remember there's a burger van there which gets rave reviews on Tripadvisor on the strength of its 'beautiful' bacon and egg baps, and 'to die for' egg baguettes. Impulsively, I decide to pay it a visit, breaking the journey in Croydon, simply because no one ever goes on a cycling tour to Croydon.

To really get the full experience, I book the Easy Hotel, which feels apt given Croydon's proximity to Gatwick Airport. I've always been intrigued by these budget airline spin-offs too; will I be required to pay extra for sheets and towels? Will those sheets and towels be orange? Will I be allowed to sleep, or will I be woken by an announcement over the tannoy every 20 minutes?

Pondering these questions as I head west, I realise there are more road cyclists in this lovely part of Kent than I've seen anywhere else: one old chap passes me at quite the clip, shouting it's a shame about the wind as he goes. I almost call after him that if he thinks this is wind he should try the west coast of Scotland. My fellow riders all but disappear, however, when my route ducks under the M25, through a dark, graffitied tunnel of the kind one might get dragged from in a body bag, before spitting me out on the straggling fringes of suburbia, a place where isolated pubs have become Indian restaurants and garden centres are the main form of agriculture.

I dip into the London Borough of Bromley and passing my first familiar red-and-white London bus stop, feel a lurching pang of nostalgia for the hills of Wales and the yawning skies of Lincolnshire – though it can't be denied that it's nice to find myself in a dedicated cycle and bus lane for once.

The Easy Hotel has set up shop in a filthy-windowed former office block not far from East Croydon station. Everything about it is indeed white and orange. Most guests seem to be working on the many construction sites nearby, and the receptionist, faced with a queue of tired people without the ID he apparently requires to check us in (are we actually boarding a flight or what, man? someone demands at one point) is momentarily silenced when I ask if I can take Eddy up to the room.

'No one's ever asked me that before,' he says finally, wincing as the front door opens to a blast of horns and sirens from outside. 'This is mad today. I normally work nights. Yeah, why not, I don't care, innit.'

It's a tight squeeze given that the room has just enough space to get out of bed, but as usual, I feel better with the bike up here rather than locked outside – and tonight, Croydon is popping. I'm not sure I've ever been anywhere with so much energy; when I venture out for dinner I feel like someone arriving from another century.

The Dutchie, a Caribbean basement bar and restaurant, is not the kind of place you go for a quiet meal either – in fact, I'm the only solo diner, but not one member of the extremely cheerful staff makes me feel weird about being on my own. When I order a Paradise cocktail because I'm too embarrassed to ask for the cyan-coloured Sex in the Bush, I receive two, 'because it's happy hour'. Fair enough, I think, not about to complain.

Emboldened, when the waiter delivers my chickpea curry with fried roti, I pump him for information on Caribbean-style breakfasts – they don't do them here, he says, but this, something like this – he points at my plate – you could eat for breakfast. 'In Trinidad they call them doubles.' Saltfish and ackee too, or bakes, or porridge, 'corn porridge' he clarifies. 'But there are a lot of islands, you know.'

The cocktails, and the rum with which I chase down my curry goat, have the effect of making Croydon, with its high-rises and glittering lights, look positively futuristic. I'm glad I came, but I'm also relieved to be back in my snug orange pod, looking out at it through double-glazed grime.

———◆◆———

I wake to the unwelcome realisation that it's my last full day on the road. Eschewing the delights of the Easy Coffee machine, I lift Eddy over a pile of sick on the hotel doorstep and set sail for breakfast in Leatherhead, feeling melancholy already, trying hard to relish, and remember, every last detail.

Croydon's traffic gradually ebbs as I slip through Epsom's quietly wealthy Arts and Crafts estates, stop for a coffee at its more democratic McDonald's and then swing round the outskirts of Leatherhead in search of the correct DIY super-store. Phil U Up parks up in the car park of B&Q, fertile ground for tradesmen and time-rich retirees, though at 10.56 a.m., he and his two staff members are on their own in the trailer.

Slinging Eddy against one of the tables in the shade of a tree, I introduce myself – and ask what he'd recommend. What's the most popular breakfast, I ask? They all ponder. 'It's probably still the bacon, sausage and egg roll,' the girl says, 'isn't it, Phil?'

Sit down, he says, we'll bring you one out. Red sauce or brown? Neither, I think from sheer force of habit – and am surprised to hear myself asking for brown, saying it'll be nice with the sausage. Where did that come from? I wonder, taking a seat. Is this who I am now? A sauce person? I feel like a fundamental shift has occurred under my very nose, and frankly, I'm not sure how I feel about it.

I'm still turning it over in my mind when Phil delivers my food. He's been a chef for nearly three decades, he tells me – he went to culinary school, 'by chance' – and bought the van 13 years ago because he wanted to work for himself. They get a real range of customers, 'from builders to office staff, and travellers to regular folk' (not a few Tripadvisor reviewers admit to making up excuses to find themselves in the vicinity), and he loves the social side of it, meeting new people every single day, and making 'long-lasting friendships'.

I'm not surprised: who wouldn't want to be friends with a man who can produce something like this soft white roll, slightly chewy on the outside, pillowy within, packed with smoky griddled rashers and sausage – though as usual it's the egg, spilling joyously from under the lid, that pulls it all together. Without the slippery proteins of the white, the simple richness of the yolk, the sandwich would be too salty, too greasy, too much. With it, it's breakfast perfection.

Phil is more succinct about the secret to success: 'good-quality bacon, good-quality sausage and a runny egg'. As I spread brown sauce all over my face, I listen to the chat among the massing lunch crowd; one Irish foreman says his lads are both off today – 'reckon they're preparing for the football already'. The girl serving him is confident; the final next week will be 1–0 to England, no extra time. A cheer goes up from the waiting customers. God speed, I think, grabbing Eddy and waving goodbye. Time to make room for the next lot.

——•◆•——

Sated, I head to the nearest park, where I lie in the sun like a snake, digesting my breakfast and considering my next move. I want to stay just outside London tonight, so I can sweep triumphantly into the city like a conquering empress tomorrow, yet also close enough that I can easily meet friends cycling from the east to ride in with me. In the end I decide on Richmond, which it later transpires has been part of London since 1965 (although it's very green and doesn't, on my visit, smell of skunk, so spiritually it's very much still Surrey in my book).

In a fruitless attempt to stave off the gloom I can already feel descending with the end of my adventure, I book a hotel with a vast freestanding copper bath in the room for my final night – in fact, I ring up to make sure I get the right one (full disclosure, I also ring up because my card is declined online), just so I have something to look forward to this evening.

I could head due north from here and be there in just over an hour to really get my money's worth, but having left London from the west, it feels apt to make my route a full circle. Already nostalgic for these days spent untethered from responsibility and routine, simply turning my feet round and round and seeing where the road takes me, I decide to wring as many miles from the day as I can by riding via Windsor to wave to the Queen.

Though there are fewer graffitied mini roundabouts and car flags round here, I note more fluttering Union Jacks, and less willingness to share the road; motorists seem to be angry about something in Surrey, even – perhaps especially – when they're driving cars worth more than many people's houses. I pass the field where the Magna Carta was signed in 1215 and try to cross Windsor Great Park, only to find a stern notice prohibiting cycles 'ridden or pushed'. Pushed? What next, I think: no prams? No suitcases? I've genuinely never felt more republican in my life.

Still huffing with righteous indignation, I make a point of riding right up to the castle itself – on the public highway of course; I don't want to be hanged, drawn and quartered.

It's tempting to linger to enjoy one of the great unsung pleasures of modern life, People Posing for Selfies – but my bath is calling me. I turn the handlebars to point like a homing missile at the capital. Across the river the playing fields of Eton smell sweet, like new-mown grass, but as soon as we head east, things become rapidly less picturesque, reaching a climax of grimness when I find myself riding the Southern Perimeter Road of Heathrow Airport. With some travel restrictions still in place, passenger numbers may be down, but freight is going great guns to judge by the number of lorries and fuel tankers that buzz past my quivering elbows.

I stop at an Esso garage for a drink and a restorative ice lolly. 'Any fuel?' the man behind the counter asks, and then looks more closely at my outfit and laughs. I tell him this is my fuel, and he asks me about my ride; his response – 'Amazing! That really is something!' – makes up for the less than lovely surroundings in which I eat it, staring over the barbed wire of the fence, wondering how long you have to linger there to be deemed suspicious.

Gradually, things become smarter again. Ads for Oxbridge tutors start appearing on lampposts in place of signs for the Feltham Young Offenders Institution. A huge traffic jam in

Hampton resolves itself into chucking-out time at the flower show – groups stumbling through Bushey Park with unwieldy bags of plants, heaving their trolleys full of compost past the deer as sleek men in Lycra weave between them on thousand-pound carbon-fibre bikes, making grimy me feel like a beast of work in comparison.

It's a warm day in Richmond, and to say I don't fit the hotel aesthetic is like saying Lance Armstrong wouldn't go down well at the World Anti-doping Agency Christmas bash – it's the kind of place where the walls are all painted in colours like Housemaid's Knee, and the staff waft around in vegan trainers. It's very much not the kind of place where people turn up in sweaty baked-bean-print tops or store their bikes in their rooms, though they do let me leave Eddy on the river terrace, safely out of sight of the other guests, for free, which, given that car parking is £18 a day, feels like a bit of a bargain.

The room, of course, could comfortably accommodate a whole bike shop. I tip my panniers out on an acre of clean carpet and immediately regret it as the sticky mustard jar rolls over and topples an artful display of vintage hardbacks, tied together, somewhat mysteriously, with baler twine.

❖❖

Tea Break: A FIVE-STAR BREAKFAST

Hotels are, of course, the home of the grand breakfast; the natural inheritors of the country house crown, a place where we all feel justified in lingering over a plate of eggs, rather than simply grabbing an apple from the lobby as we pass.

One of London's grandest examples, the Savoy, even has its own signature omelette, named for the Edwardian novelist Arnold Bennett. A regular diner, and occasional guest at the hotel, Staffordshire-born Bennett,* who mentions oatcakes only once in his novels, based two of his books in similarly large, luxurious establishments, though he was keen to stress that neither were based on the Savoy in particular.

Who originally created the dish is unclear, the Savoy's archivist admits, but 'apparently Bennett requested the omelette in other restaurants beyond the Savoy, leading to his permanent association with this particular recipe'. It has, however, become indelibly linked to them too, and I'm desperate to try it in situ.

Once again, Lucinda delivers, agreeing to accompany me (and Wilf) to the Strand for the night, just so I can order room service the next morning. When it arrives, the dog is so over-excited I actually have to scoop him up, and receive a desperate flailing paw in the face for my trouble, so hard does he fall for the white-jacketed chap with the trolley of food.

There's a strangulated woof from the carpet as I lift the cloche on the little copper gratin pan, and behold my breakfast burnished gold under the grill and garnished with a single plump tomato. A decadent tangle of smoked fish, salty, buttery hollandaise and cheesy, buttery béchamel on top of rich, buttery scrambled eggs, it bears little resemblance to the

---

* An interesting fact: though largely overlooked today in favour of more modish contemporaries like Virginia Woolf and James Joyce, Bennett was so popular in his lifetime that, according to the BBC, 'when he lay dying from typhoid in his flat at Chiltern Court above Baker Street station in 1931, London's city authorities laid straw on the streets to dull the noise. It was testament to his status as a great national figure.'

classic omelette, and is a surprisingly rich dish for a hypochondriac who was, by his own account, fixated on his own 'intestinal caprices'.

Fortunately I have no such issues, though even I feel a little bit unusual after polishing off most of the dish with a little help from Wilf, who graciously accepts a couple of flakes of pearlescent haddock in his bowl. It's silky, and savoury, and utterly delicious – and all the better enjoyed in one's pyjamas with a view of people scurrying to work outside.

❖❖

OMELETTE ARNOLD BENNETT

A recipe based on that used at the Savoy: it's not the fastest of breakfast dishes (though you could at least make the béchamel in advance), but as you're unlikely to want to eat again for at least a year, it's actually quite an efficient use of your time.

It makes one large omelette, as that's considerably less trouble in a home kitchen, but if you're feeling as competent as Savoy cooks, use four small omelette pans instead. You'll have leftover sauce, but it's tricky to make them in much smaller quantities – you can always bring them to the table for the really joyfully gluttonous.

Serves 4–6
300ml milk
300g smoked skinless haddock fillets, preferably finnan haddie
50ml double cream
12 eggs
2 tbsp butter
20g grated Parmesan
Chives, snipped, to serve

For the béchamel

2 cloves
½ onion, peeled
500ml milk
1 bay leaf
15g butter
20g flour or cornflour
Salt, to taste

For the hollandaise

125g cold butter
2 large egg yolks
¼ lemon

1 Start by making the béchamel. Stick the cloves in the onion, and put it in a small saucepan with the milk and the bay leaf. Bring to a simmer, take off the heat, cover and set aside for at least 20 minutes.

2 Melt the butter in a medium saucepan over a medium heat, and whisk in the flour. Cook, stirring, until it begins to smell toasty, but without letting it brown. After removing the onion and bay leaf, slowly pour the infused milk onto the butter and flour mixture, whisking all the time to incorporate, then cook over a low heat until thickened. Season to taste and keep warm if using immediately.

3 Make the hollandaise by cutting the cold butter into large cubes. Put into a small, heavy-based pan with the egg yolks and 2 tablespoons of cold water. Place over a very low heat and stir continuously until the butter melts and the sauce thickens – don't be tempted to turn the heat up or you'll scramble the eggs. (Note, if it starts to curdle you might be able to save it by plunging the pan into a sink of cold

water, so it doesn't hurt to have that ready just in case.) Squeeze in the lemon juice and season to taste. Keep warm – putting it into a covered, heatproof bowl set above a pan of hot water is a good way to do this.

4 To assemble, heat the milk in a wide saucepan until it comes to a simmer, then add the fish, cover, turn off the heat and leave for 7–10 minutes or until it comes easily away from the skin. Meanwhile, lightly whip the cream. Remove the haddock from the pan and break into large flakes.

5 Whisk together the eggs, and season lightly. Heat the butter in a frying pan over a medium-high heat and add the eggs and half the fish. Cook, stirring constantly, until just set, then slide out onto a heatproof plate and heat the grill to high.

6 Mix together 300ml béchamel and 75ml hollandaise. Fold in the cream. Add the remaining haddock and spoon this on top of the omelette. Sprinkle with the cheese.

7 Put the omelette under the grill until lightly browned, then pat yourself on the back and serve topped with chives.

After failing to make the most of one vast bath back in Staffordshire, I'm determined to realise my considerable investment this time, so, having cashed in my welcome drink on the terrace, I head out, still unshowered, in search of a picnic. Seven-course tasting menus are all very well, but nothing quite beats the idea of drinking wine in the bath.

I go to pay my respects to the Thames, smaller here, trapped neatly within high stone walls, and then turn and walk into town, passing a bar playing 'Three Lions', passed by a car trailing strains of 'Sweet Caroline' in its wake – truly the whole country has gone football mad.

Richmond feels to me like the spiritual home of the M&S food hall and it's not long before I locate one and empty it of picnic's greatest hits, including those big green buttery olives that always taste Super Luxe, a tub of chocolate cornflake cakes and, most importantly, a bottle of white burgundy. (Sorry, but I couldn't bring myself to go for a hard-boiled egg in a plastic pot, however high it is in protein.)

A detour to Tesco for ice, and I'm all set for my big night in, striding slightly self-consciously with my carrier bag past reception, where people in expensive neutrals are arriving for dinner. Shutting the curtains in case any tipsy Richmond types stray into the garden below, I stick the wine in the sink with the ice, strip and draw a bath.

Let me tell you, I feel very fancy indeed as I swipe a glass – an actual wine glass! – from the mini bar and lay out the snacks. Then, of course, the practical problems emerge. The bath is so deep it's hard to reach in and out of it, so I move a table closer. The water is so warm that my glass steams up immediately and I have to add an ice cube. And, unlike my bath at home, where the hot water has to be topped up every 10 minutes, this thing feels like lying in a copper cauldron. I remember what Martin Grant told me about copper's conductive properties back in Arbroath, and it begins to make sense – it's like being made into marmalade.

Stubbornly, having paid a remarkable amount for this moment, I manage to remain in the scalding water for approximately 25 minutes, and then, with a core temperature approximating that of a freshly baked stottie, I give up. Slathering myself with expensive body lotion, I lie like an Emmett's ham on the huge bed, and put away rather more of the chocolate cornflake cakes than wine experts might think desirable with a Montagny Premier Cru.

As I munch, I consider the egg; the simple greasy joy of the fried egg sandwich, the more refined pleasures of the Benedict family – there seems no end to the humble egg's talents on the breakfast table. Astonishingly versatile, easy to prepare and endlessly good value for money, they're also, I happen to know after years writing about such things, very nutritious.* In fact, go to work on an egg is more than just a great advertising slogan: there's evidence that protein-rich foods like eggs do indeed keep us feeling fuller for longer than more carb-heavy breakfasts . . . though personally I believe the two go rather well together.

If there's an unsung star of the British breakfast table, I'd say it was the egg, I think tipsily – equally at home in the fanciest dining room as it is in the most rough and ready truck stop, it's a true national icon.

I begin to feel quite emotional about its simple beauty. Clearly I'm out of practice with drinking wine. Finally, with a couple of inches left in the bottle, I admit defeat: I need my beauty sleep because tomorrow, after 46 days apart, I'm going to be reunited with the dog. I'm so excited I can barely sleep.

Ridden: 96.55km
Climbed: 415m
Breakfasts eaten: 2 (eggs Benedict; egg, bacon
and sausage bap)

---

* Eggs are a complete source of readily digestible protein – which means they contain all eight amino acids we need to function, as well as most vitamins with the exception of C (sorted by adding some tomato, or a glass of orange juice on the side).

RED SAUCE OR BROWN?

Phil: 'Brown sauce, on a sausage egg crusty roll.'

Kaj: 'Ketsuppi. Though I prefer cold cuts, pickled fish and yoghurt.'

Wilf: 'Is baconnaise an option?'

20
RICHMOND TO WESTMINSTER
Bubble and Squeak

What mortals Bubble call and Squeak,
When midst the Frying-pan in accents savage,
The Beef so surly quarrels with the Cabbage.
– Peter Pindar Wolcott (1738–1819)

I throw open the heavy curtains the next morning with as much theatricality as I can muster with my second and last hangover of the trip, and eye the river at the bottom of the garden, flowing east towards home. After seven weeks on the road, it's finally time for me to do the same.

My feelings about this are muddled: on the one hand I'm giddily excited to see friends, and most of all Wilf, who has existed only on my phone for the past seven weeks. I'm looking forward to having a big mug of tea on my own sofa too, made by me, just the way I like it . . . but I'm going to miss slipping in and out of people's lives, always waking up somewhere new, never knowing quite what the day will hold – and, of course, the excuse to eat as many breakfasts as takes my fancy in the name of research.

Pulling on the clean kit I've been saving for the occasion, I hoist Eddy up to street level and, swallowing hard, attach the cheery yellow panniers for one last time. Unable to shake old habits, I detour past the Scandinavian bakery for sustenance, remembering the cardamom bun I shared with Ali on that rainy morning in Edinburgh, and then begin the familiar ride through Richmond Park, the towers of the City of London now visible on the horizon, fallow deer placidly occupying the foreground. The usual gangs in Lycra whizz past discussing equity investments – I do this route a lot, sometimes bringing Wilf for a walk, sometimes just for the pleasure of stretching my legs, and I have no need for a sat nav from here on in.

I'm thinking instead, as I pedal a well-worn groove through south-west London, of what I've learnt from the last couple of months. I embarked on this trip back in May assuming riding around the UK would be hard, that we don't have a cycling culture, or even much infrastructure, and I'd feel vulnerable on the roads here. It's true that, thanks to our relatively dense population, roads tended to be busier than those in France, but there are more, and better signed, cycle routes than I'd expected, and drivers, outside the Home Counties anyway, have been surprisingly generous, even courteous. (I think fondly of the Cornish bus that thanked us for letting it pass with a sonorous triple toot of the horn.)

People, whether on trains, in hotels or simply by the side of the road, have been, for the most part, pretty friendly – and occasionally, really unnecessarily kind – reminding me that if you take the time to chat, or even just to smile as you pass, we Brits aren't always as bad as we like to make out.

Food, if not always quite as sophisticated as across the Channel, has certainly been more plentiful,* and I can confirm that the UK is still capable of furnishing the hungry traveller with a cracking breakfast – a proper rib-sticking thing, hewn of porridge oats and puddings, pikelets and preserves.

I may never lose my horror of beans touching yolk, or my disdain for chips before noon, but I can now see the merits of scrambled eggs on a fry-up, and might even concede that hash browns aren't the worst thing in the world (though I still maintain they've got nothing on an honest tattie scone).

Yet though I started this trip with a fiercely romantic idea of the cultural importance of the great British breakfast, I'm finishing convinced we should stop treating it as some sort of sacred culinary cow, in need of constant policing. That first bite of Ned's fried macaroni cheese in Devon was enough to persuade me that some rules were made to be broken.

Fun as it is to argue about black versus white pudding, or tinned versus fresh tomatoes, there isn't, and never has been, a definitive version of the Full English or Ulster Fry to adhere to – I love them, and I'll keep on eating them, and insisting my way is the right way, but deep down I now know they're just random collections of ingredients on a plate, less than a century old, and no more bound to any particular meal than dal and rice, or bread and butter.

Indeed, it strikes me that the very term 'all-day breakfast' exposes the inherent absurdity of trying to keep food in such pigeonholes. Not so very long ago, anything was fair game on

---

* Special thanks to the landlady of the King William in Catcott, Somerset, who knocked us up a mid-afternoon cheese toastie and chips when her chef was on a break.

the British breakfast table, from mushroom curry to spaghetti alla Milanese.* If variety is the spice of life, our increasingly narrow menu – cereals and toast in the week, bacon and eggs at the weekend – is in need of some serious seasoning.

It would probably help if we got over our fixation with the Edwardian country house breakfast too – a moment enjoyed by approximately 3 per cent of the population, well beyond living memory – and liberated things like kippers and kedgeree, hog's pudding and laverbread from their shiny silver chafing dishes before they go the same way as plus-fours and under-parlourmaids.

They're living foods, not historical curiosities to be locked away in a special box that's only opened on the occasional weekend morning, when you've got time for a leisurely breakfast. Play around with them, eat them when you like, how you like; make kipper vindaloo or hog's pudding ravioli; the use it or lose it mantra applies here just as much as it does to your local butcher, baker and candlestick maker. If we're not buying these foods then they'll disappear. And that would be a far worse crime, I think, swerving abruptly to avoid a pigeon, than microwaving a bowl of porridge.

Instant porridge reminds me suddenly of lovely Charlie, up in Carrbridge, and all the other people I met along the way. I'm grateful for their collective generosity in this strangest of years, marked by Brexit and Covid. Some were visibly delighted with the digital trade lockdown brought, others, more reliant on the hospitality industry, clearly felt their business was teetering on a knife edge – but regardless, there are many easier ways to make a living than smoking fish and stuffing sausages, and they all deserve to be celebrated.

---

* Both suggestions in *Fifty Breakfasts* by Colonel Kenney Herbert (1894).

Of course, I remind myself, the landscape is still shifting beneath all our feet. Eating habits continue to change; no one knows if things will go back to the way they were pre-pandemic, or if more of us will find ourselves working from home more often, something that, anecdotally, appears to increase our enthusiasm for the concept of breakfast.

Will this be the start of a new golden age – or will we all be back bolting cereal bars at our desks by the time you read this? It's impossible to say, but I hope the last year, if nothing else, has reminded us to stop, and take a minute to enjoy our food, whatever day of the week it is. Breakfast is for life, kids, not just for weekends.

A thin infant wail from the pavement as I descend Putney High Street brings me back down to earth, reminding me to look out for Anna and Emma by the bridge. Both had children too small to leave last time around, but they've been keen to join me on this expedition, and insisted on riding all the way from Bethnal Green to meet me on my final morning. I'm impressed, honoured and a bit teary as they hove into view, grinning like idiots.

'Are we allowed to hug now?' Emma says, throwing her arms around me as I hastily swallow the last of my Scandinavian bun. I guess so, I say. Oh God, I think I'm going to cry.

'Don't cry,' Anna says, ever the voice of reason, 'Ride. I looked at the Regency Café website and it closes at noon today.'

I need no further prompting. I'm not quite sure who we're meeting at the Regency, but I do know that Gemma is definitely on her way, and she's bringing Wilf McWilf of the Clan McWilf, Emperor of Terriers, Prince of Dogs, with her.

I lead my maids of honour down the New Kings Road and along the Embankment, past the Chelsea Pensioners and the wedding cake of the Albert Bridge, the Tate in Pimlico and then, just as the Houses of Parliament hove into view, cut up to the café, where Martha is waiting, busy on her phone as usual. 'Oh my God, there's a huge queue,' she says, grabbing me and squealing. 'I can't believe you made it. How WAS IT?'

◆◆◆

Tea Break:
THE GREASY SPOON

Surprisingly, the first greasy spoon to feature in print, back in 1906, refers to a disreputable restaurant in Paris, though the term is apparently an American one – regardless of its origins, it's shaken off its pejorative connotations of smeary cutlery and dirty plates to simply refer to any caff* which will serve you up a fry-up. Not all purveyors of fried goods are greasy spoons – the fish and chip or chicken shop would never be classed as such – and not all places serving a fry-up either. Some are very much restaurants. It's hard to put into words . . . but you'll know a greasy spoon when you see one. The best way I can describe it is to say that a greasy spoon feels homely.

Though the stereotypical example has the bright, wipe-clean style of the post-war period, in fact they're much older, the remnants of fashionable seventeenth- and eighteenth-century coffee houses, given over in the Victorian era to serving 'thick

---

*   Rather than a café, a word that stubbornly retains its faint pretentions to continental grandeur.

slices of bread and butter . . . eggs, rashers of bacon, chops, kidneys and cold beef and ham' to working people at all times of the day. (Another contemporary observer glosses this as 'eggs which are musty, bacon which is rusty, steaks which are tough, and chops which are tainted'.)

Their heyday was, however, between and just after the wars, when they were one of very few options for eating out – 'At the end of the Second World War, catering was a kind of visual and nutritional desert between the works canteen and the Ritz,' according to one source – a step down from the more respectable Lyons tea rooms, but offering somewhere warm to sit in the same way as a pub (which, in those days, was a place you went to drink, rather than eat). In fact, a large part of their appeal was their function as a cheap meeting spot: Quentin Crisp called them 'layabout cafés . . . marvellous places where you could sit through lunch and tea and supper without ordering anything more than one cup of coffee'.

Offering familiar fare at all times of day – bacon and eggs, sausages, omelettes, buttered toast – they were a home from home, a place where you could buy a little space for yourself for the price of a cuppa, where there were no airs and graces on the part of either staff or customers.

Often run by immigrants, the greasy spoon's range has always been eclectic, from the macaroni and gelato offered by the Verrecchia family at the University Café in Glasgow to the shish kebabs and stuffed aubergines served up by the Turkish owners of my local greasy spoon – alongside the tea and fry-ups naturally.

These classic caffs began to go into a sharp decline in the 1990s, as American-style coffee shops, with their soft lighting and comfortable chairs, pushed rents up and made them feel old-fashioned and unsophisticated in comparison. Many of the country's best-loved examples have disappeared over the last two decades, to be replaced by soulless chains. The coffee may be better, the food (occasionally) more adventurous – but the atmosphere is irreplaceable.

●●●

The quality of the Regency's breakfast is clear from the line that leads down the pavement, though that may also have something to do with the interior, a post-war utilitarian riot of tiles, linoleum, framed photos of cup-winning Spurs teams and old boxing posters framed by neat gingham curtains. A frequent backdrop for fashion shoots, films (including a somewhat traumatic scene in 2004's *Layer Cake*) and Instagram posts, it attracts a diverse clientele of tourists, hipsters and men who just want to read the paper in peace.

Like any great local, however, it has its unwritten rules, the most important of which is that no one is allowed to sit down until they've ordered, which means that the queue moves surprisingly quickly as we horse trade menu items. We're all having the full breakfast, obviously – eggs, bacon, sausage, beans or tomatoes (tomatoes for me, thank you), bread or toast (does anyone go for bread?), tea or coffee (tea), but do we really need all the extras? I say we do, but eventually I agree to compromise and barter a little of my bubble and squeak for Anna's black pudding and Emma's sacrilegious hash browns. We're in south-east England, so no other puddings are on offer, and Martha's chips are her own problem.

Just as I'm ordering, and Marco at the counter is pouring me a tea from a vast institutional urn, Australian Claire, who saw me off and has come to see me home, walks in through the wrong door. There's a one-way system in place thanks to Covid, and she has clearly not read the signs.

'OI! WRONG DOOR!' Marco booms. Since the pandemic, they've installed perspex screens across the counter and, to compensate, a microphone, which makes what was always a shouty process positively deafening. Everyone turns to stare at Claire, who, confused, approaches, still smiling uncertainly. 'LADY IN GREEN! GO BACK OUT AND IN THE RIGHT WAY! YES, YOU!' he bellows. She's mortified, and retraces her steps, appearing shamefaced a minute or so later at my elbow. In the meantime, Marco has apologised to a second Claire instead. 'Sorry about that, love. It's all this social distancing. Don't mind me.'

She shrugs, more important things on her mind than being mistaken for someone else entirely, and asks if they have Marmite. (They do.)

BUBBLE AND SQUEAK

Really, all you need to know is that bubble and squeak, in its modern incarnation, is a hash of leftover vegetables, fried until crisp and served very hot. Mashed potato and cabbage are the usual suspects here, but like so many such recipes, bubble is very adaptable – just about anything goes, as long as it's not too wet. That said, if you don't have potatoes on hand, I'd suggest including something else starchy as a base. (Alternatively, you could take bubble back to its roots, and replace the spuds with leftover roast beef. Not such a great choice on a fry-up perhaps.) This is dreamy with a fried egg on top, and is particularly delicious cooked in bacon dripping if you're of the bacon-eating persuasion.

Serves 4

125g sliced cabbage, Brussels sprouts or other greens (or use leftovers)
2 tbsp butter
2 spring onions, white and green parts, roughly chopped (discard the dry tops)
350g mashed potato (about 450g potatoes, boiled and mashed)

1 If your cabbage isn't already cooked, steam or boil it until just tender, then drain very well.
2 Heat the butter in a large frying pan over a medium heat and add the spring onions. Cook for a minute or so, then add the remaining ingredients and toss to combine. Season well, then turn up the heat and fry until beginning to crisp.
3 Alternatively, if you'd like a bubble and squeak cake, instead of heating the mixture through in a large pan, heat a tablespoon of oil in a small frying pan over a medium-high heat and fry it in there instead, pushing it down into one compact round. Cook for about 6 minutes, then turn over (a plate will be useful here) and repeat (or shape into individual cakes, as preferred).

We squash into a little formica booth, and await our summons, though there's something I'm looking forward to even more than my breakfast. Suddenly a large furry object appears in my eyeline, hoisted up to the window and looking furious about it. I scramble past the people who've come all this way to meet me, rush out of the wrong door, oblivious to Marco's distress, and lunge at Wilf, who immediately slips behind Gemma's legs. Clearly we have some making up to do.

He's not allowed inside, I say apologetically, but I'll be as quick as I can, and I'll bring out some bacon.

For him or me? Gemma asks, as I return through the correct entrance, just in time to hear my order sung out – BREAKFAST WITH TOMATOES, TOAST, BUBBLE! – a plate higgledy-piggledy with charred tomato, nicely browned back bacon, an almost perfect egg (I think they must poach them in advance, then fry them, so they're runny, but also a little rubbery) and a great heap of bubble and squeak, my favourite breed of breakfast potato. It's a beautiful thing to come home t—

YOU WANT RED SAUCE OR BROWN SAUCE, DARLIN'?

After seven weeks on the road, I finally know the right answer.

'Brown, please, mate,' I say. 'Always brown.'

Ridden: 26.32km
Climbed: 134m
Breakfasts eaten: 2 (a raisin bun; a corker of a Full English)

RED SAUCE OR BROWN?

Emma: 'Red sauce and mustard on my bacon sarnie.'

Anna: 'BROWN SAUCE for me. Thank you. And very crispy bacon. (Oh, you weren't asking about bacon.)'

Australian Claire: 'Maybe a touch of brown sauce but happy without. Still traumatised by the man shouting at me for coming in the wrong door at the café and then shouting "red sauce, brown sauce" at me when I ordered my breakfast.'

Other Claire: 'Marmite.'

THE FINAL FRY

The Full English, Scottish, Welsh and Ulster Fry are wonderful things, but even better is a home nations mash-up: a breakfast super-group if you will. OK, it involves sacrifices – though if you have potato bread AND bubble and squeak I won't judge you, and you can even replace the tomatoes with beans if you must, but frankly I think this is pretty much perfect as is. (Tinned plum tomatoes are more than acceptable outside tomato season.)

Serves 4

4 sausages of your choice
Oil or dripping, to grease
2 large ripe tomatoes
A pinch of sugar
4 soda farls (page 167)
Bubble and squeak or potato bread (page 365/168)
4 rashers of streaky bacon
4 slices of black pudding
4 slices of white/hog's/groats pudding (page 67 if you'd like to make your own) or haggis
4 lavercakes (page 84)
Eggs of your choice (I'd recommend scrambled, page 338)
Sauce of your choice (page 30–33 if you'd like to make your own)

1 Heat the oven to 200°C/180°C fan/gas 6. Put the sausages on a greased baking tray in the oven. Cut the tomatoes in half, put them on a greased tray and season with salt, pepper and a pinch of sugar. Bake for about 30 minutes, until the tomatoes are soft but still hold their

shape, and the sausages are well browned, leaving them in a bit longer if they're not quite there. (Note, if you're not baking fresh tomatoes, then you can fry the sausages in a little fat first instead, before you do the bacon, but if you have the oven on anyway, this will save some time.)

2 Meanwhile make the farls and/or the bubble and squeak. Once the sausages and tomatoes are ready, turn the oven off, but put the farls and/or bubble and squeak in there to keep warm while you cook the meat.

3 Heat a large, greased frying pan and fry the bacon until it begins to render its fat, then add the puddings and lavercakes and fry until golden on both sides (you may need to do this in batches). Put into the oven to keep warm while you make the eggs.

4 Fry the eggs in the same pan, or scramble or poach them in a fresh pan.

5 Divide the ingredients between plates, and serve with butter and sauce on the side – and perhaps some toast, because why not?

◆——————◆

Vital Statistics

Red sauce: 31

Brown sauce: 24

No sauce: 4

Other sauce: Butter (2), mustard (2), marmalade (1), date and lime chutney (2), barbecue sauce (1), sweet chilli sauce (1), Marmite (1), Worcestershire sauce (1)

Total breakfasts eaten: 47.5

Favourite breakfast: All the ones with Wilf

Distance cycled: 2,388km (54km more than in France)

Total ascent: 19,416m (3,741m less than in France: no Alps)

Top speed: 71.3kph coming down Peak Hill Tor on Dartmoor (21.3kph faster than in France)

Average speed: 17kph (1.6kph faster than in France)

Punctures: 1 (same as in France)

Minutes before Wilf forgave me for going away: 4,320 (coinciding neatly with the Egg McMuffin trip)

ACKNOWLEDGEMENTS

After the last couple of years, it's hard to know where to begin with the thank yous, but given none of this would have happened without the heroic efforts of Sarah Ballard and Eli Keren at United Agents, and Katya Shipster at HarperCollins, to get it over the line before everyone went home for 12 months, I'm going to start there. Thank you all for believing in the idea, and me, and for your unflagging enthusiasm in the face of cruel circumstance – without you, I'd still be sitting on the sofa looking at the map.

Thank you to Sarah Hammond and all the design and production team at HarperCollins for making it look beautiful, and not blinking in the face of my digital disasters, to Annie Lee for saving me from my own mistakes, and to Jess, Hattie, Kara and all the marketing, publicity and sales teams for bringing the vital question of red sauce versus brown sauce to the attention of the nation.

I'm grateful beyond belief to all the people who helped bring this book together – who welcomed me despite the pandemic, and gave up their time to talk to me: Guy Tullberg, Mary Quicke, Sally Lugg, Kate Jones, Marion and Graham Dunn, Rob Rattray, Captain Beany, Paul Desmond, Tracey Jeffery, Andrew Ramsay, James Hacon and Rory, Charlie Miller, Heather Davidson and Fiona McMullen, Martin Grant, Gary at Alex Spink, Maunika Gowardhan, Bharat and Brudo the beagle, Abi Sawyer and Kate Halloran, Grant Harper, Mark Thomas, Phil Furlonger, David Yip and Junny Shek, as well as Sam Brice, Jack Clarke, Judith Carville, Ren Behan and all the many people who advised on matters like what South Africans really have for breakfast and whether crab appam is a thing. In fact, thanks to all the lovely people on Instagram and Twitter (and yes, they do exist) who helped with suggestions and offered endless moral support, even without Wilf as inducement. Not forgetting Jenny for sending me to Iceland and Georgina Hancock for getting me out, Keith and Ann for saving my bacon on the puncture front, Mike Brent the physio for getting me back up and sort of running, crack medical team Nurse Nathalie and Doctor Rob, and ScotRail's kindest conductor for helping make my marmalade dreams come true.

Huge gratitude to the people who came along for the ride, or gave me a bed and a stiff drink or a cake en route: Caroline (semi-professional lifesaver), Lucy, Ned and Juliet (you're all coming along next time), Gemma (still my favourite wife), Pam and John (maker of the best G&Ts east of Land's End), Tess (a million times over), Tor, Faith (that cake!), Stefan, Rhian, Ann and Eurfyl, Tia and Jerry-Lee, everyone at Hoar Cross Hall, the ever-intrepid Lucinda, Marie my Manx correspondent, lovely Harry and Jay, Bellsie and Charlie, Posy and Pete and kids, the Edinburgh crew Rosie, Craig, Finlay, Harry, Sofia and Teddy, History-Alice-and-Ali, Dan and Anna, Sam and Gareth, Alex, Sandy, Hamish and Bob (and Doug for owl identification), Tim, Al and Liberty, Matt and Caroline, and Emma, Anna, the Two Claires and Martha. Thanks for cheering me up, making me laugh like a drain and never failing to ask if I've started on the next one yet. (Bob, and everyone at Feast, I owe you all for your patience, even if I haven't managed to get Bob in a gold lamé jacket this time.)

Kaj, *kiitos* for looking after my beloved so well, and ensuring I continue to be a great disappointment to him, and to the BCUs for the lols and fridge cake during those long months of lockdown – genuinely not sure what I would have done without you girls, but sorry, Meek is still mine. Thanks to Mum and Dad for the Deluxe Beach-side Writing Retreat, and Adrian, Debbie, Amelia and Seb for welcoming me to Portugal and feeding me wine when I was a writing zombie . . . and of course, thanks to Wilf, for being the world's best writing companion. Now we can go out for a proper walk, I promise.